Praise for
Help for the Harried Homeschooler

"Christine teaches us how to teach our children while keeping our sanity!"

—JONNI MCCOY, author of *Miserly Moms, Frugal Families* and
Miserly Meals

"This is a work of impressive clarity, overriding intelligence, and magnificent common sense. Not only is Christine Field a pleasure to read, she has something powerfully useful to say. Trust me, the time you spend with this book won't be wasted."

—JOHN TAYLOR GATTO, author of numerous books, including
Dumbing Us Down, A Different Kind of Teacher, and
The Complete Idiot's Guide to Homeschooling

"Bursting with warmth, wit, and wisdom, *H~~ ~~d Home-schooler* provides practical help a~~ ~~hooling moms."

—ELLEN BANKS ELWELL, ~~ ~~
Idea Book

"Christine Field has done it again, producing a practical, down-to-earth, helpful, and well-organized collection of fifteen all-you-need-to-know chapters in *Help for the Harried Homeschooler.* This book is sure to be a great encouragement to novice and veteran homeschoolers alike. I've homeschooled for nine years, and I learned a great deal in my reading of Christine's book. I highly recommend it."

—RHONDA BARFIELD, author of *Real Life Homeschooling,*
Eat Healthy for $50 a Week, and *15-Minute Cooking*

"Posing problems, suggesting solutions, compiling other authors' sage advice, citing personal examples and biblical answers, Christine helps homeschooling moms find practical solutions to organizational, time, and stress-related problems."

—KYM WRIGHT, author of *Women: Living Life on Purpose*,
and the Learn and Do Unit Studies

"*Help for the Harried Homeschooler* provides valuable encouragement for the vital endeavor of homeschooling. Christine is as helpful as an understanding friend at your kitchen table, making difficult tasks seem achievable. In these pages, veteran and novice homeschoolers will find new resolve to joyfully educate their children."

—MARTHA RUPPERT, homeschooling mom and author of
The Dating Trap

"Christine has put together myriad helps that would take years of experience to realize. This is a great blessing for the new and overwhelmed homeschoolers, including fathers."

—DR. BRIAN RAY, president of the National Home Education
Research Institute

help for the
harried
homeschooler

help for the harried homeschooler

A Practical Guide to
Balancing Your Child's Education
with the Rest of Your Life

Christine M. Field

WATERBROOK
PRESS

Help for the Harried Homeschooler
PUBLISHED BY WATERBROOK PRESS
12265 Oracle Boulevard, Suite 200
Colorado Springs, Colorado 80921

All Scripture quotations, unless otherwise indicated, are taken from the *Holy Bible, New International Version*®. NIV®. Copyright © 1973, 1978, 1984 by International Bible Society. Used by permission of Zondervan Publishing House. All rights reserved. Scripture quotations marked (KJV) are taken from the *King James Version*.

ISBN 978-0-87788-794-2

Published in the United States by WaterBrook Multnomah, an imprint of the Crown Publishing Group, a division of Random House Inc., New York.

WATERBROOK and its deer colophon are registered trademarks of Random House Inc.

Library of Congress Cataloging-in-Publication Data
Field, Christine M., 1956-
    Help for the harried homeschooler : a practical guide to balancing your child's education with the rest of your life / Christine M. Field.—1st ed.
        p. cm.
    ISBN 0-87788-794-2
        1. Home schooling—Handbooks, manuals, etc. 2. Education—Parent participation—Handbooks, manuals, etc. I. Title.

LC40 .F56 2001
371.04'2—dc21

                                                                                    2001049350

Printed in the United States of America
2010

10 9 8 7 6 5

Contents

Introduction 1

PART I: HOMESCHOOL BASICS

1. Balance 7
   The Key to Homeschool Sanity

2. Chaos Control 23
   Getting and Staying Organized

3. Discipline 39
   Train Up a Child

PART II: IN THE HOMESCHOOL CLASSROOM

4. Structure vs. Freedom 63
   The Great Homeschooling Debate

5. Too Much of a Good Thing 81
   Making Curriculum Choices

6. Beyond Academics 93
   Character and Life Skills Training

7. The One-Room Schoolhouse All Over Again 109
   Teaching Multiple Ages

8. Evaluation 123
   Setting and Meeting Standards in Your Homeschool

PART III: FAMILY ISSUES AND THE HOMESCHOOL

9. The Family Circus 141
   Quibbling Siblings and Tireless Toddlers

10. What's a Daddy to Do? 159
    The Impact of Homeschooling on Your Marriage

11. Sane Socialization 181
    School Ties vs. Family Ties

PART IV: PERSONAL ISSUES AND THE HOMESCHOOL

12. When Your World Falls Apart 199
    Homeschooling Through Crises

13. "You're Going to Ruin Those Kids!" 217
    Dealing with Disapproval

14. To Walk and Not Grow Weary 233
    Handling Discouragement

15. New Life in the Valley of Dry Bones 247
    Learning from Burnout

Afterword: The Rewards of Homeschooling 267

Notes 273

Introduction

In my former profession as a criminal prosecutor, I was often called upon to make decisions involving matters of great weight. I decided whether or not to arrest a suspect, whether or not to press criminal charges, whether to prosecute the accused or decline prosecution. Although a judge did the sentencing in any given case, my recommendation was given great consideration. The power of "guilty" or "not guilty," liberty or confinement, sometimes even life or death, was in my hands.

Yet I can honestly say that as weighty as those decisions were, as complex as my responsibilities, they pale in comparison to the decisions and responsibilities I face as a homeschooler.

Before I ever thought about homeschooling, when I considered the quality of the education I wanted for my children I focused on a number of things: the qualifications of the teachers, the prestige of the school, the academic rigor, the array of activities available to complement the academic program. I used my own education as a basis for evaluation. I had both learned well and had a great deal of fun throughout my years in school. Why wouldn't I expect my children's educational experience to be the same?

But I grew up in a different generation. For part of my education, I attended a religious school. I lived in a neighborhood of families who were actively involved with one another, and most of my classmates came from intact, God-fearing homes. The world is different than it was when I was growing up. Society is different. Comparing my own educational experience with what the world had to offer my children was comparing apples with oranges. I realized not long after sending my oldest daughter off to school that preparing my children for the future is an entirely different matter than the task my parents faced with me and my siblings a generation ago.

And so I brought my daughter home. Suddenly the quality of her education became wholly my responsibility. What she learned, when she learned, how she learned—all of it was up to me. By bringing her home I agreed not only to train her academically, but to prepare her for the world in every way: character training, life skills training, social training, spiritual training. When we teach our children at home, who they become is entirely in our hands. Talk about weighty!

If I had understood all the ramifications of my decision, if I had known the work and worry and struggles that lay ahead, would I have made the same decision? For all the time and effort I've put into the education of our four children, for all the sacrifices my husband, Mark, and I have made in our personal lives, for all the ways it has changed the rhythm of our days and will yet change us, the answer must be a resounding yes! Nothing I've ever done has been so satisfying. Nothing has felt more important. Nothing has taught me more.

Remember those Dreft detergent commercials in which a young mother dressed in a beautiful white gown gently rocks her baby while pristine white curtains billow out behind her? Is that a picture of your house? It certainly isn't a picture of mine—Ringling Brothers and Barnum and Bailey would be more like it! There is a lot of love and enthusiasm in our home but not too many quiet moments with my sitting around in a beautiful white gown.

I was not prepared for some of the things I have had to give up because I homeschool my children. So many pursuits and simple pleasures have been put on the shelf: women's Bible study at church, crafting, having free time to simply goof off. My days are so much more complex than I ever dreamed they could be as a stay-at-home mom.

There are times, I admit, when I resent the extent of my personal sacrifice. But there are other times when the sacrifices are minor compared to the payoff: the pleasure of our children's company (most of the time!), the thrill of witnessing learning and discovery, the peace of knowing our children are safe and protected, the joy of watching them grow, the assurance of watching their souls develop. For all that Mark and I have given up, we have gained our children's hearts. I know we are not alone in this experience.

My friend Patsy has homeschooled all six of her children. Emily, her second born, recently graduated from high school. Mother and daughter were out and about running errands one day not long ago when the topic of homeschooling came up between them. "Mom," said Emily, "people think homeschooling is so hard. But you know, it is the easiest way to get the results you want."

Patsy was startled and pleased by Emily's insight. She thought about all the hard work of running a house, birthing babies, chasing toddlers, teaching reading, finding tutors, driving to lessons, training, disciplining, praying... And then she looked over at her lovely girl, modestly dressed, with a bright, healthy mind and a heart that belonged to Jesus. "How true!" she told Emily, silently thanking God for leading their family to homeschool.

Their conversation went on to contrast their family's homeschool experience with their observation of other families whose children had been educated in a traditional school. The hearts of many of those children had been won to the world by their secular education or their peers. "How much harder life is for those parents who must undo the damage, battle an ungrateful, disobedient child, and fear [for their child's] future," Patsy wrote in response to a questionnaire I prepared for writing this book. "How much better it is to not be afraid of the work of homeschool, [to] put your energies into the struggle to get up every day and persevere with the teaching and the housework and the toddlers."

It isn't easy, this homeschooling journey, but it's worth the price we pay. I know. So do the many homeschoolers from across the country who contributed their stories and insights to this book. My prayer is that you, whether a seasoned traveler on this bumpy road or a tenderfoot just setting out, will recognize your own experience in these pages. May you find comfort in knowing that you are not alone, and may you find both encouragement and practical solutions to the common problems homeschoolers face.

> *"And let us not be weary in well doing: for in due season we shall reap, if we faint not."*
> GALATIANS 6:9, KJV

PART I

***

homeschool basics

CHAPTER ONE

Balance

The Key to Homeschool Sanity

Eleven-year-old Clare threw down her pencil in frustration. "Mom, I just don't get this long division! What's wrong with me?"

I looked up from the stack of mail I was sorting through and reached across the table for her notebook. "Nothing's wrong with you, Clare. Let's see what—"

"Momma?" three-year-old Daniel whimpered as he tugged on my pant leg. I looked down. With lower lip extended and his eyes about to brim over, he lifted his arms in desperate appeal.

Caitlin, my nine-year-old, raced into the room as I bent down to pick up Daniel. "Mommy, will you help me find some more sticks and branches? Please?" An injured mourning dove had taken refuge outside our living room window, and Caitlin, determined to nurse it back to health, was in the middle of building a cage for its care.

The phone rang before I could answer her. Clare picked it up, said, "Hello," and handed it to me. "It's Mrs. Stewart. Mom, do I have to finish my math right now?"

"Christine?" Denise Stewart's voice came over the phone. "Just calling to confirm dinner tonight. Is there anything I can bring?"

Dinner! I *had* to get started on that broccoli salad, or it wouldn't have time to marinate. "No, I've got everything I need. But thanks for asking, Denise. We'll see you about six, then?"

I've got to get to that scum in the downstairs bathroom before the Stewarts get here, I reminded myself, staring down at Clare's notebook and trying to focus. "Okay, Clare, what is it you don't understand?"

"Everything!"

I felt a hesitant touch on my arm. "Mommy." My six-year-old, Grace, looked up at me with soulful eyes. "I really need to talk to you."

I gently stroked her hair. "About Melissa?" Melissa had informed Grace yesterday that she didn't want to be Grace's best friend anymore.

Grace nodded, and I offered a quick, silent prayer for her hurting heart.

"Daniel stinks," Clare announced, screwing up her face and holding her nose.

He did. Literally. What's more, he was leaking all over me. I jumped up, holding him at arm's length. "Oh, Daniel!"

And I still hadn't put that load of laundry in—the one with my other pair of jeans *and* the skirt and blouse I was planning to wear for dinner tonight.

"Mom," Caitlin whined, "if we don't go now, it's gonna be too dark to look for stuff."

I glanced at my watch. Good grief, where had the time gone? Mark would be home any minute, and the front room was littered with books and toys. I liked to have things picked up before he arrived, but this time it wasn't going to happen. Had I reminded him this morning that the Stewarts were coming over? Maybe not. He'd mentioned a whole long list of work and family concerns he wanted to talk about over dinner.

"I give up," Clare said in disgust, once again throwing her pencil down. "Who needs long division anyhow?"

Does this real-life Field family scenario sound familiar? Do you know what it's like to be pulled in a dozen different directions at once? If you're a homeschooling mom like me, I can almost guarantee you do.

On most days, simply being a mom is hectic enough. But as dedicated homeschoolers, on any given day we aren't simply moms. We're Mom Multiplied: mother, teacher, disciplinarian, wife, hostess, cook, maid, laundress, prayer warrior, social director, church member, consumer, banker, bookkeeper, nurse, storyteller, community member, and more. At the same time we're individuals with needs, desires, and dreams of our own.

Our job reminds me of the feats of the plate spinner on the old *Ed Sullivan Show*. He could balance several plates on his upright sticks and keep all of them spinning, rarely breaking one. Once in a while one would start to wobble, and he would quickly tap it to set it right. The difference is that in my life, plates seem to be falling and flying across the room more often than not!

So how do we keep all our plates spinning at once? How do we manage our time and energy in such a way that everything that needs to get done *gets* done—without giving us ulcers and making us crazy? How do we choose what role to play, what need to fill, what action to take right now, this moment?

Making Choices

An acquaintance who is a former minister left the church after nearly twenty years of service. He struggled for years with balancing the demands of a congregation, career, and kids. He jokingly refers to his experience as "burning out for Jesus."

Unless we're careful to manage our personal resources appropriately, we face the prospect of "burning out for homeschool." This is not what God calls us to do. He never asks us to do more than he equips us for. We get ourselves into trouble, I believe, when we try to do his work our way instead of depending on him for strength and wisdom.

We also have problems when we impose our own definitions on God's calling. Does being a good homeschooler mean being a gourmet cook and a Vacation Bible School teacher and a community volunteer? Perhaps God never meant for us to be spinning all those plates at once. Perhaps we can afford to let a few of them fall so we can keep the truly important ones going. We can't do it all. We can't have it all.

I used to think I could. In fact, by the world's standards, there was a time when I did. I had a nice law practice, an office, a loyal secretary, and tons of clients who depended on me. But…

I had two little girls waiting at the baby-sitter's who were depending on me too. I had a husband who vaguely remembered what it was like to get some care and attention from me.

I've had it all—and having it all felt like having nothing at all.

Now, in terms of "things," I have very little. But my life is rich beyond my wildest imagination. I've learned the truth of Matthew 6:21: "Where your treasure is, there your heart will be also." I praise the Lord for placing my heart first with him, then at home with my family.

Balance begins with accepting our limitations. Our time and energy are finite. When I'm fully involved in homeschooling my children, sometimes my hands are too busy for sewing or baking bread from scratch. Sometimes the photo albums have to wait to be updated. Sometimes the beds don't get made and the laundry goes longer than I would like. While I am finite, household tasks, it seems, are infinite! However much I do at home, there's always more I *could* do.

Outside our homes too, there are many worthwhile activities we could engage in. Perhaps the needs of the church gnaw at your conscience, or the call for neighborhood or community volunteers tugs at your heart. I constantly have to remind myself that a need, however compelling, does not constitute a call. Jesus himself didn't minister one to one to every person he encountered. He didn't heal every afflicted person. He chose to do only the work that his Father had given him.

What is the work the Father has given you? The more clear you are about your calling, the easier it will be to make choices about where to spend your time and energy. "After God and my family, homeschooling comes next in my line of priorities," says Montana homeschooler Tina. If an activity promises to take her away from those three priorities, she can say no without feeling guilty.

Shari, who homeschools in Illinois, agrees. "Once I grasped what God had called me to do, it made saying no a lot easier," she says. Staying focused on her mission, "the ministry of motherhood and teaching," keeps her content with her life as a homeschooling mom.

Another tool to help you stay balanced is to submit each new decision to a three-part test recommended by Dr. James Dobson: (1) Is this activity worthy of my time? (2) What will I have to eliminate to make room for it? (3) What will be its impact on our family life?[1]

Kat, a homeschooler from California, offers this additional advice for deciding whether or not to add another element, however worthwhile, to her already busy life: She puts off answering any request for her time or resources for several days. "I pray about it, check with my husband, and sometimes ask my children what they think about it," she says. "Then, [within] the next day or so, I call the person and am able to say yes or no." And no, she adds, is a word she uses much more often than she once did.

Many things I have wanted to do—or thought I wanted to do—have fallen by the wayside when I've subjected them to this level of scrutiny. Know your mission. Consider your family's needs. Pray. While there may not always be time to do everything we want to do, there is always time to do those things to which God has truly called us.

As for the many decisions I must make each day about where to spend my time and energy, I have a simple guideline: What is God's idea about what I should do this day? this hour? this moment?

In those small decisions, I believe, lies the essence of gaining balance as a homeschooler. When we surrender our need to control every aspect of our lives, when we see ourselves instead as instruments through which God desires to work—then and only then will we able to tread the homeschool journey with confidence, knowing that he will guide us each step of the way.

After a large storm hit our area recently, my first thought was to go out in the yard to gather up the fallen branches. My oldest daughter had another idea: "Mommy, let's stay on the couch and pray." At her bidding, we prayed for Daddy and others who were out in the storm. We asked God to keep all of us safe. I whispered my own silent prayer of gratitude for the great God who gave me this sensitive daughter to remind me to put his priorities first in my life.

The storm passed and the yard eventually got cleaned up. I was so grateful I had not missed this glimpse into my daughter's precious heart in order to do some chore! God used her to help me choose wisely.

Managing Time

"Even after I've weeded out the nonessentials, there isn't enough time in the day," sighs a harried homeschooler. "How can I ever get everything done that needs to be done in only twenty-four hours?"

Yes, one day includes only twenty-four hours. A mere sixty minutes compose one hour. One minute equals the briefest sixty seconds. No one can argue with those definitions. Yet for the most part, time is a matter of perception. In an article called "Beat the Clock," the *Chicago Tribune* reported that "the gist of scholarly research on time and its perception is this: The more events there are in a given time and the more a brain is engaged and its curiosity fed, the longer the time will seem and the greater will be the fulfillment."[2]

So homeschoolers should feel awfully fulfilled, right?

Not necessarily so. The report goes on to reveal that after studying 10,000 Americans and their schedules for three decades, John P. Robinson of the University of Maryland at College Park and Geoffrey Godbey of Pennsylvania State University at University Park determined that Americans have about forty hours of leisure time a week now, versus thirty-five in 1965. It just doesn't feel like it. "The thief is perception," the article concludes. "People are losing time only in their minds, but the perception feels more real than the reality."[3] In other words, we feel more rushed because we *perceive* that we have less time.

In my previous professional life, I took pride in a busy schedule. Then, lots of appointments and a heavy caseload were signs of success. My perspective has changed 180 degrees. Now, over-busyness means I'm probably not managing my time well. If every waking moment is filled with activity of one kind or another, I'm not balanced. I'm risking "burning out for homeschool."

Dr. Richard Swenson, in his book *The Overload Syndrome*, warns: "Beware of the presumption of overextending. What happens if we are out on a limb, doing one hundred and fifty percent of what we ought and then get into trouble? We cry out to God, 'Help!' But God replies, 'When you come back to where you belong, then I will help you. Remember: *You* are the creature. *I* am God. Use My power, not your own.'"[4]

Time in the homeschooling family will always be at a premium. Some moms simply accept the fact that during the years they spend teaching their children at home, they won't have time for many things they might otherwise enjoy. Ellen Stanclift, who homeschools in Maine, says that she is not willing to sacrifice her relationship with her children to gain time for other activities, nor does she feel resentful because she doesn't have much free time. "I truly love being with my children, and I also know that this is but one season of my life," she says, adding, "My children are excellent companions, and we all have fun together."

Barbara Fackler, a homeschooler from Illinois, notes that there have been times when both she and her husband, who are both self-employed, have had to turn down work in the interests of homeschooling. "But the cost of lost work is hardly missed over the course of a year and is certainly less costly than private school or continuing in an educational system [that] does not meet the needs of our child," she says. "How can the value of a few days' work be compared with the value of a good education? One is a minor financial inconvenience; the other holds lifelong consequences."

Homeschooler Luanne Shackelford is another mom who accepts the limits on her time during this season in her life. "My time is something I can give my children now in a way that I won't be able to give them later," she says. "I can be with them [now] and teach them godly values. I can use situations in our everyday life to illustrate Biblical truth. I will never have this time again. Many things can wait, but kids grow up."[5]

While homeschooling is an enormous time commitment, some moms have found, to their surprise, that teaching their children at home frees up their time. My friend Jeanne, who prior to homeschooling had one child in school, one in preschool, and a napping toddler, says the biggest change for her was that suddenly she was in control of her time again. Being in charge of her own schedule "created more hours in my day," she explains. "And it certainly has freed me from the stress and impatience that are inevitable when one tries to mix deadlines and small children."

Other homeschooling moms whose schedules are no longer dictated by the local school system find that having more freedom makes them *feel* as if they have more time, whether or not they really do. Suzanne, who home-schools an only child, says that not having to worry about her daughter getting to school the next morning allows the whole family "more freedom to enjoy impromptu walks on the prairie path, evening musicals, or an event in Chicago" they otherwise would have had to forgo. Another mom, in Arizona, says that trying to keep track of her children's schooling was making her "a nervous wreck." Now that she homeschools and doesn't have the hassles of "finding costumes for the Christmas play [or] searching for lunch money, lost shoes, and permission slips," she has gained not only time but peace of mind, she says.

A Mother First or a Teacher First?

Perhaps the most crucial roles we must balance as homeschoolers are those of mom and teacher. A friend told me recently, "The part I don't like about being my children's teacher is that I feel I do a lot less mothering. I'm always having to be on top of them, trying to move things along, have them get their work done. I feel like 'Sergeant Mom.'"

One of the things I worried about when I first decided to homeschool was whether being my children's teacher would change my relationship with them. My prayer was that I could successfully integrate being a loving mom with being a good teacher.

Since then I've discovered that the education part of homeschooling fits in beautifully with the living part of life. As their mom, I know my children better than anyone. I know what motivates them, I know *how* to motivate them when they are less than enthusiastic, and I know when it's time to back off because we've been working too hard.

One of the homeschoolers I surveyed for this book noted, "If I sent [my children] to school, *that* would change our relationship!" I know exactly how she feels. So does Trish, who homeschools in Missouri. Trish believes that sending her son off to school every day has much more potential to change their relationship than does teaching him at home. In fact, she views her son's education as an extension of her parental duty to recognize and encourage his abilities.

Some homeschoolers believe that teaching their children at home does change the relationship between them—in positive ways. As a result of homeschooling, Tina, in Montana, sees each of her children as "a whole person, not just as a child." She also is in a position to know "what they are learning, how they learn it, and what they are struggling with," she says. "If they were in government school, I would miss so much of knowing who they are."

Moms who have always homeschooled experience this congruence of roles from the beginning, like Merre in Missouri, who has been her children's teacher from birth. "They expect and respect that [teacher] role," she says.

Those who come to homeschooling later relish the opportunity to regain their position as their children's primary influence. Deborah in California is much closer to her children than she was when they attended school away from home. "My girls come and talk to me more," she says, which she sees as especially important as her daughters get older.

Many moms celebrate the fact that homeschooling improves relationships between parent and child. My friend Cathy homeschooled two children for three years and then sent them to a private school for grades three and up. Her third child, now thirteen, has been educated solely at home. "I think [he] has more respect for me than my others did at this age," she says. Mature and cooperative, he doesn't argue about doing jobs and actually looks for ways to lighten Cathy's load.

It's interesting to hear nonhomeschoolers lament the fact that their children have suddenly "changed," that a son has an "attitude problem" or a daughter is distancing herself from her family. Many parents assume that the process by which school and peers become more important and more influential than home and family in a child's life is a part of maturation. Homeschoolers challenge this belief.

Maine homeschooler Ellen Stanclift comes to the teacher/parent question from a unique perspective: She was a public school teacher before her children were born. "Even then," she says, "I believed that the parents' relationship with their children should be first and that [parents] were the primary teachers of their children. I believed that I was merely employed to facilitate specific academic skills."

This was not a popular view among her colleagues, most of whom believed that teachers should be the primary influences in their students' lives. In addition, she encountered only a handful of parents who were eager, or even willing, to fill the primary guiding role in their children's lives.

Some of those who did take that role remain close to her to this day. "It was from these involved and dynamic individuals that I realized the incredible importance of a strong parental figure," she goes on to say. "I believe that the role of parent *as* teacher is one *all* parents should fill—not just homeschooling parents. Children need strong authority figures in their lives.… I hope that our family *does* have a stronger 'teacher/parent' role than the average American family," she concludes.

One mom I interviewed reported that when she began homeschooling, her kids seemed to measure her against their former teachers. She "dealt swiftly with that attitude of comparison," she says, making it clear that their endeavor was "entirely different." "I think being their teacher could have changed our relationship," she adds, "but I didn't allow it to." Because she approached her dual role of mom and teacher as "the most natural thing in the world," her children stopped testing her.

Therein, I believe, lies the key to balancing the roles of mom and teacher: Make teaching and learning the most natural thing in the world. Make your home a place for living, loving, and learning, and there will be no conflict in the roles you play. In the healthy, well-balanced homeschooling family, the roles of mother and teacher are lived out in harmony as we mentor our children into maturity.

In fact, more than choosing between roles, homeschooling is about blurring the lines between them. We don't have to be a mom one minute and a teacher the next. My friend Linda reads historical novels to her children while they fold the laundry. In my home, my children and I have some of our best conversations in the kitchen while I'm cooking or cleaning. Homeschooling is our major commitment, but while we are educating our children, everyday life goes on. With the right perspective, everyday events can be learning opportunities rather than a series of disjointed activities. The exciting part is that we are all living and learning together.

"Being There"

On an average day, Jesus balanced many roles. He taught, he healed, he encouraged. In the midst of his Father's business, he took time to get away to a solitary place to pray. He showed kindness and compassion to all he encountered, even when he was weary and tired from his burdens.

Homeschooling is a process that has great impact on our children and changes us in ways we never imagined. It requires commitment far beyond pledging to serve on committees or bake cookies for fund-raisers, as you may have done before you brought your children home to school. It calls us to be present in our children's lives in the most significant way possible. One of the joys of our calling is that we're not limited to asking our children when they get home from school, "How was your day?" We know how their day was. We were there.

Author Iris Krasnow left a glamorous career to raise her family. In her book *Surrendering to Motherhood* she addresses this concept of being present in our children's lives. "Being there" isn't about money or about staying home full time, she writes. Rather, "It's about an emotional and spiritual shift, a succumbing to being where you are when you are, and being there as much as possible. It's about crouching on the floor and getting delirious over the praying mantis your son has just caught instead of perusing a fax while he is yelling for your attention and you distractedly say over your shoulder: 'Oh, honey, isn't that a pretty bug.' It's about being attuned enough to notice when your kid's eyes shine so you can make your eyes shine back."[6]

"This 'Now' with the children isn't a cage," Krasnow observes. "It's the marrow. Finally, I have drilled and drilled right to the Essence."[7]

I love that—the idea of drilling to the marrow, to the very essence of life. Of being connected to life profoundly. I have moments when I experience that. I know the joy of seeing my own children's eyes light up with wonder. Yet still I struggle mightily to stay focused on the now that Krasnow writes about.

Maybe it's because too often the now feels like sheer drudgery. *Where is the joy in this?* I ask myself as I move from task to task, grumbling as I go. On a really bad day, I lash out at the children: "Why can't you take care of your stuff?" I shout. Then I look at my own disheveled room. Where do I think they learned their habits?

Reading Brother Lawrence's book *The Practice of the Presence of God* revolutionized my spiritual life. A humble monk who cooked and cleaned for the other monks in his monastery, Brother Lawrence did everything, from peeling potatoes to scrubbing pots, with a heart full of the love of God. "During your meals or during your daily duty," he wrote, "lift up your heart to Him, because even the least little remembrance will please Him. You don't have to pray out loud; He's nearer than you can imagine."[8]

God is near to us when we are changing diapers, scrubbing floors, or washing laundry. Like Brother Lawrence, we can do these things prayerfully and from our hearts. How much better an example to our children to do those tasks in love instead of with grumbling and grousing!

When we view the dailiness of life—the diapers that need to be changed, the questions that beg answers—as interruptions and distractions, we miss the greatest benefit of mothering and of homeschooling: the gift of being there to share it all. "When you stop to be where you are," Krasnow says, "then your life can really begin."[9]

In the scope of things, the relationships we build with our God and our families here on earth are what matter most. If we can keep that perspective in the midst of managing the little details of life, we will take care of those less important things swiftly and efficiently so we can concentrate on the things that matter most.

✶✶✶

Practical Pointers for Gaining Balance in Your Life

Following are a few suggestions that may help you as you balance your complex role as homeschooling mom:

- Make a list of all the tasks you perform in your home, and answer the following questions for each one: (a) Which can be done only by you? (b) Which can be done only now? (c) Which will still be there to do in ten to fifteen years? Use your answers to help you decide how you should spend today. Will you regret not having spent more time with your children? There are many things I want to do yet with my life, but my children are only children once. I will miss many great opportunities, sometimes disguised as small things, if I do not seize them now.

- Find ways to "blur the lines" between your many roles. You'll find practical ideas for doing this in many of the chapters that follow.

- Avoid putting up artificial distinctions between schooling and home life. Your home is your children's laboratory for learning.
- Stay home more often. Leave blank spots on your family social/activities calendar. Pursue leisure activities at home as a family.
- Encourage your children in productive at-home pursuits such as crafts or hobbies.
- If your personal reading time is limited, go first to the Bible. You'll find more expert advice you need for life, child rearing, and education than in any number of the latest bestsellers.
- Practice being there in every aspect of your life, no matter what role you are playing.
- Focus on your mission. Remember: The world has many needs, but so does your immediate family. You are not called to meet everyone's needs.
- Whatever else you do, build loving relationships with your children. Letting your children know they are loved is of far greater significance than any academic subject you might teach.

✳✳✳

Homeschooling is more than an educational choice. It's a lifestyle. Recognizing that fact helps put the many demands on our time and our personal resources in perspective—and may be our key to success as we manage the myriad roles of Mom Multiplied.

CHAPTER TWO

Chaos Control

Getting and Staying Organized

The alarm woke me up with a start. It couldn't be time to get up already, could it?

Groaning, I fumbled for the clock and turned off the buzzer. I wanted nothing more than to pull the pillow over my head, snuggle deeper into the mattress, and go back to sleep for the rest of the day.

That or run away.

My head throbbed from lack of sleep. I'd been up till eleven o'clock doing chores—though looking around, nobody would have guessed it. Dragging myself out of bed, I found my slippers using the Braille system, threw a sweater over my p.j.'s, and shuffled toward the kitchen. Maybe a cup of coffee would help.

I tripped over a dollhouse in the middle of the family room floor, catching myself just short of falling headlong into a pile of dirty laundry. *I'll pick up before the kids wake up*, I thought to myself.

But Daniel was perched on the couch, his pajamas sagging and a stain spreading out on the upholstery beneath him. "Juice, Momma!" he screamed. Over his shoulder I could see into the laundry room, where even more piles of laundry awaited me.

Clare, rumpled and sleepy-eyed, wandered into the kitchen a moment later. "Hey, Mom. Where's breakfast?"

"Coming." I pushed aside my lesson plan book—coffee-stained and nearly empty—to make room on the counter. Now what had I done with the coffee filters?

Clare switched on the radio. "Warm and sunny," a cheerful voice—too cheerful this early in the morning—announced. "Look for another beautiful day!"

Make that another long *day,* I thought. Another day of endless chores. For me *and* for the kids, who were behind in math and grammar.

But they've been so cooperative lately, I told myself. *And we could all use some sunshine and fresh air.* Shouldn't we seize the day and dig some joy out of the fresh spring weather? Or should we plug along with our chores and our lessons?

Six-year-old Grace ambled into the kitchen a few minutes later, clutching a book to her chest. *Frog and Toad,* I noticed. The one we'd been reading together at bedtime. "Mommy, could you read one more chapter? It's so good!"

Soon she wouldn't fit in my lap anymore, I reminded myself, feeling a sudden ache. Grabbing a cup of coffee, I asked my eleven-year-old to change the baby and whisked Grace and her book off to a quiet corner. The rest would get done. Eventually.

A lot of life is maintenance. Dailiness. Meals have to be cooked, laundry has to be cleaned, toys have to be picked up, diapers have to be changed. As homeschoolers, if we want to keep our sanity, we've got to be organized.

On the other hand, joy often comes from seizing the day—or even better, the moment. How do we walk the tightrope between order and flexibility without plunging over the side either into rigidity or chaos?

For me, the routine tasks, the ones that require little thought, are the ones I try to approach in an organized manner. Those things that require my heart and my mind—like relationships and important lessons—I try to be prayerfully flexible about.

The frustration caused by disorganization is a major stumbling block for many homeschoolers. Spending time organizing your time, your schedule, and your household chores may mean the difference between your survival as a homeschooler and throwing in the towel.

Don't confuse orderliness with rigidity or inflexibility. Having a plan isn't a prison; it's a lifesaver. Organization and routine also help our children feel secure. When our surroundings are reasonably orderly and our children know what to expect from the day, they feel safe and grounded—and more able to focus on the task at hand, whatever that might be.

If you like the way things are going in your home, if you feel as if you're accomplishing what needs to be done, if your children are productive and self-motivated, then you probably don't need an organizational overhaul.

On the other hand, if you are stressed out, if your children are whiny and at loose ends, if you can't even remember your goals for the year, then an organizational overhaul is probably long overdue.

Getting Your House in Order

I'm not a stranger to chaos. I sometimes hesitate to invite people to my home. It is furnished haphazardly; the walls scream with artwork, progress charts, reminder lists, and papers; and the house and yard are scattered with toys and projects in various stages of completion.

On the other hand, my home reflects the fact that children are in residence. The books, toys, and projects that are often out are a testimony to the active minds and imaginations of my children. If my house were spotless and barren, it would be dull indeed. Instead, it is brimming with life and all that life brings. It is a place of creativity and learning. It is *our* home, filled with *our* children.

Kate Theriot of the Homeschooler's Curriculum Swap, an active Internet bulletin board homeschoolers can use to buy and sell used curriculum, says that the first "casualty" when she began teaching her children at home was housekeeping. "I had been pretty meticulous before," she says. "Now I turn a blind eye to the food on the floor, inches of dust on the furniture and things all over the house. When six people occupy the same space nearly twenty-four hours a day, there is no conceivable way to *get* it straight and *keep* it that way more than a few minutes."

Sound familiar? Here's how Kate deals with it: "I settle for clean clothes and dishes, decent meals rather than gourmet, and things more or less where we can find them.

"The kids 'help' clean the house," she adds, "but they don't do it half as well as it needs to be done. So I settle for their efforts and look forward to the day when I can get it clean [the way] I like it."

What standards should we settle for? That depends. What can you live with? What can your husband and your children live with? I know homeschooling moms who knock themselves out to clean their houses when the others in the house may care only about having a hot meal on the table and a path cleared through the toys. Ask your family what level of order they need in the home in order to function effectively. Don't do more than what needs to be done. Does it really matter if the attic is cleaned this year? Or is it more important to sit and read a book with your child? Which is of eternal significance?

Clearly, our housekeeping standards loosen when homeschooling is added to the equation of daily life. Before I started teaching my children at home, having a clean house was a priority. Now my priority for my family is that we are living and learning together. The day I get my house "clean the way I like it" will probably be the day my last child leaves home. Until then I've learned, like Kate, to "settle." I want to cherish my children's presence while they are here—even if the house is a mess!

Complete chaos is rarely an effective environment for learning, however—or for teaching. If frustration over household chores is affecting your ability to teach and your children's ability to learn, it's time to do something about it.

How does the wise woman get her house in order? The task begins with analysis. Contemplate the following questions as you think about the tasks that need to be taken care of in the daily management of a home. Consider meal planning and preparation, household chores, laundry, and clutter control:

- Who is doing which tasks now?
- Which tasks usually cause arguments?
- Which tasks drive you absolutely crazy?
- What isn't working well?
- In light of your answers to those questions, what needs to be done differently?

With a general analysis completed, you're ready to make some decisions. For each of those areas you're unhappy with, you have several options:

- Continue to do the task yourself the way you have always done it.
- Learn to do it better, more efficiently, and with less stress.
- Assign someone else in the family to do it.
- Hire someone outside the family to do it.

Before you decide which strategy is best for you and your family, consider the ideas in the following sections.

Meal Planning and Preparation

In our house, we refer to the cluster of activities around planning meals, grocery shopping, and cooking as "fooding." It is a time-consuming task; the average mother at home plans, shops for, and cooks about a thousand meals per year! Because fooding is so time consuming and so essential to family life, we should do all we can to make it an efficient, healthy, and manageable task.

Menu planning is a sensible place to begin. Taking a chunk of time to create several menu plans at once has a number of benefits:

1. It saves time in the long run. You'll build up a data bank of winning menu plans you can rotate on a regular basis.

2. It reduces trips to the store. If you make a shopping list to go with every menu plan, one trip to the store is all you'll need for the span of time you've planned for—except for trips for fresh ingredients.

3. It saves money. At the end of a long day, you are less likely to choose costly takeout or restaurant food if you have a menu planned and all the ingredients on hand. You can also take advantage of sales to cook in bulk or to cook multiple portions.

4. It relieves stress. Saving time, trips to the grocery store, and money are all great stress reducers!

How to begin? Go through your cookbooks. Look through your recipes. If the volume is overwhelming, practice a little "recipe management." Which cookbooks and recipes are you really using? I once took some of my cookbooks on vacation and sorted and organized recipes while sitting on the deck at the lake.

I use the notebook method to organize my recipes. If you have recipes from lots of different sources, this is a nice idea. Put them into notebooks, slipping each sheet into a plastic cover. Sort them with dividers. When I got around to organizing this way, I realized that I had multiple recipes for the same thing. How many meat loaf recipes do you need? Keep the one you like best and throw the rest away!

Use your notebook to plan a week's menu. Note every ingredient on an accompanying shopping list. Photocopy the list and place several copies in a plastic sleeve for later use.

I like to cook; I just hate having to do it all the time. Here are some ideas to help you spend less time in the kitchen—and more time with your kids:

- Cook in multiples. Never make one of anything. When you are preparing soups, stews, chili, meatloaf, and spaghetti sauce, make two or three extra portions and freeze them. Soon you will have several weeks of spare meals ready in the freezer.
- Cook by protein type. If you buy a quantity of chicken or ground beef, cook it all at once and package three or four portions to freeze and use later.
- Buy a bread machine and the biggest Crockpot you can find. These appliances are special gifts for homeschooling moms. At least twice a week during the winter, I spend twenty minutes in the morning, assembling Crockpot ingredients and loading the automatic bread machine. These days seem to go the smoothest.
- Make a perpetual shopping list of staple items. Write down the items in the order they are displayed in your market. Make multiple copies of this list. I keep mine on a clipboard where I can also keep coupons so I remember to use them.

Many families use healthy cooking as a curriculum to teach their children. Spending time in the kitchen with your kids is not only great family time but is also making an investment in their independence. In some families, the older children actually bear much of the burden of meal preparation, thus freeing Mom for teaching and training the younger kids. In our home, my preteens take turns doing lunch duty, and I am then freed to invest that time with the younger children.

Household Chores

When you are home all day, the house will never be clean. Get used to it, and wait for the day the last kid moves out! One friend quipped that the only time her house gets cleaned is when she's expecting company. When the children see things are picked up, they ask, "Who's coming, Mom?"

Speaking of children—make sure they know that housework is everyone's work. Everyone lives in your house. Everyone is responsible for taking care of it. Helping maintain a clean and healthy home is a service you each perform for one another.

We explain to our children that they are required to do things around the house because they belong to a family, and a family works together. Serving one another is a manifestation of love.

Instilling an attitude of healthy service in our children may be one of the most important legacies we pass on to them. How many power struggles can we help our sons and daughters avoid in their future relationships if we teach them that love and service are intertwined? With the right training now, perhaps in the future they won't argue with their spouses about whose turn it is to change the baby or who has washed the most dishes. Instead, they will do what needs to be done out of love.

Isn't it interesting that our children *want* to do chores when it is least convenient for us—like when they're two years old and have few skills? Young children are the most eager to help out around the house, and they are also the most inconvenient to train. But if we are faithful to work with them at age two, by the time they're six or seven, they can be a genuine help.

With our young children, Mark and I have always used the "five fingers for little folks" approach. I draw the child's hand on a piece of paper and write one morning chore on each finger: Eat breakfast and clean up after yourself, get dressed, brush your teeth and wash your hands and face, make your bed, pick up your room. Then instead of having to ask whether he or she did each job, we simply ask, "Did you do all your fingers?"

We have also used picture charts with prereaders. At the top of each column we draw a picture of a toothbrush, a neatly made bed, etc. The child checks off each task as he or she completes it, or even better, pastes a star on the chart.[1]

Some other good ideas to help keep the house neat and clean:

- Tidy in short bursts at intervals throughout the day.
- Have one or two tidy-up times in the day, such as before school and before dinner.
- Set a timer for fifteen minutes and have everyone work until the buzzer goes off.
- Play "21 Pick Up." This idea comes from Kat, who homeschools in California. She sets the timer for a random number of minutes, "sometimes ten, sometimes three," in which time everyone has to quickly pick up and put away twenty-one items.
- Do major chores on a schedule so they don't back up. For example, schedule laundry on Monday and Thursday, a major cleaning of bathrooms on Tuesday, a major cleaning of the kitchen on Wednesday.
- "Power clean" several times a year. This may take a few days, depending on the size of your house. Once the cleaning is done, keep on a schedule of maintenance.
- Keep a set of index cards, each listing a job that needs to be done on a regular schedule. Rotate the cards as you do some maintenance each day.
- Deep clean one room per day.

Don't forget, the world won't come to an end if the house isn't perfectly tidy. Sometimes, as I noted earlier, we are our own worst taskmasters. Maybe it's time to lower your standards. I used to think my husband expected a consistently clean house, but when we had a serious talk about it, he told me he would rather I spend my energy with the children than on cleaning.

Whose standards are you trying to keep?

Laundry

A speaker at a conference I attended quipped, "Doing the laundry is like the love of God. It's everlasting." That would be funny if it wasn't true! For families with children, laundry is never done. For homeschooling families in particular, it must be done as efficiently as possible. Consider these pointers:

- Do the laundry at the same time you are doing something else. (Q: Do you know how to tell a veteran homeschooler? A: Her lessons are timed by the buzzer on the dryer!) My friend Linda reads her read-aloud books to the children while they fold the family's laundry. (This would also work during dish washing.)
- Give each child his or her own laundry basket. You can wash the clothes and return them to the child in the same basket. Even very young children can take full responsibility for their own laundry.
- Have a sorting table in the laundry area. Make all family members responsible for depositing and retrieving their own laundry.
- Limit the size of each family member's wardrobe. It is a law of housekeeping in our age of abundance that the more clothing you have, the more laundry you wash. Take a clothing inventory for each member of your family, noting current sizes on the list. Take these lists with you to stores and garage sales when you're shopping. If Susie already has fifty-two pairs of shorts, she probably doesn't need another—no matter how cute they are!

Clutter

Clutter is like a gnat circling around your head. You swat it, but unless you get it, it buzzes around and continues to annoy you. And just when you think you've got clutter under control, things start to pile up again. The gnat is back, once again circling your head.

Clutter stems from having too much *stuff.* Our possessions keep us busy cleaning, sorting, and otherwise maintaining. At times it feels as if *they* own *us!* When you are tempted to buy a new item, ask yourself if you will really use it. Do you already have something similar? Could you borrow the item from a friend until you decide if it's something you don't want to live without?

If the item is an article of clothing, consider carefully whether it's something you'll wear on a regular basis. When I worked outside the home, I had a closet full of store-bought clothes of which I wore only a small fraction. After leaving the work force, I began to shop at garage sales and consignment shops, and before long I had a closet full of used clothing—of which I wore only a small fraction. The end results were the same: I had a collection that kept me busy cleaning, sorting, and maintaining.

One way to get ahead of the clutter game is to allow yourself a new item only after disposing of something you already have. If you already own more than you know what to do with, try the three-bag decluttering strategy. One bag is for items to throw away, the second is for items to give away, and the third is for items you're not sure you want to get rid of. After disposing of bags one and two, put bag three away for six months. If you haven't missed the items in that length of time, you can safely give this bag away as well.

Kate Theriot of the Homeschooler's Curriculum Swap has an excellent idea for preventive maintenance of clutter in the homeschool. She keeps all the textbooks and other teaching materials she's using for the year in one room, organized by subject so they are easy to find and easy to keep track of. "I insist on all books and supplies being put away when the children are finished so that the room isn't always a mess of papers and books," she says.

The task of decluttering an entire house can seem overwhelming. Here are some options for breaking down the job:

- Clean out one drawer per day. You can easily clean out a kitchen drawer while you are talking on the phone, or a bedroom drawer while you are watching the news.

- Schedule one room per week for a major decluttering and cleaning. After the entire house is done, keep a maintenance schedule so things don't get out of hand again.

- For the truly brave: Commit a chunk of time (at least a week) to give your house a makeover. This level of decluttering is hard to do while keeping up with your homeschooling responsibilities and the daily maintenance involved in raising a family. But if your house has gotten away from you, it may be your only choice. Get the kids involved—you'll have lots of opportunities for interesting discussions. If you feel guilty about their missing schoolwork, set aside an hour each evening to read aloud. If, on the other hand, getting the kids to help out seems more overwhelming than the task at hand, consider sending them to Grandma's for the week!

- Get some attractive storage containers to encourage you in your work. Sometimes a new way to look at managing your clutter will inspire you to really get a handle on it.

- To truly delegate the task of decluttering, hire a closet organizer to help you. Or have that friend from church or your support group who is *so* organized give you some tips. Your public library will have some fine books about home organization too. One of my favorites is *Confessions of a Happily Organized Family* by Deniece Schofield (Cincinnati: Writer's Digest Books, 1984).

Once your household is organized, you'll have an easier time organizing your homeschooling day.

"A Rut to Run In"

When your home is the center of learning, learning is more than phonics. Homeschooling is about teaching and learning in the midst of life, which is not always predictable. Children get sick, the phone rings with people who need your help, and family and friends experience crises. You can count on your own share of crises as well.

Kathryn, who homeschools in New Hampshire, believes that phone calls, visitors, and other interruptions of daily life actually enhance her day. Instead of seeing interruptions as nuisances, she thinks of them as opportunities for her to enjoy the social contact and for her children to practice independent learning and self-control. "Being flexible is very important," she says.

Nevertheless, a schedule can help the homeschooler prioritize tasks, stay focused, and relieve the stress of daily decision making. An effective schedule can do so without compromising the freedom and flexibility a mom like Kathryn treasures.

I like Debra Bell's description of a schedule in *The Ultimate Guide to Homeschooling*: "a rut to run in."[2] A rut isn't always appealing, but it will always keep you on course.

To help you create a homeschool schedule, consider these pointers:

- Concentrate on flow. Schedule blocks of time for daily activities, but don't worry about being rigidly tied to the clock. What's important is that you—and your children—know what comes next.

- Schedule a quiet time at midday. Give yourself *and* your kids a chance to recharge.
- Minimize disruptions in your day. Buy an answering machine. Make a sign for your door that reads, "Homeschooling: Do Not Disturb."
- Don't forget the weekends. Schedule family field trips. Get Dad involved. Weekends are for family learning.
- Post an activity chart where everyone can see it. If you have more than one child, make sure each knows who does what, when. See chapter 7 for scheduling tips when you're teaching several children.

✳✳✳

More Practical Pointers to Organize Your Life for Homeschooling

- Set aside time each week for planning. Organize lessons and teaching tools. Make menu plans, grocery lists, chore charts, and to-do lists. Write down appointments where you can't miss them.
- Buy or create an organizer. Have a section for each area of your life. Mine has sections for a family calendar, to-do lists, menu plans, shopping lists, chore lists, lesson plans, and writing projects.
- Place a box with hanging file folders, customized to your family and your needs, near the telephone. My box has, among other things, files for medical records, homeschool support group newsletters, and calling lists.
- Assign specified study areas and compartments for school materials. You will save hours looking for lost books, pencils, and papers.

- Plan your outside activities around homeschooling, not the other way around. School isn't something we jam into the day around everything else. It's our priority. If you find yourself doing way too much "car schooling," stay home more.
- Develop daily school and chore checklists, and keep them on a clipboard. A few times a day, check with each child to assess: Is it done? Is it on time? Is it neat and accurate? I've used checklists successfully for both my children and myself!
- During the summer, take an hour a day to plan out your school year so it won't creep up on you in August. Use this time to do your reading, curriculum shopping, thinking, goal setting, and decluttering.
- Set your own standards for housekeeping. Remember, no mom, no family, no system is perfect. What may be clean and organized for a mom with one child who attends school seven hours a day will not look like what is clean and organized for a homeschooling mom with several children. As long as you are homeschooling, your home will look like a homeschool home. Don't make yourself crazy trying to make it look like *House Beautiful.* The housework will never be done. Enjoy the process, or you will miss the joy.

✳✳✳

"God is not a God of disorder but of peace," said the apostle Paul (1 Corinthians 14:33). God scheduled Creation. He orders the seasons. And he can help us make sense of our days. There is hope for the organizationally challenged!

CHAPTER THREE

Discipline

Train Up a Child

I usually let the answering machine pick up phone messages during the school day, but on this particular day I was expecting several important calls. I was on a committee for a homeschool student recognition night and had to firm up some details with other moms.

The phone rang steadily throughout the morning. Each time, I jumped up and hurried to answer it in the next room. "You kids keep working, I'll just be a minute," I'd say on my way out the door.

But "just a minute" wasn't enough with one of my callers. Things had to be settled, and the conversation went on for several minutes. I tried to block out the sounds from the next room, where my children were talking and giggling, clearly having abandoned the work I'd left them to. Then I heard a loud rumble as someone dumped the huge box of LEGOs out on the schoolroom floor. I covered the phone and yelled over my shoulder, "Clare! Caitlin! Just because I'm on the phone, that doesn't mean you can goof off! Get back to your schoolwork. *Now!*

"Sorry," I apologized to my caller. "You'd think they could sit still for five minutes without my having to stand over them like an armed guard. Sometimes I wonder if they'll ever learn!"

I know I'm not the only one who feels this way sometimes. "How can I teach my child when she won't listen to me?" frustrated homeschoolers ask.

"You can't," says Gayle, who homeschools in Texas. "Your first order of business in homeschooling is to develop the child's responsibility to respond to your direction. If the child doesn't have that skill, he won't learn from you." Kate Theriot from the Homeschooler's Curriculum Swap agrees: "You must deal with the heart issues first. You must have [your child's] obedience before you can teach him much of anything."

They're right. Until we earn our children's respect and obedience as authority figures, teaching and learning are beside the point. If we can't control our children's behavior, they will not learn. That doesn't mean we should give up homeschooling and send our children to public school if they're not responding to us, although, I confess, I've fantasized about sending my children off to school for a while so someone else could deal with their behavior!

Dual-Role Discipline

Does our dual role as parents and teachers make disciplining our children more difficult? Jonni McCoy, author of *Miserly Moms,* said in a survey for this book that she thinks she's "a bit more disciplinarian" than she would be if her children went to an outside school. "I sometimes wish I could be the good guy, comforting [my kids] from the other teacher," she says. But other homeschooling moms feel there is tremendous blessing in being an all-day disciplinarian to their children.

A mom of twins from North Carolina says the dual role "strengthens and improves [our] relationship. When you spend this much time together, you must be always working on the relationship, working out any problems." Lily, an Oklahoma homeschooler, likes the fact that her children are getting consistent discipline, instead of one set of rules for home and another for school. "Because we are Christians, we believe that there is only one set of rules—God's rules," she says. "And these rules apply all the time, in any place. These rules don't change if the teacher's back is turned or because 'everyone else is doing it' or if they're not the 'cool' thing to do. I'm thankful for the opportunity to instill our Christian values in our children on a consistent basis."

Denise, an Illinois homeschooler, likes being the main authority in her sons' lives because based on her intimate knowledge of their character and personalities she is able to predict their behavior and attitudes. She is also immediately aware of unexpected language and undesirable behaviors because "I know where they are and what they are doing all the time. If something does come up, I can trace the source pretty quickly and 'fix' it." Because she is both their parent and their teacher, she says, her sons are accountable to her in both academic and social arenas.

Establish Lines of Authority

Most homeschoolers agree that in our dual role as teachers and parents, we have far greater opportunity to establish and maintain lines of authority than we would in either role alone. With that opportunity comes great responsibility, as the ability of our children to respond positively to parental guidance may be, in the words of Gayle, in Texas, "the first and foremost skill that will ensure [their] future success."

It won't matter how smart or well educated our children are if they will not respond to authority. "Far more important than reading, writing, and arithmetic," Gayle concludes, "is your relationship with your child as his authority, his teacher, his mentor, and his guide in life. Do whatever it takes to establish this."

The question is how. It's never been easy, and it may be more difficult now than it was even a generation ago. "Our culture has lost its way with respect to parenting," writes Tedd Tripp in his wonderful book *Shepherding a Child's Heart.* "We are a rudderless ship without a compass. We lack both a sense of direction and the capacity to direct ourselves."[1] Tripp believes that because our generation threw off authority in the rebellious culture of the 1960s and 1970s, we don't understand the concept of authority. We didn't accept authority then, and we don't know how to wield it now—in part because we don't know where our authority over our children comes from.

As Christians, we have an advantage. The Bible makes it clear that our authority comes from God. We don't discipline our children to suit our whims. We do it because God tells us to. We do it not to make our children do what we want them to, but to encourage them to do what God wants them to—in Tripp's words, "to empower them to be self-controlled people living freely under the authority of God."[2] We require obedience from our children because we are called by God to do so and because they are called to obey and honor us. Scripture is abundantly clear about this:

- "These commandments that I give you today are to be upon your hearts. Impress them on your children. Talk about them when you sit at home and when you walk along the road, when you lie down and when you get up" (Deuteronomy 6:6-7).
- "Train a child in the way he should go, and when he is old he will not turn from it" (Proverbs 22:6).
- "The rod of correction imparts wisdom, but a child left to himself disgraces his mother" (Proverbs 29:15).
- "Honor your father and your mother, so that you may live long in the land the LORD your God is giving you" (Exodus 20:12).

You are the authority in your homeschool because God is the authority in your life.

It took me years to recognize God as the authority in my own life.

Remember the old Abbott and Costello comedy routine "Who's on First?" In a delightful verbal convolution, the duo tries to determine who's on first, second, and third bases in a baseball game. The problem is that the players are named Who, What, and Where. The confusion created by their dialogue as they try to sort things out sounds a lot like our lives as homeschoolers.

My life would have been much easier if, at an earlier age, I had resolved who was "on first" in my life. I am a child of that rebellious generation Tripp talks about that tossed out the entire concept of authority. When I was a child, I thought adults were stupid. We all did, I suppose, and in my case, my parents were too old and too tired (I am the youngest of eight) to fight with me. I was a rebellious child, a rotten teen, a marginal young adult, and a drifting adult.

Throughout my life I chose an accelerated path of self-will. I never accepted my parents' authority, and I never accepted God's authority. God was a kind of vending machine; I inserted my requests, and depending on whether or not he was in working order, I received or did not receive my desires. I had religion, but I did not have relationship.

As my life spun out of control with myself at the helm, I began to question God's purposes. Why would he allow so many bad things to happen to me? I didn't see the connection between my own self-will and the adversity I faced, and I continued to seek control over every aspect of my life. Going to law school and becoming a trial lawyer only fed my need for control.

But God had lessons in store for me I could never have envisioned. Raising children, aside from being one of the greatest blessings in my life, also matured me and helped me sort through many things. Taking care of a tiny baby made me realize there were things I *couldn't* control. And having a second baby seventeen months later convinced me I was not in control of anything!

It was at this point that I became willing to submit everything in my life to the Lord. Not all of it at once—my notorious self-will would not allow that. Submission came in small steps over a period of time, until I finally reached a place in my life where I sought most of all to please God.

In our family now, we have all come to accept that we must submit to God—mom, dad, children. It's the way God set things up in the world. Children must honor and obey their parents because God ordained that parents have authority. Parents in turn must love and serve their children, a balance that keeps us from trying to shove our authority down our children's throats. Children, too, are to serve one another in love.

Why Discipline?

Contrary to popular belief, discipline is not for the purpose of changing behavior. Parents often get sidetracked by their children's behavior, but actions are not the real issue. "The basic issue," says Tedd Tripp, "is always what is going on in the heart." Effective discipline concerns itself not with a child's behavior, but with the attitudes of heart that drive the behavior. A change in behavior that does not stem from a change in heart, Tripp says, is like the hypocrisy that Jesus condemned in the Pharisees.[3]

The distinction is not merely academic. There is real danger in putting our children's behavior ahead of their hearts. I always get nervous when I encounter perfectly behaved children; I wonder what is going on under the surface of their smooth, unruffled exteriors. What will they be like in ten years? Have they been browbeaten into good behavior while their hearts quietly plot rebellion?

Good behavior is convenient for us as parents, but we must not confuse it with a will submitted to God. Discipline is not about rules; we can teach a monkey to obey rules. It is about relationship—our relationship with God, our relationship with our children, ultimately our children's relationship with God. Because God loves us, he disciplines us (see Hebrews 12:5-6). It is the process by which he conforms our character to the character of Christ. Because we love our children, we discipline them—for the same purpose: that they too might become more like Christ.

Children are born to seek first their own pleasure and satisfaction. They function on the basis of getting what they want, when they want it. Our job as parents is often contrary to their goal: We are to give them what they *need*. We have two choices when our goals collide: We can give in to our children and keep them at an arrested stage of development, or we can lead them to maturity by taking on the task of discipline.

For the Christian parent, discipline is, in essence, *discipleship*. We start the process when our children are born, and while our physical authority stops when they go out on their own, we continue to disciple them as long as we live. Parenting is the ultimate form of discipleship. As we seek to follow Christ in our own lives, our children learn to follow him. If we live our lives with integrity twenty-four hours a day, seven days a week, 365 days a year, they will see and learn. Submitting ourselves to God's authority is the power behind our own authority.

Our Children, Ourselves

As mothers, we set the tone for our home. We can make it a pleasant place to be or a miserable one, both for ourselves and our children. We can make it a place where good behavior flourishes, or we can unwittingly create an atmosphere in which misbehavior makes our home a war zone.

Homeschooling forces us to confront a great many discipline and personality issues—and not just our children's. Sometimes God uses the behavior of our children to address our own issues. Are we angry? bitter? envious? lacking in patience, perhaps? Difficult children are often sent to us by a God who has something to teach us about ourselves.

Many times, we contribute to our children's behavior problems by our own actions. Yelling, for instance, increases tension exponentially and can exacerbate problem behavior. Low expectations for our children's behavior can become a self-fulfilling prophecy. Children may take advantage of inconsistency in our standards and expectations to get away with as much as they can. Sometimes, personality clashes between parent and child can get out of hand. And like it or not, your children may be catching some of their negative attitudes from you! Let's look more closely at these five possibilities.

Yelling. I never knew the depth of my anger until I had children. I've already told you about my issues with control; I wanted, always, to be in charge of what happened and didn't happen in my life. Children, I discovered, didn't care about my agenda.

That made me mad! At times, I found that the slightest offense could blow the lid off my self-control. I'd yell at my children, trying to regain control of an out-of-control situation. All I accomplished, of course, was to prove to my children that *I* was out of control.

In a little book called *When You Feel Like Screaming: Help for Frustrated Mothers,* Pat Holt and Grace Ketterman, M.D., write that the major reasons mothers lose their cool are too much stress and too many demands on their time.[4] That pretty much sums up life for a homeschooling mom, doesn't it?

Yelling might make us feel better—for a nanosecond—but it makes our children angry, sad, and hurt, which can escalate an already explosive situation. "A gentle answer turns away wrath, but a harsh word stirs up anger," Proverbs 15:1 reminds us. "A fool's mouth is his undoing, and his lips are a snare to his soul," warns Proverbs 18:7. "He who guards his lips guards his life, but he who speaks rashly will come to ruin," Proverbs 13:3 admonishes.

The more we yell, the more we yell. Have you ever noticed that? The enemy would like nothing better than for us to yell so much that our children's hearts close up to us and to God. Yelling is a spirit quencher.

When you're frustrated and about to blow, take a deep breath and count to ten. Physically leave the room if you must. Collect your emotions, give your nasty feelings to God and submit your heart to Christ. Then go back to whatever precipitated the potential outburst and turn it into a teaching opportunity. What caused the friction? What action can you take to handle the problem?

Low expectations. In George Bernard Shaw's play *Pygmalion,* a professor takes in a Cockney flower girl, trains her in the social graces, and ultimately passes her off as a duchess. By changing what people expect of her, the flower girl changes the way people treat her. The theory is that we tip people off to what we expect from them. They respond to our cues by adjusting their behavior to match our expectations.

Educational researchers Robert Rosenthal and Lenore Jacobson wrote about the so-called "Pygmalion Effect" in *Pygmalion in the Classroom.* Teachers in several classrooms were told that 20 percent of their students, identified by name, were intellectually superior. In reality, the children were randomly selected and represented the average children in each classroom. Yet the identified students showed an increase in their IQ scores over the course of that school year, and their teachers reported them to be "more appealing, more affectionate and better adjusted"![15]

What if you tried this experiment on your own children? Think of them as well-behaved children; start treating them that way. Expect much, and they will give their best effort. Expect little, and they will likely meet those expectations as well. Like the characters in Shaw's play, they will change their behavior to meet your expectations.

Inconsistency. Many discipline problems can be traced to lack of consistency in our standards and expectations. No system works unless it is adhered to consistently. Sometimes I think I am doing my children a favor when I slack off the rules a bit, but lowering my standards usually backfires and causes more behavioral problems. When I'm inconsistent, the kids notice and try to get away with more, and then I have to nag and retrain them. We must let our children know that a standard is a standard, anywhere, anytime, under any circumstances.

We must also be consistent in meting out consequences for misbehavior. A child who misbehaves and receives no consequence has little incentive to change his behavior. Decide on appropriate consequences for infractions of your house rules (you'll find ideas later in this chapter), and then apply them!

Personality clashes. Do you have a child whose personality just rubs you the wrong way? Do you have difficulty accepting a child for some other reason? Sadly, we tend to deal with such children harshly. We often detach from them emotionally—when closeness is what they crave and what we need.

We can work on our children's behavior and attitudes, but we cannot change their personalities. My friend and fellow author Kym Wright realized at a certain point in her family's life that she could not overhaul her children's "natural, God-given personalities." She could train them in respect, responsibility, and obedience, but trying to change their personalities, she decided, would be "as much a sin as not training them at all."

"Trying to change someone's basic personality is almost like playing God," Kym writes. "We do not think God did a very good job, so we need to one-up him. We have to accept [our children] *as they are.* We can work within that framework to mold them more to Christ's image, but we have to accept them as they are right now. It is important for our peace and for the child's view of himself."[6]

I love to read about the way Jesus related to children. He always blessed and welcomed them. He held their hands, looked at them, touched them. We read in Matthew 19:14-15 that "Jesus said, 'Let the little children come to me, and do not hinder them, for the kingdom of heaven belongs to such as these.' When he had placed his hands on them, he went on from there." Then again in Mark 10:13-16, "People were bringing little children to Jesus to have him touch them, but the disciples rebuked them. When Jesus saw this, he was indignant. He said to them, 'Let the little children come to me, and do not hinder them, for the kingdom of God belongs to such as these. I tell you the truth, anyone who will not receive the kingdom of God like a little child will never enter it.' And he took the children in his arms, put his hands on them and blessed them."

We can make the same kind of connection with our children by accepting them as God made them. All children need someone who hears and understands them, but difficult children need connection even more than most, especially as they grow older. Detaching from them only causes more problems—and more pain.

Find ways to connect with your difficult child. Explore her personality strengths, her likes and dislikes. Find out what delights her and share in that delight. Your love will grow, and your child will know she is loved.

Modeling negative attitudes. "The first step in child training is to decide what you want your child to become and then become that very person yourself," write Michael and Debi Pearl, the wise authors of *No Greater Joy.* "The second principle of child training is [not to] complain or be surprised when they turn out to be just like you."[7]

Our children learn their attitudes toward obedience and service from *us*. Are we teaching them to follow Christ? Are we modeling integrity? Check your own approach to life, God, instruction, correction. How many times have you heard a child sigh or make a negative comment and then realized she heard it first from you?

"Discontented parents breed discontented children," according to the Pearls. "Your attitude is the root of the family attitude tree. A bitter root cannot produce sweet fruit." Although we are responsible for our children's attitudes, we need not attempt to change them; we need only change ourselves. "Since [your children's] attitudes are reflections of your own," say the Pearls, "you need only change your attitude, and the reflections will change."⁸

If you see your children reflecting actions and attitudes you're not happy with, go to the source. Ask God to change you. If they have a positive role model, your children will fall in line.

Discipline How-Tos

Teaching subject matter is the easy part of homeschooling. Addressing issues of the heart is much more difficult—and more important in the long run than anything else we do as parents and homeschoolers. If my children grow up to be rocket scientists but have no love for the Lord in their hearts, if they refuse to obey him, then I will have failed them.

As God has disciplined me in my life, I have come to realize that discipline grows from love. A God who had no love for me would allow me to sin myself into oblivion. In the same way, letting my child run amok is not love. It is irresponsible.

How do we carry out God's charge to train our children in the way they should go? First, as already discussed, every family member must understand that God is in authority over all of us. Our children must accept that our job is to train them to accept both God's authority and the authority he has granted us as parents. It is crucial that children come to appreciate the fact that when they disobey their parents, they are disobeying the higher authority to which we are all accountable.

Second, we need to establish clear expectations, based on biblical values, for our children's behavior. Third, we must establish consequences for our children's actions and consistently enforce them. Fourth, along the way, we need to reinforce positive choices and behavior with verbal encouragement and other rewards. Fifth, when required, we need to give gentle correction. Finally, and perhaps most important, we need to be in constant prayer for our children and their spiritual growth.

1. Establish and Enforce Clear Lines of Authority in Your Home and Your Homeschool

If you believe you are all accountable to God, let your children see *you* obeying and honoring God with your life. Then expect them to obey both you and God. Remind them often what you expect from them—the same things God expects from you: a good attitude, careful listening, thoughtfulness, doing your best work, not complaining.

Illinois homeschooler Denise has been able to establish very clear lines of authority in her family's homeschool. "What I say goes," she says. She attributes her children's obedience to two factors. First, her children know that her *no* always means no and her *yes* always means yes. Second, she has learned that the best way to gain her children's respect is "not so much to respect them, but to respect their father." When the line of authority in their household is clearly established, Denise's authority holds more weight with her children. Denise's acceptance of Dad's authority gives the children a healthy model for accepting hers.

2. Establish Clear Expectations Based on Biblical Values

Your children must understand what is acceptable and what is unacceptable behavior. To this end, be clear; be as specific as possible; and frame your expectations in positive terms, as principles rather than rules. For instance, telling a child, "Don't hit your sister" is not nearly as effective as telling her, "In our family we treat each other with respect. It is not respectful to hit another person, no matter how angry we are."

The phrase "in our family" is powerful. It sets a standard clearly and in a positive manner. It gives children a concrete guideline. It unifies the family.

"In our family, we honor God. All of our behavior is measured against this standard."

"In our family, we love one another. That means we treat each other with gentleness and kindness."

"In our family we all work first so we can all play together later."

It may be worthwhile to set school lessons aside for a few days or even several weeks to work on basic attitudes and behaviors with your children. Create a set of "In our family" statements based on your own beliefs and priorities. Be consistent and cheerful. Set reasonable expectations that your children can reach, and don't expect every annoying behavior to change overnight.

Give your children both limits and increasing freedom; your goal for them is increased self-discipline and self-control, not merely passive obedience. You want them to know how to handle themselves when you or another authority figure is not around.

Don't get too hung up on a system. Remember that you are working on a discipling relationship. Sometimes we put too much trust in a method of discipline and don't leave room for our relationships with our children, for their relationship with God, and for our own relationship with God. Theories and methods don't move our children toward maturity and don't conform us all more perfectly to God's will. God himself does.

3. Establish Consequences and Consistently Enforce Them

What if your child does not choose to cooperate? The grandest of plans are worth nothing if your child is not on board. Only when consequences are stated clearly and in detail and carried out consistently are your limits worth anything at all. "Boy, you're in trouble!" is never as effective as, "If you hit your brother, you can't play with your friends later on. In our family, first we show love and respect for one another; then we can show it to our friends." To be truly effective, the consequence must be carried out immediately and with calm objectivity rather than in anger.

There are two types of consequences. Natural consequences are those that would occur without your intervention. If your child goes out without a coat, she will get cold. Logical consequences are those that you construct or provide to make some rational sense. For example, for a while we used a confiscation box to deal with items left cluttering the living room. If Mom picked something up, the child could redeem the item from the box for a ten-cent fine. We explained this to the children by pointing out that if we left our car parked illegally, it would be towed and we would have to pay a hefty fine to redeem it. The principle at work is that our carelessness with our possessions has a consequence—the item is lost, or a fine must be paid for its redemption.

Choosing appropriate consequences is an art. Author Elizabeth Crary suggests the following guidelines: (1) The consequence should be reasonable. (2) It should be enforceable. (3) It should be clearly related to the offense. (4) It should be consistent with nurturing care. (5) Anger, resentment, and retaliation have no place in an appropriate consequence.[9]

Consequences should also be based on what's important to your child. You want to create some discomfort for her; this mild discomfort or inconvenience is often an incentive to remember and obey. You know your child; what privileges would she least want to forfeit as a consequence to undesired behavior? A particular television show, computer time, playing with friends, video games, free time?

Children can often be your best source of ideas for appropriate consequences. We had our first family meeting to talk about expectations and consequences when our oldest two were about four and five years old. At that time the undesired behaviors we were dealing with were slapping, leaving bikes out, and yelling. We asked the children what would be an appropriate response on our part to each of these infractions of our household rules.

Here's what they came up with: If they left their bikes out, the bike would be hung up in the garage out of reach for three days. If they yelled unnecessarily, they would have to go to their room for ten minutes. If they slapped a sibling, they would serve a time-out. With the rules posted on a chart in full view, we would merely point to the chart when an infraction occurred, and our children would take their punishment. After all, the consequence was their own idea.

Remembering that the purpose of consequences is to help children learn, not to punish them, look over the following list of consequences we've come up with in our family, and use them as examples for constructing your own:

- Not clearing dishes off the table—child clears everyone's dishes for that meal.
- Not meeting reasonable daily study goals before Dad gets home—child must forfeit play time after dinner to complete work.
- Kitchen not cleaned after meal—child must clean kitchen after meals for the rest of the day, whether or not it is his or her turn to do so.
- Goofing off instead of doing schoolwork—child must complete assignments before doing some discretionary, fun activity.
- School goals for the week not met—child cannot participate in weekend fun activities.
- Messy room—child stays in room until it is cleaned or cannot invite a friend over until the room is clean. The principle is that in our family, we take pride in our home.

When an infraction occurs, don't nag and harangue. Just ask the child, "What choice are you making?" This forces him to be accountable for his actions. Give him two choices: "Either do your work in a responsible, cheerful fashion, or you are choosing to forfeit tonight's family movie." Stress the fact that he is making a choice. Don't nag or yell; just state the consequence and *enforce it*.

When our children mess up, our tendency is to want to rescue them. Our daughter forgets to take her required T-shirt to co-op gym class, so we rush home to get it for her. Our son leaves his display for the co-op history fair until the last minute, so we stay up half the night helping him assemble it. But rescuing our children from the consequences of their actions is shortsighted. We may be their hero for the moment, but long term, we are teaching them that it's okay not to follow through on their responsibilities.

4. Reinforce Positive Choices and Behavior

Your children need to know when they are making good choices. Just as important, they need to know that *you* know when they are making good choices. Praise them verbally, or reward them in other ways to encourage positive choices and behavior. Recently, our daughter was invited to go to a movie with a friend. On her own, she decided the movie was inappropriate and informed us she wasn't going. We praised her for making such a wise choice without our input and told her it was a measure of her maturity.

Some other ideas:

- Proverbs 1:9 says obedience to God's Word will be a garland to grace your head and a chain to adorn your neck. If your young child has been particularly cooperative, make her a crown or necklace to honor her.

- Exodus 20:12 says that children who honor their parents will live long in the land. Let your responsive child stay up later than usual.

- Isaiah 1:19 says that those who obey the Lord will eat the best of the land. Take your obedient child out for a special meal with you.

5. Give Gentle Correction When Required

Parents are enjoined in Scripture to treat their children gently. "Fathers, do not exasperate your children; instead bring them up in the training and instruction of the Lord," Paul instructed in Ephesians 6:4. And again in Colossians 3:21, "Fathers, do not embitter your children, or they will become discouraged."

My husband is the police chief in the town where we live. He instructs his officers to be pleasant and well mannered when they are issuing tickets for driving offenses. We should have the same attitude when we mete out correction to our kids. Criticism and harsh correction lead to rebellion and discouragement. Gentle correction leads to a heart more conformed to God. "The wise in heart are called discerning, and pleasant words promote instruction," says Proverbs 16:21. Children respond to pleasant words much more readily and cheerfully than they do to harsh words.

6. Pray for Your Children

Pray for your children the way Moses prayed for his people. He did not demand action from God; instead, he prayed that his people would be restored to a right relationship with God. When the Lord's anger burned against the people, Moses implored him, "Turn from your fierce anger; relent and do not bring disaster on your people," and the Lord was merciful and spared them harm (see Exodus 32:11-14.) When our kids screw up, they need restoration of their relationship with you and their relationship with God. Make that your prayer, and know that "the prayer of a righteous man is powerful and effective" (James 5:16). God wants nothing less than the best for you and your child.

How long will it take before we see fruit in our children's lives? A week, a month, a year, a few years? It takes time for our children's character to develop, just as it took time for us to mature in our faith. The results are God's. Our responsibility is to be consistent in our training as we discipline them and disciple them to become followers of Christ.

✳✳✳

Practical Pointers for Promoting Discipline in the Homeschool

- Remember that effective discipline focuses on principles and relationships, not rules. A rule says, "Don't kill." The principle is, "Love your neighbor." A rule says, "Don't be disrespectful." The principle is, "Honor your father and mother."
- Make sure your children know they are loved, whether or not their performance pleases you. I can recall spanking my daughter Grace, then praying with her about her behavior. She responded by praying that Mommy would stop being so mean! We were locked in a power struggle that required God's healing touch on both our hearts to bring us back to one another in love.
- Be clear on the point of your discipline. Discipline is to conform our children to the character of Christ and to help them submit themselves to the will of God.
- Be gentle. Our discipline should draw our children closer to our hearts. Remember how Jesus always drew little ones close to himself.
- Don't set up behavior problems. Avoid yelling, expect good behavior, be consistent. Don't detach from the child who rubs you the wrong way. Ask God what he wants to teach you through your difficult child, and model positive attitudes and behavior.

- Invent ways to have positive encounters with a difficult child—even if you don't feel like it! Let him or her choose an activity for you to do together. Be fully present, mentally and spiritually.
- Understand and submit to the lines of authority in your life.
- Remind your children that we are all accountable to God for our behavior—mom, dad, children. When your children dislike your correction, make sure they know whom they are mad at. Are they mad at you or at the God who made you their parent?
- Take your cue from the way God deals with us when we need discipline: with compassion, not harshly or indifferently. "As a father has compassion on his children, so the LORD has compassion on those who fear him" (Psalm 103:13).
- Study your children to find out what they delight in. Then join in those activities to strengthen your bond with them. Even if you hate tea parties or playing in the dirt, try doing these things with your children in small doses. Enter into their world.
- Nurture trust by accepting what your child has to say. Is he free to talk to you about anything, or do you shut him down? Only by taking the time to allow conversation to flow freely will you know your child's thoughts, fears, perceptions, and insights.
- If you're unsure about appropriate limits and consequences for your children's behavior, the Doorposts IF/THEN chart or Gregg Harris's "21 Rules of the House" might help you. These commercial products are available through your homeschool product distributor.
- Write out a list of principles to guide you in your discipline. Post it inside a kitchen or bathroom cabinet. Refer to it often. It might read something like this:
  1. Effective discipline always comes from the heart.
  2. It honors God; it is not for my convenience.

3. It is gentle rather than harsh.
4. It preserves my child's dignity.
5. It recognizes good behavior.
6. It inspires self-control and confidence.
7. It trains my child above all things to follow Christ.

✳✳✳

"No discipline seems pleasant at the time, but painful," the writer of Hebrews tells us. "Later on, however, it produces a harvest of righteousness and peace for those who have been trained by it" (12:11). As Christian homeschoolers, we have both great opportunity and great responsibility to train our children through discipline. Nothing is more important to their success—or the success of our homeschool.

PART II

**

in the homeschool classroom

CHAPTER FOUR

Structure vs. Freedom

The Great Homeschooling Debate

Recently at the grocery store I bumped into a woman who was excited to learn I was a homeschooler. "My daughter in Michigan homeschools," she told me. "It's so cute—every morning after breakfast, she helps my granddaughter into her coat and hat and mittens, kisses her good-bye, and sends her out the back door."

I looked at her blankly. "Why would she do that?"

"Why, so when Marnie comes back in the front door she knows she's at school," Grandma said, as if surprised I couldn't figure out such a simple thing.

There is no question that this Michigan mom-turned-teacher is doing school at home! On the other hand, I know a family who appears never to "do school" in the traditional sense. Their house is jammed with books and other resources, and their children spend a lot of time reading or working on projects—they have animals, gardens, science experiments, and art projects everywhere. But "going to school" isn't a separate experience from the rest of their home life.

These two families illustrate a great debate among homeschoolers. At one extreme are parents who seek to tightly control every aspect of their children's education, from what they study to when and how they study it to whom they study with. The focus is on structure. The motivation is to give their children a rich, complete education, with all the i's dotted and all the t's crossed.

At the other extreme are parents who let their children choose their own educational program, from what they want to study to when they want to learn to read. The focus is on freedom. Their motivation, too, is to give their children a rich educational experience—but without the burden of expectations. Childhood, these parents believe, should be a time for fun.

Which approach is "right"? Either, neither, or both!

Most of us grew up believing that education looked a certain way. It took place in a defined space and time. In the Catholic school I attended for a number of years, for instance, much of my learning was by rote. It was the way traditional education played out.

When I was in high school in the '70s, however, schools began to bite at the apple of the school-without-walls theory—even religious schools. Educators were much more receptive to trying alternative ways of learning. I remember convincing my high school principal to start an elective class called "Creation!" She even allowed me to administer the class. Students submitted proposals for some creative work they wanted to do, and we met on a regular basis to work on our projects. At the end of the semester, we had an exposition. A group of girls sang songs that were popular on the radio at the time—I remember something from the Supremes. Others exhibited artwork or read poetry.

I also convinced the nuns to let me write poetry under the trees on the boulevard for my English class. Any misgivings they had seemed to dissolve when I published my first poem that year and then went on to publish several others.

Experience has taught me that life itself is education. I am educating myself when I read, watch videos, talk to people, or work on the computer. So why do I still sometimes get the notion that my children have to be sitting in rows of desks in a classroomlike setting in order for real learning to occur? Was I so programmed by those early years that school still looks like that to me?

I know from my own experience that too much structure can be demotivating. I remember attempting to play with building blocks with my daughter when I was a young parent. She would be having a grand experience stacking, unstacking, arranging, and rearranging her blocks (and, yes, dipping them into her milk at times!). Then I would come along and suggest we build a city or construct a tower. My daughter would immediately lose interest and wander away. She didn't care about the goal I wanted to impose. She wanted to explore!

Too little structure, however, can be unproductive. I've witnessed totally unstructured homeschool programs in which the child wandered from one nonproductive pursuit to another, never really learning or accomplishing anything. Children, some more than others, need guidance, suggestions, and a creative atmosphere to spark their imaginations.

As the creative creatures of a creative God, we need to remember there are no set-in-stone formulas for effective homeschooling. We don't rely on methods anyway; we rely on the Holy Spirit. With that in mind, I believe it is possible to homeschool with integrity while preserving our children's spirit and individuality. To totally leave our children's education to their whims is irresponsible, but if our relationships with them are solid, with strong emotional and spiritual ties, we can make decisions together about how our home education program will proceed. A parent who seeks first to know, accept, and love her children's hearts will have no trouble gaining cooperation in training their minds.

Finding Balance

The heart of homeschooling is one of tremendous freedom. We are free to teach how we wish, what we wish, when we wish. But with our freedom we need the balance of structure—both for our children's sake and our own. "Nothing ever gets done if you don't have a schedule," says a homeschooler from Arizona. "On the other hand, it is stressful to operate a family like a military academy. It takes the joy out."

Finding the right balance between freedom and structure for your homeschool may take some time. Opinions and approaches abound, and probably no single one will be right for your family. When my husband and I were new parents, we listened to and read a lot of advice about parenting, but when it came to making decisions, we took what made the most sense for our family and set aside the rest. New homeschoolers go through the same process. We must take what works and leave the rest behind.

What works probably won't be the same for every child, in every situation, at every point in your homeschooling journey. Each child is different. One may need a rigorous schedule, while another can be given weekly assignments and left to work on his or her own. As children mature and grow in their abilities and skills, their need for structure and freedom may change as well. Margaret, who homeschools preschoolers in Georgia, currently stresses freedom in her approach. "The only structure we have is naptime!" she says. "I figure eventually we'll cover all the nursery rhymes, songs, stories, colors, shapes, letters, and numbers that a structured program would, but without the stress." When she adds more academics to her program, Margaret may have to add more structure as well.

What works in your homeschool may change based on your own abilities and skills as well as your children's. Kate Theriot of the Homeschooler's Curriculum Swap has been using a packaged curriculum, "with a few minor changes," for several years. "God clearly led us to it," she says.

Initially, she had tried an unstructured approach but had been unhappy with her children's academic performance. The packaged curriculum was right for Kate's homeschool for four years, but she's already decided that next year "we will be much freer again." Why? In part because she has learned "how to have structure without chaos [and] freedom without loss of learning," she says.

How do real-life homeschoolers balance freedom and structure in their programs? Many start with a structured approach, either because it feels more comfortable or because they want to instill a solid work ethic in their children. As they mature and gain confidence, they may relax and begin to incorporate more child-led learning. Others begin with a totally child-centered approach and switch to greater accountability when they sense the child requires it.

Some homeschoolers cover their academic subjects in detail in a fairly structured morning program, then use the afternoons for field trips and child-directed projects. Some give their children an entire week's worth of structured assignments on Monday and allow them the freedom to pursue their studies independently. If they don't complete the work by Friday afternoon—neatly and correctly—they finish it on Saturday. If all their work is done by Thursday afternoon, they get to take Friday off. This approach works best with older students who are capable of self-direction.

My friend Connie has a "barometer" to help her determine if she's giving her children too much freedom in their education: If she has to "pick up the pieces" after every learning experience because her kids don't get it on their own, she knows she has to bring more structure to her teaching. But if her children are learning and seem to be proud of the job they're doing, the level of structure she's giving them is correct.

My friend Sue is the kind of person who finds freedom and peace in structure, so it's natural she would favor a structured approach to educating her children. Other homeschoolers simply feel they have no real choice.

Kimberly, who homeschools with a chronic illness, says that "more structure, despite it going against my grain, is better for me and my crew." A child with a learning disability, in order to learn at all, might also require a structured environment.

Jonni McCoy, author of *Miserly Moms,* tried an unstructured approach when she first began homeschooling, but found her children weren't learning everything they needed to learn. "Delight-directed school sounds good," she says, "but [it] leaves out the essentials for certain careers and college learning. I mean, who delights in trigonometry? But it still has to be done."

Too much structure, however, can be stifling. One homeschooling mom from Illinois notes that in an "overly rigid environment," her children feel restricted and pent up, and it shows in their behavior. But when they have enough unstructured time, "their creativity flourishes and they make some incredible discoveries." Janet, another homeschooling mom, agrees: "The need for the homeschooling mom to be in 100 percent control does not work in my house," she says. For one thing, when she listens to her son's needs, he listens better to her direction. "Listening to his heart has helped me be a better teacher," Janet claims. She has also learned to accept that sometimes "he just has to do what he has to do, so to speak, and that's the reality of living."

Lily, who homeschools in Oklahoma, started out with the "school at home" approach, but nobody was happy with it. "God has shown us daily that our children have a natural curiosity and love for learning," she says. "They initiate much more education that I could ever plan for them." A California homeschooler concurs; sometimes she will start to begin her "schooling" and find that her boys are already doing something educational!

These moms have discovered an important concept: Children are naturally curious and full of excitement about learning. My own children constantly startle and delight me with their innovation. My daughter Clare, for instance, recently taped a multitude of magnets to her feet to see if she could climb the refrigerator! And my daughter Caitlin is forever redesigning our guinea pig and rabbit cages to make them more interesting for the animals.

Whether we sit down with our children to review a stack of letter cards or simply make materials and projects available so they can explore on their own, they are soaking up knowledge and practicing skills. In fact, supplying materials to your children without attempting to direct their play encourages creativity—along with some highly complicated messes as a result of their brain cells firing full time!

When my children are struggling with motivation, I try to remember the block-building incident I described earlier. Am I seeking to be too directive? With four children at different levels, the accountability built into a structured approach helps keep our homeschool on track. Yet my kids seem to learn best when Mark and I consult with them about what to study and how to study it. When my daughter chooses to read an entire chapter in one sitting instead of breaking it up over three days, for example, she feels more ownership of her learning experience. As a result, she does her work more cheerfully—and learns better as well. Kate Theriot finds the same to be true in her homeschool. "My children lose interest when things are force-fed," she says. "I see their interest levels soar when they are learning something they pursued on their own."

"It has been said that variety is the spice of life," writes Jessica Hulcy, cocreator of KONOS, one of the first comprehensive unit study curricula available to homeschoolers. "I propose that balance is the meat and potatoes of life."[1]

I like that. Circumstances won't always allow our children to do as they wish, and Mark and I have no qualms about functioning as a "benevolent dictatorship" to help prepare them for those times; on the other hand, we honor their choices as much as possible and make sure we give them plenty of time and resources to pursue their own creative interests.

If you, too, lean toward structure in your educational approach, be sure to stay flexible. Use your children's interests to keep them engaged in learning. In my home, a Vacation Bible School bird camp led to continued exploration, including building bird houses and using field guides to identify local birds. My daughters' ballet lessons inspired reading about the history of dance and watching videos of the major ballets. And a dead squirrel in the horse trough led Missouri homeschooler Merre to an unplanned biology lesson that included a dissection! "Our routine is flexible enough to accommodate a squirrel [that] had drowned in the horse trough," she says, "but structured enough to require daily violin practice, devotions, Bible history, chores, and daily academics."

Finding the right balance between freedom and structure in your homeschool requires intimate knowledge both of yourself and your children. Know your own heart, and strive to know, accept, and love your children's hearts.

Six Approaches to Teaching

Various approaches to teaching incorporate varying levels of structure and freedom. Read the descriptions below and consider the ideas for implementing each approach. Which ones excite you? Which stimulate your own imagination? If you're excited about what you're teaching, your kids will be excited too!

Few people follow a single approach to educate their children; no one exactly fits any one approach, and no one approach, no matter how highly touted, fits every family. You may want to use the Charlotte Mason approach for literature and a Saxon textbook for math. Maybe the "unschool" approach feels right for science and history, but you'd rather use a programmed text for spelling and grammar. Experiment. Use what works for you without feeling bound to adopt the entire concept. You'll end up with an approach that will be just right for you and your family—and uniquely yours.

The Traditional Approach

"Doing school at home" is the traditional approach to homeschooling. Teacher moms use textbooks, workbooks, and other tools similar to those found in traditional classrooms. The traditional approach also includes the use of "work texts." The student studies lessons, does assignments, and takes tests for a subject all in a single workbook. Such work texts allow for independent learning, self-checking, and self-testing. Many fine Christian publishers supply this type of curricula, with varying doctrinal emphases.

The traditional approach works well for families who need a schedule, a plan, and perhaps some accountability. It also allows for concrete measures of accomplishment. Most homeschoolers take this approach toward at least some subjects; math and phonics, in particular, seem to lend themselves to the traditional approach.

Some of the major suppliers of traditional materials and work texts are A Beka Book (877-223-5226), Bob Jones University Press (800-845-5731), Rod and Staff Publishers (606-522-4348), Christian Liberty Academy (800-348-0899), Alpha Omega (800-401-9931), Christian Light Education (540-434-0768), and School of Tomorrow (800-925-7777).

The major homeschooling magazine that features traditional methods is *The Teaching Home,* Box 20219, Portland, OR 97294. The phone number to call for sample copies or subscriptions is 503-253-9633.

The downside of the traditional approach: It may not meet the needs of every child, especially children who don't do well with "book-learning" or with independent learning. It is often rote rather than hands-on learning, although any creative mom could throw in experiments or field trips here and there to liven things up a bit. Some would say that proponents of this approach view the child as a container to be filled with knowledge—rather than a dynamic force that interacts with knowledge in order to learn.

Unschooling

The "unschooling" approach to education is based on the work of American educator John Holt in the 1970s. Holt believed that a child's natural curiosity and desire to learn were stifled by traditional schooling. He advocated an unstructured approach that allowed children to pursue their own interests. Many Christian unschoolers prefer to be identified by the term "relaxed home educators."

Unschooling "demands a great deal of faith and trust by the parent," writes author and unschooling advocate Mary Griffith. Most parents who use this approach, she says, are amazed by the amount of actual learning that occurs when children are basically in charge of their own education. And because it is undertaken at the child's instigation, "it is neither rote nor boring, and is understood more deeply and retained far longer" than parent-assigned learning.[2]

In practice, unschoolers unschool to varying degrees. Some allow learning to be completely driven by the child. Others take a structured approach to the basics and unschool the other subjects. At the heart of this approach is providing the child with an interesting environment filled with books, resources, and caring adults who will interact with him or her in meaningful ways.

The major magazine that covers unschooling issues is *Growing Without Schooling,* Holt Associates, 2269 Massachusetts Ave., Cambridge, MA 02140. For more information, visit the magazine's Web site at http://www.holtgws.com or refer to one of these excellent books on the topic: *The Unschooling Handbook* (Prima Publishing, 1998) by Mary Griffith or *The Relaxed Homeschool* (Ambleside Educational Press, 1994) by Mary Hood.

The downside of the unschooling approach: Because this approach is very child-centered, subjects important to your child's future may be glossed over or even skipped. It is also more difficult, some believe, to assess whether the child is really learning. In addition, unschooling can be labor- and time-intensive, as it requires parents to plan and ferret out resources rather than depend on a set curriculum.

The Classical Approach

The classical approach to education focuses on teaching children the tools of learning. In the early *grammar phase*, the emphasis is on the mastery of facts. In addition to reading, writing, arithmetic, Latin, and Bible memory, the child might learn the classifications of plants and animals and how to distinguish rocks and other specimens. In the *dialectic phase*, the child is taught the rules of logic and learns how to reason. He asks how and why things happen and learns from his inquiry how to draw logical conclusions. A student is usually ready for this stage between the ages of ten and twelve. In the final *rhetoric phase*, usually encountered around age fifteen, the child hones verbal and written skills in order to be able to communicate and express himself.

The three phases of a classical education are called the Trivium, and the newsletter featuring the approach is *Trivium Pursuit*, PMB 168, 139 Colorado St., Muscatine, IA 52761. For more information, see the Web site at www.triviumpursuit.com or call 309-537-3641. The must-read books on the classical approach are *Recovering the Lost Tools of Learning* (Good News Publishers, 1991) by Douglas Wilson and *The Well-Trained Mind* (W. W. Norton & Co., 1999) by Jessie Wise and Susan Wise Bauer.

The downside to the classical approach: Some homeschoolers see this approach as overemphasizing ancient disciplines and classical language and literature. It is also difficult—though not impossible—to find a packaged curriculum that closely adheres to the classical approach, and parents often have to do some scholarly research of their own, as well as shop for appropriate resources, in order to pull a curriculum together.

Charlotte Mason and Living Books

Charlotte Mason was a late nineteenth-century British educator who abhorred textbooks and favored instead exposing children to the best sources of knowledge, which she called Living Books. Rather than having a child study a science textbook, for example, she might have encouraged him or her to take a nature walk, make observations, draw sketches, and then consult field guides to identify the plants, bugs, and animals encountered. The approach is very hands-on and real-life oriented.

The publishers who provide curriculum for the Charlotte Mason approach are Calvert School and Sonlight Curriculum. The classic books on this approach are *For the Children's Sake* (Good News Publishers, 1984) by Susan Schaeffer Macaulay, *A Charlotte Mason Companion* (Charlotte Mason Research & Supply, 1998) by Karen Andreola, and *Educating the Whole Hearted Child* (Whole Heart Ministries, 1999) by Clay and Sally Clarkson.

The downside to the Charlotte Mason/Living Books approach: Some homeschoolers see it as too focused on art, literature, and nature. Strict adherence to this approach may mean an educational program too broad for any one thing to be studied in depth.

Unit Studies

Teaching by way of unit studies involves choosing a topic and delving into it over a period of time, incorporating various disciplines. A good unit study will include aspects of social studies, science, history, the fine arts, math, language and literature, and Bible study. Because the information presented in a unit study is all interrelated—a more natural format than dividing it up into individual subject matter—children may learn it more easily and retain it longer. The advantage of this approach for a family with several children is that all ages can learn together to their level of ability.

The major suppliers of curriculum for the unit study approach are Alta Vista (800-544-1397) and KONOS (972-924-2712, e-mail: info@konos. com). One magazine I recommend that features unit studies and lesson plans is *Home Schooling Today*, P.O. Box 1425, Melrose, FL 32666. The best resource I've found for developing my own unit studies is Valerie Bendt's *How to Create Your Own Unit Study* (Common Sense Press, 1997).

The downside to the unit study approach: Some homeschoolers shy away from this approach because they worry about gaps in their child's learning and because they find it difficult to assess and document learning.

An Eclectic Approach

In reality, most homeschoolers take an eclectic approach to their children's education—some of this, a little of that. In our homeschool, we take a traditional approach to most subjects, but we supplement textbooks with "real" books and field trips. In the summertime and sometimes during the school year, we do unit studies. Some are predictable, like hatching chicks and watching caterpillars metamorphose into butterflies every spring. Some are spontaneous, such as a month-long study of arctic explorers we once did, sparked by our reading aloud of *Mr. Popper's Penguins*.

A balanced eclectic approach tries to integrate all the approaches I've described above. For a study of flowers, a unit plan might incorporate all of the following activities: reading a science or nature text (the traditional approach), studying the classification of living things (classical), taking a walk through a conservatory (eclectic), planting seeds (unit study), planning a fantasy garden (unschooling), and reading some poetry about flowers (Charlotte Mason).

Learning Styles

Knowing the teaching approach you feel most comfortable with is half the battle of choosing the right educational program for your family, with just the right balance between freedom and structure. The other half is knowing the learning style each of your children favor.

A learning style might best be described as your child's most natural and effective way of taking in and assimilating information. (He or she may or may not have one obviously strong learning style.) Understanding learning styles can help you make appropriate decisions about how much and what kind of structure will help your children best learn. Think of each of your children individually. Does he or she respond with more interest to visual, kinesthetic, or verbal cues?

The Visual Learner

A visual learner learns best from visual cues. Demonstrating a task for a visual learner, for instance, will be more effective than telling him or her how to do that task. Provide pictures, charts, or graphs; show a video about your subject matter; prepare visual aids of your own. Be creative. If you are at a loss for ideas, most public libraries have a collection of books that present teaching ideas and strategies. Use them! Do you have a teacher supply store nearby? These stores are a gold mine of supplies to stimulate the visual learner.

Cheri Fuller, learning style expert, suggests these strategies for promoting visual learning:

- Provide the child with lots of slides, maps, diagrams, and charts.
- Give him or her opportunities to draw or paint.
- Use visual objects to represent abstract ideas or concepts. To teach geography, for example, try a game like "Where in the World?" (which uses color and shape to help children

identify and locate countries) or a bright, multicolored map or puzzle.

- Use flash cards for any subject. Buy them or make your own.
- Avoid disorganization. Visual learners are easily distracted by clutter.[3]

The Kinesthetic Learner

This child learns best by doing. He or she needs direct involvement with the subject material. Fuller recommends these strategies to promote kinesthetic learning:

- Buy a big chalkboard or a large whiteboard with markers for the child to use to practice spelling words, math, etc.
- Encourage lots of drawing in preschool years; let the child dictate stories and make them into books.
- Make use of multisensory reading and writing materials (sand on a cookie sheet to trace letters, for example).
- Use common items found around the house for the child to practice counting, adding, subtracting, and multiplying (dried beans and a muffin tin, for example).
- Allow the child to bounce a basketball, clap his hands, or march around the room while practicing rote materials such as math facts or multiplication tables.
- Make up a cheer using spelling words.
- Provide a puzzle map for the child to take apart and reassemble to learn geography.[4]

In our own family, one of our kinesthetic learners simply could not grasp the concept of subtraction, no matter what I did to explain it to her. We tried using blocks and pennies, but nothing seemed to work. In desperation, I placed a line of masking tape on the floor and drew numbers on it. I had her jump forward on the line to add, and jump backward to subtract. This child needed to involve her whole body in the process of learning a new concept!

We have since used such whole-body approaches in other ways: having the children jump while reciting multiplication tables or clap while spelling, for example. In the summertime, we draw a daisy with numbered petals on our driveway. The children who are learning to count jump from petal to petal while counting.

Allow your kinesthetic learners to walk around, doodle, or manipulate Play-Doh while you are reading to them; engaging in physical activity doesn't mean they aren't listening to you. In fact, the subtle body movement makes them able to concentrate on your spoken words.

The Verbal or Auditory Learner

The auditory learner learns through verbal instruction, either from others or him- or herself. Auditory learners might benefit from recording what they need to memorize on tape; they can read it once into the recorder and play it back hundreds of times. I used this method myself after I completed law school to study for the bar exam. I read my review notes into the tape recorder and listened to them on my personal stereo.

Cheri Fuller suggests these strategies for promoting auditory learning:

- Talk with the child as much as possible.
- Provide him or her with lots of opportunities for storytelling and listening to tape recordings and music.
- Encourage verbal learners to write to pen pals, keep a journal, send stories and poems to children's magazines, and make their own books.
- Quiz orally; use a fill-in-the blank tape for review.
- Play Memory and other card games that develop visual memory skills. To play Memory, the child must remember cards that have

been viewed and then placed upside down. The child turns up pairs of cards until a match is made.[5]

If you are memorizing facts or tables, is there a way you can sing them to a familiar tune for your auditory learner? Some children respond well to rap music, so rapping math or other facts is a natural for them. During study time, auditory learners would benefit by reading aloud from their textbooks. Let them spell words out loud and repeat definitions they are learning. The combination of writing things down and also saying them is powerful.

✳✳✳

Practical Pointers for Finding a Teaching Approach that Works for You

- Do further research on the teaching approaches described in this chapter. Refer to the publishers, books, and Web sites listed for more complete information.
- Explore your options by trying out, on a limited basis, some aspect of a teaching approach that intrigues you.
- Spend some time analyzing your children's learning styles.
- Incorporate strategies for all three learning styles in every lesson. Concentrate on your child's preferred style, but give him or her an opportunity to practice other styles as well.
- Complete the family profile below and use it as a guide for deciding what educational approach fits your family best:
  1. The number of children in your home:
  2. Their ages and level of independence:
  3. Their personalities and learning styles:

4. Your personality and teaching style:
5. Your educational philosophy:
6. Your goals for your family and for each child (educational, social, and spiritual):
7. Your beliefs as a family:
8. Your unique family circumstances:
   - Do you have discipline issues in the family?
   - Is your household more organized or more relaxed?
   - Which do you and/or your children need more: variety and new experiences or stability?
9. The level of accountability to which you are called, either by law or by preference:
10. Your resources:
    - How much money do you have budgeted for curriculum?
    - How much planning and teaching time do you have available?
    - How much time and energy can your spouse contribute to planning, evaluation, and hands-on teaching?
11. Your personal sense of God's leading—perhaps most important:

Finding the proper balance between structure and freedom for your educational program and deciding on the teaching approach that works best for your family is likely to take time. Don't force it, and don't lock yourself in. Explore the options. And remember, it's okay to change your mind!

CHAPTER FIVE

Too Much of a Good Thing

Making Curriculum Choices

In my fantasy I stand alone in a nondescript church basement. In front of me sits a group of glassy-eyed men and women in folding metal chairs. They raise their faces to me, waiting. I take a deep breath and then blurt it out: "Hello. My name is Christine, and I am a bookaholic."

Murmurs rise around me. Another deep breath, and I go on to admit that I am powerless over my acquisition of books. "The opportunity to get free books, or even cheap books, is an overwhelming temptation to me," I confess. "A used book sale at the library is like a party to me."

More murmurs—none of them disapproving. My audience is merely empathizing.

"In the summertime, my eyes scan garage sales for book tables, and I don't even stop unless I see one," I rush on, as if afraid someone will try to stop me before I unburden myself completely. "The recycling center's book giveaway is a celebratory event."

The nodding heads and knowing sighs tell me I am not alone. We are all here, at the inaugural meeting of BA—Bookaholics Anonymous—because we share a common addiction. In the face of an available book, we cannot say no. "Books are beginning to occupy all the spare space in my home," I admit in closing. "I'm powerless over them. I acknowledge that I must rely on my higher power to overcome my problem."

Later, on my way home, I cry out to my higher power, "Lord, I have too many choices! What resources shall I use? How can I best teach my children? Yea, verily, yet another curriculum supplier has graced my mail-box with its educational delights. Deliver me from this temptation!"

Fantasy aside, I fear I truly am a bookaholic. The real problem with that is the complexity it adds to my life. So many books, so little time! How do I choose? How do I limit my resources? How do I know which curriculum works?

"Test everything. Hold on to the good," the apostle Paul instructed in 1 Thessalonians 5:21. *Discard the rest,* is the implication. In home-schooling as in life, deciding between "the good" and "the rest" is never easy. For one thing, our choices are rarely between good and evil. More often than not, we are left to choose between good, better, and best. Because there is so much good, we get distracted. We let overabundance trip us up.

I understand the predicament of the missionary recently returned from the field who goes to the supermarket to buy a box of cereal. The array of choices is dizzying! When we teach our children at home, we must choose not only the cereal to feed their bodies but the materials and activities to feed their hearts and minds.

In the early days of homeschooling, few curriculum suppliers would sell to individuals. Today homeschoolers are considered by publishers to be a rapidly growing marketplace. My desk is proof enough of that: It's jam-packed with *stuff.* It's piled high with catalogs, magazines, newsletters, videos, books. With so many curriculum choices, making *good* choices becomes increasingly difficult. And with so many good choices, choosing the *best* is even harder.

How Do We Choose?

It takes a certain amount of courage to begin homeschooling. When we teach our children at home, decisions about their education are entirely up to us. Yes, we have both more freedom and more control than we would if they attended a traditional school. But as always, with freedom comes enormous responsibility.

And sometimes, with responsibility comes panic!

New homeschoolers, in particular, may be dismayed by the multitude of teaching approaches and curriculum choices available. Experienced homeschoolers, in the face of discouragement or boredom—either their own or their children's—begin to wonder if a new curriculum or a different approach might not be the answer to their sighs and yawns.

"Show me what to do, how to do it, when to do it!" we plead as we tune in to one homeschooling guru or another and peruse our piles of curriculum catalogs. The fear of doing it wrong, of doing too much of this and not enough of that, of missing something important entirely, causes us to give up the freedom we so courageously snatched when we decided to teach our kids at home.

Homeschooling used to be easier. The biggest decision was "Shall we do it?" Now the biggest decision is "*How* shall we do it?" Everyone, it seems, has a different opinion, approach, or method "guaranteed to make your homeschool a success." Publishers offer dozens of curriculum choices, each one touted as the best. The number of options available to the homeschooler can be overwhelming. How on earth do we choose?

What we sometimes forget in our pursuit of the best approach to teaching and the best curriculum for our homeschool is that what works for one family won't necessarily work for the next. A family with two elementary school-aged children has different educational needs than a family with infants, toddlers, and teenagers in the mix.

The number of variations within homeschooling families is infinite, and so the process of choosing an educational approach or curriculum is complex. Remember when you read a review about a particular product or hear someone gush over a particular teaching method that your family is unique.

"One of the hardest notions for most of us parents to let go of is the idea that there is one correct solution, one right answer that will solve all the problems and answer all the questions," writes Mary Griffith, author of *The Homeschooling Handbook.*[1]

But there is no such all-encompassing answer. For me, that's part of what makes homeschooling so exciting and dynamic. I am wary of anyone, either an expert or a vendor, who tells me that *his* way is the *only* way. The "my way or no way" approach to homeschooling fails to acknowledge the glorious variety and flexibility of God's creation.

We don't want to be an A Beka family or a Sonlight family or any other "brand" of family. We want to be a family tuned into God's will for our lives. Overriding all other considerations concerning the choices my husband and I make as homeschoolers are these two questions: "Will our children learn to love God?" and "Will our children learn to love learning?"

If our curriculum fails to address either of these priorities, we are misguided. We must not allow ourselves to get so sidetracked by the "experts" that we forget the important thing—training our children's hearts for the Lord.

Buyer Beware

As you examine curriculum options, keep in mind that homeschoolers are now an official market to many curriculum publishers, all of whom want our business. Just as a vendor's advertising might be designed to sell a household appliance, a publisher's marketing efforts are designed to attract us to certain products, to sway us, to convince us to buy. If we don't approach the process with open eyes, we risk being seduced by advertisers who want our curriculum dollars.

In my case, blinders might be an even better option than open eyes! Nobody contradicts me when I say I'm a stimulation junkie. The exhilaration I feel upon entering a curriculum fair is an almost intoxicating experience. I love to look at new things and explore new ideas, and the possibilities inherent in the products on display are so tempting! Blinders would be a blessing.

One aspect of the abundant-choices problem for me is my passion for the printed word. I love to read, study, and research. Part of what attracted me to homeschooling was the educational challenge: relearning facts and skills I had forgotten, figuring out how children learn, determining ways to motivate them.

Libraries and bookstores are among my favorite places. I often browse at the library for my special time alone. The realm of ideas is tremendously exciting to me, and the easy availability of books and research tools can be my downfall. Being a homeschooler requires a measure of self-discipline and decisiveness; I cannot read and digest every available book about homeschooling, much as I may want to. I cannot try and test every new idea. There simply isn't time.

Part of my problem is my notion that the answers to life's questions can be found within the pages of books. I still sometimes cling to this mistaken notion. When I decide to lose weight, I read ten books on the subject rather than simply cutting back on what I eat. When I have a behavioral issue with my children, I read what all the experts say about the problem. When studying a particular book of the Bible, I read everything I can find that others have written about it—rather that studying the book myself and allowing the Holy Spirit to reveal himself to me.

Books are fine. But don't make them the exclusive source of answers to your questions. Pray for wisdom, and let your choices be guided by the

Holy Spirit and the one book that truly matters, the Bible. When it comes to life and learning, God is the true expert. With his Word as our basis for research, we can more wisely navigate the book aisles and curriculum catalogs—and make other choices that affect our lives as homeschoolers.

Finding Guidance

God has provided us with expert advice with regard to the teaching and training of our children:

- Ephesians 6:4 tells us to "bring them up in the training and instruction of the Lord."
- Deuteronomy 6:6-9 tells us to impress God's commandments on our children, to "talk about them when you sit at home and when you walk along the road, when you lie down and when you get up."
- Psalm 78 is an entire psalm of instruction, admonishing us to "tell the next generation the praiseworthy deeds of the LORD, his power, and the wonders he has done" (verse 4).

We are to do these things in a way that may be distinctly different from the world's way. Jeremiah 10:2 admonishes, "Do not learn the ways of the nations." Rather, we are told, "Set your minds on things above, not on earthly things" (Colossians 3:2). Our goal is children who grow in wisdom and stature, with the grace of God upon them (Luke 2:40).

For more specific guidance to help you find the curriculum that best meets your family's needs, consider the following resources:

- *Other, more experienced homeschoolers.* You can learn more from a curriculum night at a homeschool support group meeting than homeschoolers of previous generations could learn in a month of study. If you're unfamiliar with support groups in your area, you can locate one through *The Teaching Home* magazine,

www.teachinghome.com, 503-253-9633, or the Home School
Legal Defense Association, www.hslda.org, 540-338-5600.

- *Books.* You had to know a book or two would make my list! My
  favorite is Cathy Duffy's *Christian Home Educator's Curriculum
  Manual* (Westminster, Calif.: Grove Publishing, 2000). Volume 1
  is a guide to curriculum for kindergarten through sixth grade;
  volume 2 covers junior and senior high school. Duffy not only
  reviews various services and products, she also talks about which
  materials fit which learning styles (see chapter 4). Her ideas
  about how to match up your family's variables with particular
  curriculum choices is invaluable.

- *Internet sites and message boards dedicated specifically to curriculum
  reviews and opinions.* Keep in mind that when you read articles or
  posts here, you are hearing someone's opinion. Still, it is helpful
  to see how materials have been used in real settings with real children. Some sites I've found helpful:

  1. Jon's Homeschool Resource Page at http://www.
     midnightbeach.com/hs

  2. Eclectic Homeschoolers at http://www.eho.org

  3. Crosswalk: Home schooling at http://www.homeschool.
     crosswalk.com

  4. Homeschooler's Curriculum Swap at http://
     www.theswap.com

  5. Christian Homeschoolers Forum at http://
     www.gocin.com/homeschool

Whatever curriculum we choose, we will be teaching our children both
skills and *content.* Skill-related subjects, like reading, writing, and math,
continually build on prior knowledge and must be approached in a certain
order. Content subjects, on the other hand—like science and history—can
be studied in any order. Most scope and sequence charts, year-to-year

listings of all the topics covered in major subject areas from kindergarten through twelfth grade, contain quite a bit of repetition. If some aspect of history is not covered in second grade, you can rest assured it will be revisited in junior or senior high school.

Rather than focusing on specific content at any given time, focus on teaching your children to be independent learners. Our academic goal is to give them an overview of knowledge in some areas and concrete, definable skills in others. The body of knowledge is growing at such a staggering rate that none of us will ever learn everything there is to learn. If our children know *how* to learn, they will be prepared for any test life throws at them.

Don't Forget Your Relationship

Sometimes I catch myself thinking, *If this material were presented differently, my children would pay more attention*, or *If the publisher had done a better job, my kids would be excited about learning*, or *If I'd chosen a different curriculum, my children would be learning more*. But to be honest, when my children aren't learning, it's more often the result of some short circuit in my relationship with them than it is a flaw in the curriculum.

Learning, at its essence, is about relationships. Your child may learn to read from a spiffy video program or from homemade flash cards and library books. The specific teaching methods you choose to employ are a matter of personal preference, availability of materials, and style. Whether you use modern technology or "old-fashioned" teaching methods, your child will learn to read. But will he or she learn to *love* reading? When it comes to communicating a love of language to your child and making him or her a life-long reader, your attitude toward books and your relationship with your child matter more than the methods you employ.

I used to worry so much about whether I was using the right "stuff." The longer I homeschool, the more apparent it becomes that learning isn't about stuff at all. It's about talking, relating, sharing, inspiring, and loving. It's also about my basic attitude toward learning and life. I want my children to learn godly character, good habits, research skills, and some specific material, but most importantly I want them to learn to love learning. If they learn nothing else from me, that's enough.

Practical Pointers for Making Curriculum Choices

- If you haven't already done so, create a family profile using the guidelines at the end of chapter 4. Use it to evaluate the appropriateness of any "must-have" curriculum for your homeschool. Remember that what's best for Suzy Homeschooler's family is not necessarily what's best for yours.
- Don't stress out about curriculum. The content of third-grade science will probably be pretty standard, regardless of the teaching materials you choose. The question I try to ask myself is, "What can I do with my children to cause them to love what they are learning?" Filling in blanks in a workbook probably isn't enough. The same information, however, when played with and lingered over, can become something wonderful.
- Don't worry about doing every problem in a workbook. If your child understands the concept, go on to something new. If later on he needs review, review. Likewise, don't lose sleep over getting through the entire science curriculum this year. Do what you can do. What you leave out now could make a perfectly wonderful summer project.
- Once you have chosen a curriculum, give it time to work. One bad week or even a bad month is not sufficient grounds to

condemn your materials to the used-curriculum fair. Rather, ask yourself if there is something you can do to spice it up or make it more meaningful to your child. Even the most mundane science discussion can be turned into an opportunity for experimentation, trying new ideas, or presenting findings in a creative way, such as building a project, writing a book, or making a display.

- Don't depend entirely on a curriculum. Take advantage of teachable moments that present themselves daily. Incessant questions may be annoying, but they present golden learning opportunities. One day at my house, we discussed the differences between the Republican and Democratic parties. That night, my older child asked me what a condom was. I was so grateful that my children were discussing these issues with *me* and absorbing our values instead of the values of the culture.

- Take advantage of community resources to enhance your children's education. Take them to museums and galleries. Enter their writing in contests. Scour your local newspaper for library programs and community cultural events. Take them on local history, art and architecture, or garden tours.

- Shake things up a bit. If your children seem weary of learning, if you're tired of doing the same old thing the same old way, consider the following suggestions to breathe new life into your homeschool, whatever curriculum you use:

  1. If you generally use traditional teaching methods, try a unit study or a delight-directed approach to learn something new. Ask your children what they would like to study.

  2. If you usually do unit studies, try using a textbook to cover the next portion of your subject matter. Your child's brain

may be ready for a change of pace, and you may need time to catch your breath between planned learning experiences.

3. Use or design games to teach the concepts you are studying. (My favorite resources for learning games are Peggy Kaye's books: *Games for Math* (Pantheon Books, 1987), *Games for Learning* (The Noonday Press, 1991) and *Games for Reading* (The Noonday Press, 1995).

4. Make a time line and base your studies on periods of time.

5. Look for new ways to have your children present what they have learned. If they usually write papers, have them make a poster, video, or banner. Encourage them to put together a newspaper covering a particular topic as the day's scoop. Consult Dinah Zike's two books, *The Big Book of Books* and *The Big Book of Projects,* for hundreds of creative ways your children can present materials. (Contact Dinah-Might Activities, Inc., at P.O. Box 690328, San Antonio, TX 78269. Phone: 210-698-0123)

6. Read a favorite biography aloud, and encourage your children to read other biographies. *Hero Tales* by Dave and Netta Jackson is a three-volume set containing brief biographies of inspiring people, like Gladys Aylward, Martin Luther, and Mother Teresa. Other favorites of ours include *Brother Sun, Sister Moon: The Life of St. Francis* by Margaret Mayo; *Joan of Arc* by Nancy Wilson Ross; and *The Beggar's Bible* (the story of Bible translator John Wycliffe) and *The Bible Smuggler* (the story of William Tyndale) by Louis Vernon. Vernon also wrote about Martin Luther in *Thunderstorm in Church* and John Wesley in *A Heart Strangely Warmed.* All these books, as well as many biographies of famous Americans like George Washington and

Benjamin Franklin, are appropriate for all age levels and are available through Greenleaf Press, one of my favorite history resources (www.greenleafpress.com, 615-449-1617).

7. Hold a family science or history fair.

• Don't forget to take time out from curriculum just to have fun! Homeschooling is serious, hard work. It is an awesome responsibility. But it doesn't have to be *all* work. I have "fun" file folders, totally separate from my schoolwork files, for each month of the year. Into these files go craft ideas, party ideas, and recipes for seasonal goodies that I've found in magazines. (See the section entitled "Seasonal Savors" at my Web site: www. HomeFieldAdvantage.org.) When we're feeling creative (or *want* to feel creative!) or we're looking for ideas to make a gift for someone, we dip into these files. We are never at a loss for something to do. We also have something the children have dubbed "the magic closet" where we keep art and craft supplies. You might create a magic bag or a magic box if you don't have an entire closet handy—someplace to store paints and those Styrofoam egg cartons you intend to make into flowers some day. Keep art supplies and craft materials accessible for spontaneous creativity. Take the time to make your home a haven, not just a schoolhouse. Relax. Create wonderful, fun-filled, smile-provoking memories with your kids. Major in mothering and minor in the mundane stuff of life.

Remember, there is no best curriculum. What works for your homeschool will depend on what your family wants and needs. More important than any specific skill or content is that your children learn *how* to learn—and even more important, that they learn to love learning. Work toward that as your primary goal, and you can't go wrong with any curriculum.

CHAPTER SIX

Beyond Academics

Character and Life Skills Training

M y first two children spent their earliest years in a very child-
centered environment. My husband and I, as new parents, felt it
was our job to entertain them and make them happy.

As the oldest approached age seven, she could read just about any book
in the library—but she did not know how to dry dishes! We began to realize that we were not merely the cruise directors for our children's blissful
voyage through childhood. Their education doesn't stop at academics; our
job is to equip them for life.

In fact, one of the great privileges and responsibilities we have as homeschoolers is to see that our children gain the character they need to develop
good hearts as well as good minds and the skills they need to navigate
life with grace and aplomb—every bit as important as any geography,
trigonometry, or English grammar they might pick up along the way.

Character Education

"Character education is the missing link," write Dr. Raymond and Dorothy
Moore, the "grandparents" of homeschooling.[1] True, public schools have gotten

involved in character and values training in recent years. But in the interests of the separation of church and state (at least as interpreted by the current Supreme Court), such training has been carried out in a moral vacuum.

Values training without a standard is like an archer shooting off an arrow, having it land where it will, then rushing to draw a bull's-eye around the place where it landed. To an outsider, it might look as if these programs are hitting the mark, but in reality, they are hitting nothing. With only a toothless generic standard by which to measure good against bad and right against wrong, no wonder the Moores call character education the "missing link."

In our homeschools, however, we have the wonderful opportunity to instill in our children our own values. And if we use God's Word as the definitive standard for moral behavior, those values will be God's values as well. We need not settle for drawing in the target after we've shot the arrow. Our target is already drawn.

"The highest goal of teaching at its best is character education," write the Moores. "It is bringing to our children/students lessons of love [that] breed concern for others—putting [others] ahead of ourselves."[2]

What a difference from the lessons of American culture, which teaches us to look out first for number one! Success is measured in the world's eyes on the strength of our personal accomplishments, and those accomplishments become the measure of our character.

Our faith tells us what character really is: a measure of the Christlikeness in us. It is based not on our accomplishments but on our obedience. The world may tell us to visualize success and to garner the power of the universe to meet our goals, but as Christians, we know that true success is found in Christ: "My purpose," Paul wrote, "is that they [Christians] may be encouraged in heart and united in love, so that they may have the full riches of complete understanding, in order that they may know the mystery of God, namely, Christ, in whom are hidden all the treasures of wisdom and knowledge" (Colossians 2:2-3).

It's not that we don't want our children to achieve—of course we do. In fact, the child who has the advantage of the kind of hands-on character training we can provide in our homeschools "generally becomes a self-directed leader in his society," according to the Moores. "He knows where he is going and is not easily pressured by his peers."[3]

What we want our children to understand is that their accomplishments are the result of their faith, not their own strength alone. We want them to realize, too, that their value is based on the value God places on them, not on their own achievements. We are valuable because God values us and has special plans for our lives, whether or not the world thinks we are valuable. When we free ourselves and our children from the obsession to succeed in the world's eyes, we can all concentrate on helping others and finding ways to contribute to the world—a vastly different focus.

How Can We Teach Good Character?

For the Christian, good character encompasses the qualities of Christlikeness that come from a dynamic relationship with God. Scripture gives us many starting points. "His divine power has given us everything we need for life and godliness," Peter wrote in his second epistle. How? "Through our knowledge of him who called us by his own glory and goodness" (2 Peter 1:3).

Peter then listed the qualities we are to add to our character: faith, goodness, knowledge, self-control, perseverance, godliness, brotherly kindness, and love (2 Peter 1:5-7). "If you possess these qualities in increasing measure," he concluded, "they will keep you from being ineffective and unproductive in your knowledge of our Lord Jesus Christ" (verse 8).

Mastering these areas of character could take a lifetime! When we add to them the fruit of the Spirit from Galatians 5:22-23 (love, joy, peace, patience, kindness, goodness, faithfulness, gentleness, and self-control), we have a perfect outline for values training. If you really want to institute a formal character curriculum, God's Word is the best you could ask for.

Here's a simple way to develop a curriculum to help your children toward Christlikeness in their character:

1. Identify the traits you would like to see in your child.
2. Write a definition for each of those traits.
3. Find scripture related to each trait.
4. Find stories to illustrate each trait.
5. Find songs that relate to each trait.
6. Choose one trait at a time on which to focus. Discuss the trait (or lack thereof) in your family's everyday life. Encourage your children to practice that trait. Track their progress with charts and reminders. Reward the behavior.
7. On an ongoing basis, read biographies about people of good character.

Now that I've given you steps to develop an effective character curriculum, let me say this: It will be only as effective as you are. Character education is an interactive process between the parent-teacher and the child. It is more caught than taught. "It is *showing by example* that honesty, dependability, neatness, order, industry, and initiative pay richly," Raymond and Dorothy Moore maintain (emphasis mine). "It is teaching the equality of human beings by practicing the Golden Rule. It is demonstrating to children how to work and how to help, instead of waiting for things to be done for them. It is teaching them to feel needed and wanted and depended upon in order to develop a sense of self-worth."[4]

"I try not to categorize school into academics, Bible, and character issues," says homeschooler Beverly in Maryland. "God is a part of our whole life. We try to see his hand in everything we do, including academics." Indeed, in the stable, value-laden, Scripture-rich environment of the Christian home, we have the resources to raise children who will hunger to know and serve the Lord. The greatest work we do may be simply to be a good example. I've always been inspired as a parent and an at-home teacher by this anonymous poem:

I Caught Your Faith

I saw you stand
bravely for years
But saw no trace
of senseless tears

I saw you stand
calmly through stress
But caught no glimpse
of bitterness

I saw you stand
prayerful in grief
but saw no trace
of unbelief

Though you spoke well
of Jesus Christ
I caught your faith
watching your life.

As Christians, our faith is a part of everything we teach, live, breathe, think, and do. Character education is a way of life. Yet the temptation for some homeschoolers is to treat it as a subject that can be distilled in a one-hour lesson every day. We can talk about values, recite definitions, and quote Scripture all we like. But do our lives truly honor God? Do our actions follow our words? Are we Christlike in our treatment of others?

We develop character in our children as we serve as their role models and as we weave values training into everything we do. As we create an environment of love and grace where friends and family members interact with one another honestly, openly, and with integrity, we are a 24/7/365 example for our children to follow.

Nevertheless, there are some practical ways we can incorporate values training into our homeschool curriculum, even if we choose not to treat it as a separate subject. A simple starting point is to have your children copy Bible verses for penmanship practice. Talking about character issues as part of your Bible lessons is another natural. Kathryn, a homeschooler in New Hampshire, starts every day with a Scripture lesson based on what's going on between family members. "During that time we talk bunches about character," she says. "Sometimes we talk about the good character traits [we are seeing], other times the bad."

"Our reading program involves reading Bible stories," says Gayle, who homeschools in Texas. "I like to combine the Bible with academics whenever possible. Even math shows God's great orderliness of creation." She spends significant time on academics, but if Gayle sees her son's character slipping in a particular area, she has no problem letting academics go until that issue is resolved.

Ellen Stanclift, a Maine homeschooler, acknowledges the need for a strong academic program to prepare her children for higher education and adult life. But she also believes that academics without character is a lost cause. "A hugely successful but highly immoral child would not be a success to me!" she says. Ellen does follow a character curriculum, but she doesn't let it limit her; any time a character issue crops up, she addresses it.

Focusing on character education doesn't mean neglecting academics. Both are important to our children's lives. "By wisdom a house is built, and through understanding it is established; through knowledge its rooms are filled with rare and beautiful treasures" (Proverbs 24:3-4). Without knowledge, the house is empty. But without wisdom, there is no house. Build on the foundation of wisdom, then fill your children's minds with knowledge. To be successful in the ways we most want them to be successful, they need both.

Understanding Character Development

According to Dr. Kay Kuzma, author and child development specialist, character development in children follows a predictable pattern. Children under the age of two have little understanding of right and wrong, but between the ages of two and four, they begin to make decisions based on whether they will be rewarded or punished for a behavior. "The child is self-centered, and his primary thrust is to do what he wants to do," says Kuzma. "His decisions are based on whether or not he will get caught and punished."[5]

Sound familiar? Many times I have seen one or another of my children pause briefly before they take a particular action. I know exactly what they're doing: figuring out the probability of being caught!

Kids between the ages of five and ten are concerned with conformity. "They don't want to be embarrassed or made fun of," says Kuzma, and they make decisions accordingly.[6] Good role models and positive peer influence are crucial during these years. I'm always pleased when I see my children in this age group take leadership by making good decisions that other children emulate.

During the later school years, children develop their own internal moral code—not always rational in the eyes of adults—and become "almost legalistic" in following it, says Kuzma. "Children in this stage become very vulnerable to doing what authority figures tell them to do." What a respected teacher or an influential peer tells them may become gospel truth in their minds.[7] If they choose to dogmatically follow a positive authority figure, like a teacher, parents have less to worry about, but kids at this stage are just as likely to follow someone who doesn't have their best interests at heart—a dangerous situation.

Research indicates that children who have a strong religious background and find themselves in a restrictive environment tend to plateau at this level for the majority of their moral decisions, according to Kuzma. They seem stuck, unable to move on to a more sophisticated stage.[8]

The final stage of character development, to which adults aspire, is to "have an internalized set of moral principles to judge whether something is right or wrong," says Kuzma. "Individuals who make principled decisions consider questions such as: How will it affect others? What if everyone were to do this? What does God say about this behavior?"

If a child never develops an internalized moral code, Kuzma says, he or she "will be swept away by the various pressures: the pressure to win, the pressure to be accepted, the pressure for attention, the pressure for self-gratification, etc."[9]

Kuzma provides the following guidelines to encourage the development of good character in your children:

- Help them develop healthy self-images.
- Provide family standards.
- Encourage thinking about right and wrong when making decisions.
- Encourage them to make their own decisions and take responsibility for them.
- Allow them to shoulder the consequences of their decisions.
- Avoid controlling their every move.
- Don't shelter them from hardships.[10]

We have a tall order to fill in raising our children to be effective and productive Christians. But God is faithful. He gives us his divine power to accomplish his will. And in the loving environment of our homeschools, we have fertile soil to plant the seeds of godly character.

Life-Skills Education

A stool cannot stand on two legs alone. In addition to academics and character education, our children need training in life skills—the third leg on which a balanced homeschool program stands.

Life-skills education ranges from the mundane, like balancing a checkbook, to the sublime—developing a rich prayer life, for instance. Learning the skills necessary to navigate modern life in all its complexity will help our children approach adulthood with confidence and manage their careers, families, and homes with wisdom and insight. Teaching basic life skills is a way to prepare them for service to God both at home and in the workplace.

Consider these fourteen Maxims of Maturity as you plan this part of your educational program:[11]

1. Responsibility begins in small things. It's never too early—or too late—to expect your children to manage small responsibilities. Encourage your children to help out around the house, even if initially it creates more work for you; chores are the perfect training ground for a healthy work ethic. Brainstorm a list of age-appropriate chores and responsibilities and develop a systematic plan for teaching them to your children.

2. Getting along with others begins at home. There is no better place for teaching conflict resolution than the home (see chapter 9). You can also teach your children how to get along with others by having family rules and seeing that every family member follows them. Be sure they know the consequences for breaking the rules (see chapter 3). Learning good manners and etiquette in the relaxed, fun atmosphere of the home also will go far to making your children both personable and employable.

3. Everyone lives somewhere—and everyone needs to take care of that somewhere. Home should be a place to nourish ourselves and others. Make activities such as shopping, laundry, and cleaning a part of your children's everyday life. Their future spouses and employers will bless you!

4. Getting along in a great big and sometimes uncertain world requires life navigation skills. These include everything from learning to read a map to knowing the proper way to answer the telephone. Unfortunately, in this day and age, it also includes learning skills for keeping safe on the streets, handling improper touching by a stranger or relative, and guarding personal information from strangers in person or over the Internet.

5. We are given only a certain amount of time; we have to use it wisely. You can teach time organization by modeling the wise use of your own time and by helping your children manage their commitments. Never before in our history have children been so busy yet felt so empty. The activities in which they engage should provide stimulation and education, and even more important, help them develop and nurture healthy relationships.

6. We all exist in a physical space; we need to manage that space efficiently. Space organization can help teach your children that wealth does not consist in things. We are good stewards of God's gifts when we aren't overly consumed with our possessions but take care of those we have.

7. Things break and need maintenance. Children learn home maintenance and repair skills by spending time alongside mom and dad as you take care of the house. The more you teach them, the more self-reliant they'll be when they leave home.

8. Much of life involves money; either we learn to handle it or it will handle us. Teaching children the value of money must be intentional. Perhaps you will choose to give your children allowances with which to manage the expenses of their lives. You can teach them comparison shopping and wise consumerism by taking them shopping with you. They won't learn how to handle money if they never get to handle money, even if they make mistakes.

9. Each of us has only one body; we have to take care of it. Healthy bodies and healthy minds go hand in hand. Children need to know what's good for their bodies. According to the American Dietetic Association, the number of overweight children in this country has more than doubled over the last three decades.[12] By making wise choices when it comes to meal planning, you can model a healthy lifestyle and provide nutrition that will help your children grow up healthy.

10. Our brains are valuable things; we must learn to make them work at peak performance. A healthy mind is one that learns effectively. Uncovering your children's learning styles and helping them learn effective study methods for those styles will improve their academic performance and their learning potential (see chapter 4). Help them set up a study area and a study schedule to get them in the habit of learning.

11. If God is not at the center of our lives, we will be unsatisfied. Even if your children are involved in your church ministry, good spiritual habits begin at home. If they see you praying and reading the Bible, they will take family devotions seriously. If you provide them with quality devotional materials and teach them to be quiet on the inside, they will have the foundation for a firm spiritual life.

12. The more decisions we make, the better decision makers we are. Encourage your children to make small decisions from an early age. (Does Johnny choose to play with the red truck or the yellow truck?) As they grow older and life becomes more complicated, teach them to list their priorities and think about the pros and cons of any decision. If you can teach them to make good decisions when they are young, they can use the same skills to make wise decisions when the stakes are higher.

13. Life is a creative exercise; we need to develop and nourish our creativity. Whether your children end up artists or accountants, they will need to be creative. By instilling an appreciation for creative skills, we will give our children an outlet for creative expression and a chance to contribute something beautiful and personal to the world.

14. Rejoice and be glad—this day is all we have! This is the day the Lord has made—celebrate it! You can teach your children to celebrate life by embracing life yourself, by letting them see you live a life that you love. Teach them by your words and actions that life can be joyous. What better legacy can we give?

For specific ways to develop basic life skills in your children, refer to my earlier book, *Life Skills for Kids*. It's filled with practical ideas. Another great resource for life skills education is *Training Our Daughters to Be Keepers at Home*. (Unfortunately, I know of no similar resource for boys.) This book is a huge, beautiful volume, comprising a seven-year program with day-by-day lesson plans to teach homemaking skills. Designed for girls ages ten to eighteen, it is a complete course in godly womanhood, sewing, cooking, caring for the sick, making a house a home, gardening, family finances, knitting, and much, much more. A few supplemental volumes are required each year, but the book itself is over 600 pages, making it a great resource for moms and their girls. The book is available from Smiling Heart Press, P.O. Box 208, Fossil, OR 97830.

Extracurricular Activities

It seems ironic, but sometimes the hardest thing about homeschooling is staying home. I could plan an outing for each day of the week if I chose to. Scouts, AWANA, Pioneer Girls, 4-H, sports, co-op enrichment classes…

It's not a matter of choice—it's another case of too many choices! (See chapter 5.) In my life, the largest impediment to learning anything in depth has been having too much of a good thing: too many options, too many resources, too many dreams to chase. When we give our children too many choices, they will never really become masters of anything; to do any one thing well requires attention and time.

Juggling a busy schedule of extracurricular activities also adds complexity and stress to both your life and your children's. You don't need that! Many activities available for Christian homeschoolers are healthy and wholesome, but *too* many can be counterproductive. I've learned the hard way that sometimes the best use of free time is to stay home.

My husband and I have found it helpful to ask whether an activity offered outside the home could be pursued at home instead. If so, we don't need a group and a schedule and a carpool to enrich our children's lives with that experience. On the other hand, if an activity is something that would be difficult for us to provide at home, we consider it. Some reasonable outside activities I've added to our home activities include piano lessons and gym class with our homeschool co-op; I neither play the piano nor possess athletic ability, so I must rely on outside sources for these things. Carefully chosen, these adjunct activities enrich our whole program, rather than merely placing stress on our family.

We also evaluate extracurricular activities in terms of their impact on our family. Dr. James Dobson in his pamphlet *Fatigue and the Homemaker* notes that "crowded lives produce fatigue—and fatigue produces irritability—and irritability produces indifference—and indifference can be interpreted by the child as a lack of genuine affection and personal esteem."[13] Looked at from this perspective, some of the enrichment we seek to provide for our children can actually make them feel unloved!

Cutting back on outside activities, however, doesn't necessarily mean you leave your children to their own devices at home. Guess what? If there's a television in the house, they'll watch it. And if they're not allowed to watch it, they'll whine!

Children need free time. But they also need ideas for ways to fill their free time. Provide them with quality materials: educational computer games and videos, good books, craft kits, art materials, even interesting "junk." Allow them free access to these tools. I guarantee, their whining and complaints of boredom will diminish.

Keepers of the Faith is a unique family ministry that offers ideas for the productive use of free time as well as teaching tools. Project booklets for girls *(Keepers at Home)* and boys *(Contenders for the Faith)* provide suggestions and milestones for mastering skills such as needlepoint, gardening, and cooking for girls, and models, pocketknives, and electricity for boys. (My girls have completed projects from each of these booklets, by the way.) Both programs provide ideas for such things as showing appreciation to grandparents and memorizing scripture.

Although these books do not teach skills per se, they provide checklists and ideas for mastery of skills. We have used them as guides for learning many skills. An accompanying volume, *A Parents' Guide to Productive Pursuits and Practical Skills for Children,* gives parents ideas on teaching and encouraging children in skill areas. Keepers of the Faith also has a complete catalog of instruction books and kits to accompany the projects, although you could do most of them with library books and some materials from the craft store.

Motivating and extremely reasonably priced, these materials have proved a valuable resource for engaging free-time activities. For information, see the Web site at www.keepersofthefaith.com or contact Keepers of the Faith, P.O. Box 100, Ironwood, MI 49938-0100. Phone: 906-663-6881. E-mail: folks@keepersofthefaith.com.

Too much activity, even valuable activity, leaves little time for children to explore their interests and chase their daydreams. In my own life, busyness crowds out my relationship with God and with others. It definitely leads to my irritability. Is it worth it? For a homeschooler to have every hour overbooked misses the point and stresses everyone. Schedule free time—for your children's sake and for your own! Provide them with resources, let them loose, and watch them bloom.

Practical Pointers for Character Training

- Use holidays as opportunities for values education and to teach cultural mores. Don't stop at celebrating Christmas; keep Advent, become familiar with the Jewish holidays, learn about Kwanzaa and the Chinese New Year.
- Study genealogy and make a family history book.
- Foster intergenerational friendships.
- Read hero tales from the Bible to your children.
- Read stories and books about Christian heroes, available in Christian bookstores or sometimes at your local library.
- Read other value-laden books, such as William J. Bennett's *The Book of Virtues.*
- Share experiences from your own life, especially the dilemmas and hard choices you've had to make. Your personal stories are powerful!
- Create object lessons about character issues from your child's Sunday-school curriculum or from your own imagination.
- Talk to your children about hypothetical situations related to character traits you want to foster. Have them role-play possible scenarios in which they might have to make a moral choice.
- Learn and sing the old hymns of the faith.
- Give your children a concrete way to minister to the world. Bake cookies for a neighbor. Make regular trips to a nursing home to visit with the residents. Children need a way to develop a vision for serving others. The best way to do this is to have them see *you* reaching out to others.

- Encourage your children to participate in missions projects through your church.

Academics are only the beginning of what our children will need in order to successfully navigate adulthood. Homeschool provides an ideal environment to instill godly values and teach basic life skills to our kids. For many of us, the unique opportunity to provide our children with this kind of training is the reason we've chosen to teach them at home.

CHAPTER SEVEN

The One-Room Schoolhouse All Over Again

Teaching Multiple Ages

Mary manages multiples. That is, she has four children at four different levels of homeschooling. And, yes, when you're doing that, *manages* is the right word!

"My oldest is in high school," Mary reports. "She's juggling a pretty full load, and of course her subjects are separate from the younger children."

Her next two are in eighth grade and sixth grade. "They each use a different packaged curriculum because the same approach didn't work for these two," she says. So in addition to her high schooler, she supervises two additional levels of Bible, history, science, math, and language arts. "The sixth grader is studying French, while the eighth grader has a passion for Spanish," she adds.

Then there is the first grader. "He's taking a while to learn to read," Mary says, "so schooling him is time consuming."

And Mary wonders why she's so tired!

The worst year of homeschooling Mark and I ever had was the year we tried to do a full-blown, individualized program with each child. Each had a separate Bible lesson, a separate math lesson, and different topics in science and every other subject. I would dart from one child to the next, answering questions, teaching a snippet of a lesson, all the while trying to take care of the baby's needs. (The baby wasn't very stimulated or enriched that year. In fact, he was barely noticed!)

That year was unsatisfying and frustrating for all the children, and it was exhausting for me. I began to ask myself, "What am I trying to accomplish here?" and "Is this method really the best for our family?"

If our goals were to foster a love of the Lord and a love of learning, we were missing the mark. The children were only minimally interested in their lessons or in developing their relationships with God. I was so focused on getting everyone's work completed that I was skimping on my role as mom. I didn't feel very loving, and I didn't have the time to do all those little extras that a mom does to make a house a home.

Moms are often called upon to be multitaskers. My husband once told me that watching me work through my day was like running Windows 95 on the computer. The number of tasks I could juggle at the same time was staggering. But both Windows 95 and the ability to multitask are tools. We need to ask ourselves what purpose the tool is meant to serve.

Handling the challenge of teaching multiple ages is a juggling act. If we can accomplish the task with patience and grace, we will be teaching our children much about managing stress and dealing with conflict.

Guidelines for Managing Multiples

There are no easy answers to teaching a number of children of different ages in your homeschool. But consider the following ideas to make your task easier:

1. *Remember your focus.* You're where you are in your life because you're committed to loving and training your children. Always keep those priorities at the forefront of your heart and mind. Our call as moms and homeschoolers is first to love and then to teach.

2. *Work on obedience first.* You can't teach your children to read or do anything else if they won't obey you (see chapter 3). Are you "wasting" school time if you spend a week or two weeks or a month establishing rules and consequences for your children's behavior? It may feel like time spent falling behind, but you will save yourself many hours of correction time in the future. Any attempts to teach skills and content without first addressing obedience will certainly meet with frustration.

3. *Recognize that every day will be different.* I'm amused when people ask what our typical day is like. The only constant in this endeavor is the love of our faithful God. What works this semester may not work next semester. What works today may not even work tomorrow! Young children change and grow so quickly, and every change in age and ability level shifts the equilibrium of the whole family.

4. *Set a flow to the day—a sequence, not an exact schedule.* If the children know they always do certain things in a certain order, it doesn't matter if that order is followed from a 7 A.M. rising time or a 10 A.M. rising time. Have the children help design the flow of the day. (Most families find that the more rigorous academic subjects are best tackled in the morning when everyone is at his or her best.) Chart the sequence out on a poster, and have the kids decorate it with markers and stickers. When they are part of the planning, they will more likely stick with the program.

5. *Set a yearly schedule that makes sense for your family.* Even if your state requires 180 days of instruction per year, there are several ways to accomplish this:

- Teach twelve weeks, then take four weeks off, or think of it as teaching three months and then taking one month off. The months of April, August, and December seem to be the most popular "off" months for homeschooling families who follow this schedule.

- Teach six weeks, then take two weeks off. This gives you six two-month blocks in your school year.
- Teach three weeks, then take one week off each month. This works particularly well for families with lots of little ones. It's also good for new homeschoolers; knowing you have that week coming up to catch up, clean the house, and plan can keep you from feeling too overwhelmed.
- Teach forty-five four-day weeks, and enjoy three-day weekends and seven weeks off per year whenever you want them. The four-day week works very well, giving the family a weekday for running errands, going on regular field trips, or heading to the library.
- Don't forget to brainstorm possibilities for dad's involvement in your homeschool. If he commits to teaching science two evenings a week or to covering the day's Bible lesson after dinner, it will have an impact on the flow of your day.

6. Take turns with each of your children. Work with each child a few minutes at a time while the others do individual work or play quietly. Organize your physical space so you can move easily from child to child. One season we arranged three desks in a sort of triangle, and I moved quickly from one child to the next inside of it.

A big problem for us is children who goof off while mom is working with another child. Make sure your children know what they are to do while they are waiting for you. For a time, we posted a chart that read:

While waiting for Mom, I may

- move on to another problem in my current assignment,
- read a book for a book report or school project,
- do work for another subject.

Your children need to learn to take turns. This is a character issue involving self-denial. "The 'raw material' with which [parents] begin is thoroughly selfish," notes author, speaker, and worldwide mentor to many, Elisabeth Elliot. "They must gently lay the yoke of respect and consideration for others on those little children." She goes on to say that "the earlier the parents begin to make the laws of order and beauty and quietness comprehensible to their children, the sooner they will acquire good, strong notions of what is so basic to real godliness: self-denial. A Christian home should be a place of peace, and there can be no peace where there is no self-denial."[1]

Remind your children that in a traditional school classroom, they would be competing with thirty other kids, instead of just one or two, for the attention of their teacher.

7. Encourage independence. Children can begin to learn independent skills at a surprisingly early age. Even very young children can play alone for a time. Give them the tools they need to work alone. Go slowly, first giving them five minutes to work without you, then gradually increasing that time.

8. Consider a season of split scheduling. With older children and babies in the same family, a split schedule might work. One mom splits up her week this way: Her seventh grader does school three days a week and her third grader and kindergartner the other two. On the days that the younger ones do school, she works with the kindergartner for about an hour and with the third grader for two to three hours. This way she can concentrate on one child at a time, and the others keep the baby and preschooler occupied while she is teaching. Assignments that can be done independently, such as reading and penmanship, are given for homework and must be completed on the child's own time by the next school day. She begins every day with group prayer and Bible reading for all the children.

This schedule may not work if you have children learning to read. I have found that phonics and reading must be reviewed every day in order for the child to see real progress in his or her skills.

9. Set up a system of accountability. Having assignment sheets and checklists made up for every child can help ensure that independent work is completed on a daily and/or weekly basis. Spend time together in the morning on prayer, individual instruction, and the introduction of new material. Then dismiss your children to work on their independent assignments. Allow them some choice in how they approach their assignments. Some may choose to do the hardest subjects first, then the easier ones. Some may do a week's worth of work in one subject in a single day, then work on a different subject the next day. After lunch, check over each child's assignments. Make time for your children to get some physical exercise, and then have them complete the work they didn't finish in the morning.

Some families have the children be accountable to their dad. In the evening, he corrects papers and checks that all assignments are completed. This system works well if you have an older child who is bucking your authority.

As your children get older, continue to place the responsibility for learning on them. Increase their sense of control over their education. Help them set their own goals for the week. If they are involved in the planning process, they're more likely to cooperate.

Have your children correct their own work and track their progress. For example, a child can graph his reading comprehension workbook scores or chart the scores on his or her math quizzes in your record book. Talk to your children about their learning strengths and weaknesses, and decide together what work they can do on their own and what they need your help with.

If you use assignment sheets, include a daily quality-control checklist.

Have your child answer these questions: Was my work done on time? Did I check it over for errors? Did I do it neatly?

10. Study the same subject matter, adjusting the material for ages. "One of the things I learned when I was teaching public school is that even in a class of thirty children with birthdays within a few months of one another, there [were] academic differences," shares Ellen, who now homeschools two children who are two years apart. "I work with [my] children individually for language arts and math, and we teach the rest of the subjects together, with both children gaining the appropriate lesson for their age and grade."

This method works especially well for Bible, history, and science. Use a book or appropriate text geared for the oldest child as your primary resource; supplement it with other materials from the library. For example, a fourth-grade science text will probably cover insects. Read the text out loud to all your children. Have them answer the study questions orally, requiring more detail and accuracy from your older children. All the children can participate in lab activities or experiments to go along with the unit of study. For the younger children, find easier nonfiction books on the subject at the library, or provide coloring sheets related to the subject for them to work on while the older children do more in-depth work.

Tina Rice, who homeschools in Montana, teaches history, Spanish, and science to all her children together. She starts out simply enough that the youngest can understand, then leaves that child with an assignment at his or her level while she goes further with the rest of the children. "It's like being on a bus," she says. "We all start out together and the youngest gets off first, and then off goes the next."

Many homeschoolers read to all their children from the same read-aloud book. "They all like to listen," a homeschooling mom in California says. "I don't care if they play while I'm reading to them as long as they're in the same room."

11. Use packaged unit studies. If time is at a premium (which it often is when you have several children), use packaged unit studies to involve all your children in the study of a single topic. You'll want to purchase study materials to correlate with all their ages. KONOS is one publisher I can recommend.

12. Use curriculum that doesn't require major preparation on your part. My friend Denise takes this approach. "Once my kids reach seventh grade, they use A Beka Academy Video for Home Schoolers," she says. Because I love to read, write, and research, I love the idea of writing my own program, but the reality is, I don't have time. The approach that has worked best for us is to use a prepared curriculum and supplement it with good books, relevant field trips, and appropriate experiments or art projects.

13. Don't be afraid to utilize good videos—in moderation! Your public library is likely to have several titles related to the subject you are studying. In addition, many fine movies have been made of great books. Watch the movie together as a family either before or after reading the book, and gain a deeper appreciation for the story.

14. Capitalize on your children's interests. A child who is captivated by a subject can be taken on a long learning journey with that topic as his or her vehicle. Although we use a packaged curriculum, when one of our children expresses a deep interest in something, we run with his or her interest until it has been satisfied. This has resulted in some delightful forays into music, science, nature, and art.

15. Make sure each child has some downtime. One homeschooling mom shares, "After a while, so many bodies in a group tend to get a little irritating.... I make sure to split everyone up for some time every day so we can have our own space. As an example, one goes to his desk in his room, one to sit on the trampoline and read, one to the dining room table for textbook work, and one to the computer. Later we come together again in a natural way."

16. Limit outside activities. Try not to do too much running around. With so many wonderful opportunities for homeschoolers, it is a great blessing to simply stay home! (See chapter 6.) I notice that we are more peaceful and focused as a family when we stay home more. Your kids don't have to do all things all the time. A season of intense activity, like swim season, might be followed by a more lightly scheduled season. If you try to maintain an intense schedule year round, your children and your program will suffer.

17. Save complex projects for later, when all the kids are older. Building a full-scale model of an Egyptian pyramid might be a little difficult with a two-year-old underfoot! You can catch that project later, when your kids are able to take more responsibility for the projects independently.

18. Everyone does chores in the homeschooling family. Clean laundry, well-prepared meals, and a presentable house are not just the mom's responsibility (see chapter 2). Some families set aside a time in the morning and in the afternoon to do chores. We have experimented with sending some children off to do chores while I worked with other children. That way, everyone was productive. This requires some planning on my part, however. I suggest making a graph like the one below:

	Mom	Grace	Clare	Caitlin	Dan
10:00-10:30	Work with Grace	Reading	Laundry	Work with Dan	Work with Caitlin
10:30-11:00	Work with Clare & Caitlin	Play with Dan	Work with Mom	Work with Mom	Play with Grace
11:00-12:00	Work with Dan	Clean room	Work alone	Work alone	Work with Mom

By devoting some time and thought to who does what when, you'll find it much easier to meet the needs of multiple children and maintain a semblance of order in your home. The schedule doesn't have to be rigid or inflexible, but it will give you a track on which to run your day.

19. Don't forget the joy of mothering! Consider trying to carve out some mommy time where you give your children your undivided attention simply as their mother. Don't fold clothes, wash dishes, or do anything else distracting; this is their time. Have a tea party with them. Join them with paper and crayons or Play-Doh. Take these few nonschool-related moments to really enjoy just being with your kids. These are the moments that make memories.

20. Teach the children to help one another. Even a seven-year-old can tutor a five-year-old in reading or play an educational game with him or her. I sometimes give my nine-year-old the worksheets from my kindergartner's curriculum for the two to work on together. This tactic encourages closeness between siblings and gives the older child confidence in his or her burgeoning abilities. Following is a list of ideas for activities for younger children, including ways your older children can keep your preschoolers busy while stimulating their brains.

Preschool Learning Activities

- Save boxes. An empty box can be a house, and several can be a train. For a special treat for a younger child, call around to find some appliance boxes. A refrigerator box and a range box can become a castle in a kingdom.
- Provide a Pringles can or a formula can for a child to plink plastic chips into, or supply frozen-juice lids to toss into larger cans.
- Keep a riding toy or two in the house over the winter. These are great to deal with excess energy. We also picked up a small trampoline, a tunnel, and a Sit-and-Spin at a garage sale and have left these out, along with a few large balls, in our play area.

- Provide a plastic knife, a variety of cookie cutters, and a garlic press along with a generous supply of Play-Doh. The garlic press is to make Play-Doh spaghetti.
- Use magnetic letters and numbers on a cookie sheet. When your child begins to master these, trace numbers and letters on index cards and create a matching game.
- Buy newspaper end rolls or butcher paper. Leave out a sheet and a few crayons all day for your child to color when the urge strikes.
- Put some water and liquid soap in a tub, and let your child wash some plastic dishes. An especially good idea when you need to mop the floor!
- In the absence of a sandbox, pour rice into a plastic tub and give your child sand toys to play in it.
- Give your child safety scissors and a stack of old magazines to cut up. Strips of stiffer paper are great for practicing scissors skills.
- Play some good music and show your child how to "conduct" the orchestra.
- Cut out bird figures from construction paper. Let your child decorate the cut-outs and hang them from the ceiling.
- Give your child a wide-mouth jar and some pennies. Let him practice dropping the pennies into the jar.
- Tape together two toilet paper tubes for a pair of binoculars. Give your child a bird book and station him at the window to bird-watch.
- Show your child how to make a paper chain. Use appropriate seasonal colors.
- Save empty food containers to create a "grocery store." Buy a plastic grocery cart, and your child will spend hours shopping.
- Start collecting magnets of all shapes and sizes. Store them in a box with paper clips, nails, and other magnetic items.

- Give your child a paintbrush and a bucket of water to "paint" your deck or sidewalk.
- Fill a container with large nuts and bolts for your child to take apart and put together.
- Make a half-dozen beanbags in various shapes. Let your child throw them in a bucket or walk with one balanced on his or her head.
- Draw a bird's-eye view of a city on a large sheet of butcher paper. Let your child play with small cars on the roads. I have also purchased an inexpensive fabric panel with a city street scene printed on it. It folds up neatly, and with a toy car or two my son can enjoy this activity in many locations.
- Show your child how to string necklaces out of Froot Loops and long, red licorice strips.
- Make lacing or sewing cards out of cardboard or coffee can tops. Wrap some tape around the tip of some yarn for a "needle."
- Plastic cups make great stacking toys. Have a supply on hand just for this purpose.
- Let your child make a tent out of couch cushions and bed sheets. Give him or her a flashlight and a picture book to enjoy in the tent.
- Give the junk mail to your child to open, cut, draw on, and destroy. Then recycle!

The Only Child

My friend Suzanne answered a survey for this book. Her response to the question about how to handle multiple ages and stages was, "I have an only child. God bless those who have more than one level to teach!"

Some parents, however, are hesitant to homeschool because they have only one child. They fear the child will be bored or lonely without the daily companionship of other children. But consider the advantages of teaching the only child. He or she will get all your attention, and you can both really enjoy the freedom that homeschooling offers. With one child, you can easily have your school day while you go on a picnic! You will certainly have the freedom to pursue that child's interests and passions to the fullest extent possible.

It is not terribly difficult to create situations for your child to be involved with cousins, relatives, or friends from support groups. Are there aunts, uncles, or grandparents who might be willing to work with your child on crafts or home arts? Do you belong to a homeschool co-op that offers classes and activities? By joining a support group or two, you will be able to find more activities than you can possibly do!

If you homeschool an only child, enjoy the challenge and the unique opportunity you have to develop a special relationship with your child.

Practical Pointers for Teaching Multiple Ages

- Remember, every day is new! Lamentations 3:22-23 assures us, "Because of the LORD's great love we are not consumed, for his compassions never fail. They are new every morning; great is your faithfulness." I believe God gives us new parenting/schooling mercy each day as well.
- Set a flow to the day—a sequence, not an exact schedule.
- Set a yearly schedule that makes sense for your family. Some families adhere to the public school schedule, but you are not required to do so.
- Work on taking turns. If you have more than one child, they cannot all come first.

- Encourage independence.
- Consider a split schedule: Attend to babies and younger children in the mornings and devote afternoons and evenings to more serious academic work with older children while the younger children are napping.
- Encourage accountability. Create checklists and assignment sheets uniquely tailored for your family.
- Study the same subject matter, adjusting for ages.
- Use unit studies.
- Use curriculum that doesn't require major preparation on your part.
- Utilize good videos—in moderation!
- Capitalize on your children's interests. Don't be afraid to deviate from your curriculum to satisfy a child's "need to know."
- Don't stuff too many extras into your day. Staying home is easier!
- Everyone does chores in the homeschooling family. Make work and responsibility a crucial component of your program.
- Teach your children to help one another.
- Don't forget the joy of mothering! The days of childhood are fleeting. Relax.

Teaching multiple children of different ages is a juggling act that requires patience, grace, and creativity. While it can tax us to the limit, it also provides unique opportunities for our children to exercise responsibility, independence, and self-control.

CHAPTER EIGHT

Evaluation

Setting and Meeting Standards
in Your Homeschool

I don't understand it," Sharon told me, clearly concerned, after our homeschool co-op meeting one day. "At home, my son reads so smoothly and easily. But you heard him today. When he got up to read his book report, he fumbled around like he didn't know what he was doing."

"Maybe he was just nervous," I offered.

"Maybe." She shook her head, unconvinced.

"If you're really worried, you should have him tested," I told her.

A few weeks later, Sharon greeted me at co-op with a bright smile. "You won't believe this," she gushed. "Ryan is reading three grade levels above his current grade level!"

"That's great," I congratulated her. "Nothing helps like a little confirmation that you're on the right track."

At times we all wonder if our kids are doing as well as they ought to be in our homeschool. Are they learning? Is their academic progress on track? Are they developing socially and emotionally? Are they growing in character? Are your teaching methods effective? How can you know for sure?

Gauging Academic Progress

Let's look at some of the ways homeschoolers evaluate their children's progress and their own teaching. You'll recognize some of the ideas below as gauges you already use, and perhaps you'll find other ideas to help you assess the effectiveness of your homeschool even more efficiently.

- *State testing.* Some states have required testing and provide printed learning objectives for each grade level. If you are in one of these tightly regulated states, these will help you get a good handle on your children's progress.

- *Standardized achievement tests.* Even if testing is not required by your state, some homeschoolers periodically test their children with achievement tests. Some of these tests can be administered by you at home, others require a qualified administrator. If you belong to a homeschool support group, ask your leader about the availability of standardized testing. The California Achievement Test is available from Christian Liberty Academy at 800-348-0899. Visit their Web site at www.homeschools.org for more information. For other testing options, contact Bob Jones University at 800-845-5731 or www.bjup.com.

- *Advisory teaching services.* Umbrella programs such as Calvert, A Beka, Christian Liberty Academy, and others offer, along with their curriculum, test-scoring and transcript-maintenance services for your child's academic career.

- *Report cards.* Many curriculum suppliers offer a report card form for you to fill out for each child. Parents-teachers base their children's grades on subject matter tests, oral evaluations, and other tangible factors.

- *Portfolios.* Some states require portfolios of all students—public, private, or homeschooled. Missouri homeschooler Trish keeps portfolios of representative work and also maintains subject-matter notebooks for each of her children. A portfolio shows your child's growth throughout his or her academic career.

- *Core Knowledge evaluation.* The Core Knowledge series is published by Dell Publishing and can be purchased in most major bookstores. For more information, visit the Core Knowledge Web site at www.coreknowledge.org. The seven volumes of *What Your Child Needs to Know* (one for each grade from kindergarten to sixth grade) serve both as guides to appropriate learning objectives and records of your children's progress.

Less formal ways to assess academic progress include personal observation and peer-group comparison, although the latter method is not universally accepted by homeschoolers. Barbara, who homeschools in Illinois, believes that looking at what your same-grade neighbor kids are doing in school is "a good perspective builder" and can help you make sure you are covering the material your kids will need for continued education. Minnesota homeschooler Vicki, on the other hand, tries not to compare her children's academic performance with children in traditional school settings. "I know from experience that grades in schools can mean absolutely nothing," she says.

In states where formal evaluation is not required, many homeschoolers rely on their own observations to gauge their children's learning. "I think that any parent who is close to her child can get an accurate picture of how that child is doing," says Ellen, who homeschools in Maine. "Progress is easy to see." So are a child's struggles, she says, giving the teaching mom a signal to slow down and work on any "trouble spots."

One California homeschooler asks "real-life" questions to evaluate her children's math level. For example, when she and her children are standing in line at a store to pay for an item, she'll ask the kids, "If we give the man twenty dollars, how much change will we receive?" She also listens to them read aloud and looks over the letters they write to grandparents to see where their grammar and spelling might need help.

Kate Theriot of the Homeschooler's Curriculum Swap relies on both observation and intuition to assess her children's learning. "My biggest concern is where my children are in relation to where I believe they can be," she says. "I pay attention to what they are doing, and I decide whether or not they can do better or are performing at their potential."

My friend Jana judges how her kids are doing academically by how they are handling their schoolwork, how well they are reading, and how much they are enjoying the learning process.

Evaluating Other Types of Progress

Most parents, including Jana, are even more concerned about their children's growth in wisdom and character than they are in academic progress. Jana gauges spiritual growth in her kids "by their grasp of spiritual truth and how they live out their faith," she says. A mom who homeschools in Nebraska says she evaluates how her children are doing by asking herself, "Are my children more godly than they were a year ago?"

New Hampshire homeschooler Kathryn notes that parents "always need to watch carefully the attitudes in which [their children's] schoolwork is being done." Character changes can be signals that adjustments in attitude or approach might be necessary, she says.

Listening to what others have to say can often be a telling reflection of our child's development, especially when we are too close to see. "I listen to what people say about [my children]," says a homeschooling friend from California. "For example, the other day someone commented on how polite they were. You know I was just glowing all over! I knew the time I'd spent instructing them on manners had paid off."

Famed educator and ardent homeschooling supporter John Taylor Gatto offers this advice for assessing your child's social development: "You can be sure your child is 'growing socially' if he or she is curious about all kinds of people, the details of their lives, their motives; you can be sure your child is okay if he can find pleasure, satisfaction, profit in talking to all different ages, responding appropriately to the challenges and opportunities presented by those older and those younger than himself. You can be proud of your child's social growth if he relishes responsibility and looks on work as a lovely thing instead of a mere duty; if he can be alone with himself for long periods without boredom; if he confronts his own cowardice with people unlike himself and is learning to swim easily, like some noble fish, in all human environments."[1]

You might also address the following questions, developed from a number of responses to my survey of homeschoolers, to gauge your children's health in emotional and social areas:

- Do your children have outside friends? Having no friends outside the family could indicate a problem.

- Do they need you less? Do they feel secure without having to be with you all the time?

- Are they becoming more independent, or do they depend on others for things they could do for themselves? "When you find yourself being responsible for your child's habits, work, cleanliness, etc.," Kate Theriot warns, "it's time to back off, establish firm consequences for not performing duties, and stick to [those consequences]."

- Are they making increasingly wise choices? Denise, who homeschools in Illinois, says we need to be aware of the way we are helping and hindering our children's ability to make their own decisions. We have to let them be individuals, give them choices when we can, and make sure not to "smother" them. "Let them make some choices, within limits, and live with the consequences," she says.

- What feedback do you get from trusted others? Missouri homeschooler Merre says, "I often ask my close friends to evaluate my interactions between my children and me and to tell me when they see problems developing. An outside, objective, honest viewpoint helps keep me on track."

One sign for me that my children are advancing appropriately in emotional and social areas is that I can watch them in social and work-related situations without being disappointed or embarrassed by their behavior or their level of maturity. (Of course, I *never* disappoint or embarrass them!)

Assessing Your Educational Program

Evaluating your children's progress isn't merely for you to know how your children are doing; it's also for you to gauge the effectiveness of your educational program. As you track your children's progress, take time to assess your program as well.

The best educational program is flexible enough to meet your family's and your children's particular needs. If you're doing something that isn't working, try something else. Read an article or a borrowed book about an approach that differs from yours, maybe something you've heard about that sounds intriguing. Examine your own educational baggage, too—your homeschool doesn't have to resemble Brother Leo's Latin class from your past. Take into account your child's learning style and your own teaching style. Celebrate the uniqueness of your family, and let your program reflect that uniqueness.

Sit down with your husband, and ask yourselves the following questions about your educational program:

- Have we chosen the best for our family, not necessarily the best as recommended by the experts?
- Are we keeping the big picture in focus—why we homeschool and what our goals are?
- Do we see progress, however slight, in our children's character growth?
- Are the children being productive? Do they cheerfully perform even the less exciting tasks?
- Does our home learning environment encourage each child to pursue his or her talent? Do we allow time in our schedule, for instance, for piano lessons and room in the budget for art supplies?
- Do we seek, as a family, to honor the everyday teachable aspects of life, such as preparing meals, doing chores, planning a garden?
- Do we allow the children free reading materials of their own choice? Are we paying attention to those choices to uncover life-long learning interests?
- Do we remember that learning is our lifestyle, not just what we do during the hours of our school day?

Another way to evaluate your educational program is to measure it against the vision you had for your children and family when you first began homeschooling—the pattern or blueprint you first set out to realize.

Would a builder lay the foundation for a house without having studied the blueprints? Would a seamstress cut her fabric without knowing what kind of garment she was making? They both begin their projects with the end in mind. The builder's blueprint and the seamstress's pattern serve both as inspiration and guide.

So too in our homeschool journey must we keep the end in mind. What is the finished product we desire? What do we want out children to be in maturity? If only accountants or actuaries, we might as well leave their education to professional trainers. But if we want to raise up adults who love learning, who seek to develop their unique talents and abilities, who hunger for the knowledge and fellowship of God, we must carefully nurture their minds and souls while they are young.

One reason Jesus lived a life in such balance was that he knew his vision. He knew he was about his father's business. He knew the role that the Father had called him to. He had a mission—and his actions were always consistent with that mission: "For the Son of Man came to seek and to save what was lost" (Luke 19:10). Everything he did was done to further that mission.

Can we say that of our lives? Do we know the role God has called us to play? Have we defined our mission as we train up our children?

When we first considered homeschooling, we had good reasons. Unless those reasons are fresh in our minds, we'll be hard pressed to know if we're meeting our goals! Revisiting our original vision for homeschooling is a valuable exercise to help us make sure we are doing what we set out to do. Perhaps you'll recognize some of your reasons in the list below.

1. Some families choose to homeschool to keep the faith. They view their calling as a matter of obedience to Deuteronomy 6:6-7: "These commandments that I give you today are to be upon your hearts. Impress them on your children. Talk about them when you sit at home and when you walk along the road, when you lie down and when you get up." Homeschooling mom Colleen says that her goal is "to raise children in the fear and admonition of the Lord who are educated, able to debate the basics of their faith, and can be an influence in the world around them." Kat, who homeschools in California, says, "Our goal is to have children grow up to live godly lives and evangelize the world for Christ." Texas homeschooler Gayle Ash agrees: "Our personal and specific goal for Stephen is that he will be a mighty man of God and a blessing to his people.... His education is designed to be a tool to serve God, something he can use to serve God and bless God's people."

2. Others choose to homeschool in order to preserve family values. Home-schooling parents get to spend the best (and the worst!) hours of the day with their children, which provides an opportunity to pour their values and beliefs into them. "One of the overriding goals for our homeschool is to promote family unity," says Beverly, who homeschools in Maryland. My friend Connie teaches her children at home because in a world "set up to keep the children's heart from the father and the father's heart from the children," homeschooling creates a bond between her husband and children. Kansas City homeschooler Grace and her husband find great joy and encouragement in being the primary vessels for transmitting values to the next generation. "It amazes me how far my family has come—their spiritual growth and the closeness they share with one another," she says.

3. Some homeschool as a way to take back responsibility for their children. Parents who choose to provide hands-on training for their children's growth and personal development value the responsibility God has given them in this area. When we send our children to school, we shift that responsibility to others who may or may not have their best interests at heart. Lily, an Oklahoma homeschooler, has chosen homeschooling as the best way to develop self-discipline and motivation in her children so they'll be able to be productive in any field they might enter. "Mostly, we hope to see our children grow into healthy, emotionally secure adults who are well equipped to make choices they're prepared to live with," she says. She sees her calling as an awesome responsibility she doesn't wish to delegate to even the most well-meaning of strangers.

4. Others homeschool to provide their children with an excellent education. If you educate your children at home to provide them with a uniquely tailored, superior academic experience, you are not alone. Georgia homeschooler Margaret Sanders, for example, has as her goal raising "confident, independent, respectful children with a love of learning and a good foundation in the liberal arts." Studies on the academic achievement of homeschoolers are impressive. In a *Wall Street Journal* article about how homeschoolers defy stereotypes, journalist Daniel Golden reports that homeschoolers have bettered the national averages on the ACT for the past three years running, doing particularly well in English and reading compared to their public-school peers. On the SAT, which began its tracking last year, homeschoolers scored an average of sixty-seven points above the national average.[2] Often, they achieve this level of excellence with less stress and less wasted time than their publicly educated peers.

5. Some parents homeschool their children for social reasons. The socialization of homeschooled children is the subject of great debate and speculation (see chapter 11). Some nonhomeschoolers view parents who educate their children at home as overprotective or even elitist. But many parents who homeschool believe children learn communication and relationship skills better in the age-integrated home environment than in an age-segregated, randomly socialized school setting. And, contrary to the popular belief that homeschooled children are socially reclusive, the National Home Education Research Institute reports that they are involved in an average of 5.2 activities outside the home.[3]

6. Others homeschool out of concern for their children's safety. In May 1999, the Josephson Institute of Ethics released data from a survey of twenty thousand middle and high school students concerning youth violence. Of the students surveyed, 47 percent of all middle school students and 43 percent of all high school students said they did not feel safe at school, and 24 percent of male high school students and 18 percent of male middle schoolers said they had taken a weapon to school at least once in the past year.[4] These survey results were obtained *prior to* the massacre at Columbine High School in April 1999. School violence is enough to give any parent pause.

7. Some families homeschool because they value the creative possibilities of a homeschool setting. Homeschooled children experience a freedom to explore that cannot be matched in any classroom setting, no matter how progressive. Parents are uniquely qualified to meet the individual needs of their children while expanding their horizons in limitless ways. In the homeschool, the joy of learning need not be subject to schedules or a prescribed curriculum. When my children wanted to study birds or weather patterns, they did not have to wait for the topic to appear in the curriculum. We have the freedom to follow their intellectual interests.

Whatever your reasons for choosing home education, you did so with a vision for your children and their future. Do you remember that vision? "Where there is no vision, the people perish," Proverbs 29:18 (KJV) tells us. Where there is no vision, the homeschool will perish as well. If you have not thought through your vision and written it down, take time to do that now. Ask yourself where you want to go, how you will get there, and how you will know you have arrived. As a family, create a mission statement—not a statement of family goals, which may change from one school term to the next, but a statement of the foundation upon which your goals will be based.

To help my own family easily remember our mission statement, we constructed it so that the first letter of each point spells out a word, SIDES. Here it is:

As a homeschooling family, we are committed to

Strength in family relationships
Intimacy with Jesus
Depth in spirituality
Excellence in academics and life preparation
Sanity in social and emotional realms

Those are the ideals to which the Field family holds. Our mission statement is the mark for which we aim in everything we do as a homeschooling family. What are your ideals? Whether you are a new homeschooler or are beginning a fresh season of homeschooling, take the time now to clarify and focus your reasons for doing what you do. You might want to refer to the biblical principles Dr. James Dobson lays out in his book *The New Hide or Seek,* principles that he calls "the key to God's value system for humankind: devotion to God; love for others; respect for authority; obedience to divine commandments; self-discipline and self-control; and humbleness of spirit."[5]

Having a vision for your homeschool and devising a mission statement that reflects your vision will keep you encouraged and on track. Hold any activity, book, educational approach, or teaching method up to your mission statement, and you will see clearly whether or not it hits the mark. If it moves your family toward your ideals, it deserves to be part of your homeschool. If not, it's time for a change.

Measuring Your Success as a Teacher

Forget the kids and the educational program for a moment. Do you sometimes wonder what kind of performance evaluation *you'd* be getting if the school principal dropped into your classroom for an unannounced visit or even a planned one? Every homeschooler wonders at one point or another if she is really cut out to be her children's teacher.

I am often told, "Oh, I could never do *that!*" when I reveal my status as a homeschooling mom. You've probably heard it too. The implication is that we're either superhuman or insane. If they only knew!

What *does* it take to be a good homeschooler? How do we know if we've really got what it takes? How do we know we're serving our children well?

One thing we know it doesn't take is a tremendous amount of education. In their helpful book *Homeschooling: Answers to Questions Parents Most Often Ask,* homeschool specialists Deborah McIntire and Robert Windham quote from the Home School Legal Defense Association's *Homeschool Court Report:* "Possessing a teaching credential is not a prerequisite to successful home education, and a parent's level of education is a minimal predictor of his or her success as a home educator."[6]

McIntire and Windham observe, "Obviously…a parent who is only semi-literate would have a difficult time teaching a child to master reading. On the other hand, it is not necessary to be a quantum physicist to succeed at home education. Our experience in a supervisory role with home educators has shown that parental commitment and love of learning are more important than years of schooling. We have seen parents with advanced degrees burn out after less than a year while parents with only a high school education successfully homeschool for years."[7]

When we homeschool, we pledge to be present for our children physically, emotionally, and spiritually. It is a huge commitment that requires, more than any special abilities or training, willingness to work, dedication, sacrifice, and a real desire that our children discover the joy of learning.

If God has called you to homeschool, he doesn't care whether you are highly educated. He cares that you are obedient to obey his call. If you obey, he will equip you. Don't worry that you don't have the necessary qualifications to teach your children. You have God's Spirit, who will teach you everything you need to know. "I will instruct you and teach you in the way you should go; I will counsel you and watch over you," he promises (Psalm 32:8).

God is the only "principal" to whom you are accountable, and if you are in obedience to him, you're doing fine. He guarantees it.

Practical Pointers to Gauge the Success of Your Homeschool

- Research the options for academic evaluation. Read articles in homeschooling magazines. Talk to other homeschoolers about what works best for them.
- Make sure you know what your state requires for academic evaluation.
- Use more than one form of evaluation, both formal and informal.
- Pay attention to indicators of your children's emotional and social development.
- Thoughtfully answer the following questions to clarify your vision for your homeschool:
  1. How do you view your children? To whom are you accountable for their upbringing? *Read Psalm 127:3.*
  2. What are you responsible for teaching your children? *Read Deuteronomy 6:6-9.*
  3. What is the purpose for which we have been given God's Word? *Read 2 Timothy 3:16-17.*
  4. Do you desire to place God first in your home?
  5. Do you value family unity?
  6. Can you provide healthy socialization experiences for your children?
  7. Are you equipped to handle the individual needs of each child?
  8. Do you value independent thinking and creativity?
  9. Do you want your spouse to be actively involved in child training?
  10. What goals do you have for your children? (For example, to

love God, to aspire to goodness and faithfulness, to acquire knowledge.)

11. What do you hope to achieve in your homeschool in the next year? in five years? in ten years?

12. How do you hope to achieve your vision?

13. How will you know when you have achieved it?

- Write a family mission statement based on your answers to the questions above. Your mission statement helps you define who you are, what you do, why you do it, who you serve, and what resources you are committed to dedicate to your work. Think of it as your family constitution. Use it to help you evaluate decisions and choose options.

- Relax and enjoy the privilege of the homeschooling journey. Remember that if God has called you, he will equip you.

Perhaps you've heard the old expression that says if you don't know where you are going, just about any train will get you there. As Christian homeschoolers, we know where we are going. Our primary goal is to raise godly children for God's glory and purposes. Along the way, we have the Bible as a spiritual touch point to help us see if they—and we—are hitting the mark. But we need some reference points in the world to evaluate their progress in other areas. Formal and informal assessments, portfolios, and the opinions of others can give us some of this crucial feedback.

PART III

family issues and the homeschool

CHAPTER NINE

The Family Circus

Quibbling Siblings and Tireless Toddlers

I don't remember now what the fight was all about. Knowing my daughters, I think it might have been something as simple and innocuous as a hiccup or an accidental poke.

I'd left my older children at the dining room table working on independent projects while I got my two-year-old down for his afternoon nap. Just as I tiptoed out of Daniel's room, the dining room erupted. I raced to the scene to find Clare and Caitlin faced off in the middle of the room, fists clenched and their faces red with fury.

"Girls!" I reprimanded.

"She slapped me!" Caitlin screamed.

"She karate-kicked me!" Clare yelled back.

"To your rooms, both of you," I told them firmly. "We'll talk about this when you've both calmed down."

Sound at all familiar? I know my daughters love each other, but sometimes their fights are downright hateful. They scream and claw like wild animals. The younger ones see the older ones going at it and follow suit. My son has been known to bite when he's frustrated, and my youngest daughter loves to bait her older sisters into a fight.

One of our goals in homeschooling is to encourage deep friendships among our children, but some days I doubt they will even be speaking to one another in ten years! Other times, when I see them playing or working together and actually enjoying themselves, I know with all my heart that the bonds they are forming now will endure into adulthood.

As a homeschooling mom from Nebraska puts it, "Friends will come and go, but family will always be there." From early on she's taught her children how important it is that they be friends with one another.

Homeschoolers have extra reason to nurture friendships within the family. Unlike most families, we spend all day together. Every day. We have to get along!

Teach Your Children How to Fight

Your children may not fully appreciate it now, but learning to get along with siblings is great training for marriage, employment, and just about any other endeavor they will ever set their hands to. Getting along with others is an essential skill for getting along in life.

For a healthy marriage, learning to resolve conflicts with siblings at an early age may be the most valuable training your child will receive, says marriage expert John Gottman, Ph.D. "A lasting marriage results from a couple's ability to resolve the conflicts that are inevitable in any relationship," he notes. "Many couples tend to equate a low level of conflict with happiness and believe the claim 'we never fight' is a sign of marital health. But I believe we grow in our relationships by reconciling our differences."[1]

Daily life with children presents many opportunities to practice conflict resolution. Learning to fight with self-control and respect for the other party may take years, but without a healthy example at home, it may not be learned at all.

"Any parenting plan needs to include ways for children to practice disagreeing agreeably," says counselor and author Dr. Bob Barnes.[2] Early training in conflict resolution teaches children how to negotiate and compromise, he says—again, good preparation for marriage. Then he goes on to tell how one family resolved an ongoing conflict between the parents and the children. The kids were constantly whining for treats and special goodies, always asking for more, more, more with no recognition that these things cost money.

The parents explained that ice cream cones and sodas add up over a month's time, and the family decided together to set aside a certain amount each month for such indulgences. The children had to agree among themselves on how and when to spend the money. Once the allotment was spent, by agreement of the parties, it was gone for the month. The children learned a great deal about negotiation and compromise from the exercise, and their parents didn't have to listen to any more nagging for treats.

Rather than teach children the art of fighting, parents too often intervene as mediators to solve problems between their children. A more meaningful approach, especially as the children get older, is to encourage dialogue to help them come to resolution on their own. "What's a better way to solve this problem?" you might ask to get them started. Then listen to them as they work it out. Stay available to offer helpful suggestions and to monitor the discussion, but put the burden for resolving their differences on your children, without expressing any interest in who's "right" or "wrong."

One way to help your children learn negotiating skills is to assign them a large chore, such as cleaning out the garage, and leave them to work out the division of labor. They are usually quite capable of coming to a satisfactory resolution, especially when mom and dad aren't butting in with suggestions.

Another good way to let your children practice compromise is to have them decide among themselves what television programs to watch. If you allow them an hour a day of television time, let them work out whose favorites take precedence on any given day. I'm a firm believer that children should never have their own televisions or computers; they miss out on too many wonderful opportunities to practice their negotiating skills!

Other things we have purposely done to encourage cooperation between our children may seem minor but have been effective in helping them learn how to negotiate. For example, lightweight scooters are all the rage with children today. We own one—and only one. This forces the children to take turns and work out getting their share of its use. On weekends, we have the children decide what activities they'd like to do, an exercise that requires discussion and sometimes compromise. Often we will buy only one copy of a book that more than one child wants or needs. Why? To force them to cooperate and negotiate the time they each get to read it.

In my house, having to share something with a sibling—whether it's the parents' time, a bedroom, toys, or clothing—can be a major source of conflict. Having to share requires children to negotiate and compromise. It also encourages loving and responsible habits and attitudes, such as acceptance, patience, taking turns, and leaving things in good condition for the next person.

The most significant friends we make in life are those who live with us. Other friends and acquaintances come and go, but your children will be siblings forever. Help them to be friends with one another as well.

Practice Kindness

Have you ever caught yourself in the following scenario? The kids are acting out, deliberately disobeying, or simply not doing what you want them to do. Maybe they've been trying you all day. You're tired, you have a headache, and you just can't take it any more! You let loose, yelling that if they don't shape up in the next five minutes, you're going to—

The phone rings before you have a chance to get specific with your threat. (Or maybe after.) You take a deep breath, pick up the phone, and are instantly sweet and charming to whoever is on the line, effortlessly putting aside your anger at the children. Once you hang up, however, you immediately launch back into your diatribe.

Do you know what you've communicated to your children, however unwittingly? That putting on a nice face for outsiders is important, but it's okay to be mean to one another in the home.

We're all human. We get tired, we get angry, and sometimes we say and do hurtful things. When I realize that I've been hypocritical, I ask God to forgive me. When I know that I've been less than kind to my children, I apologize to them. I can't expect them to be kind to one another if I don't practice kindness with them. Being kind within the home is just as important—no, *more* important—as being kind to strangers and others outside the home.

On their own initiative, our children have expressed great kindness to one another. I've seen one of my daughters make her sister, who wasn't feeling well, a get-well card. I've seen another purchase a little trinket out of her own money just because she knew it would make a sibling happy. My children are learning the joy that generous, unconditional giving brings. Believe me, when they exhibit that type of behavior, they receive hearty praise!

Children who gain the ability to set aside their own needs and reach out to help others in need are learning to be good citizens as well as good family members. But teaching children to be aware of the needs around them isn't easy. Dr. Barnes notes in his book *Ready for Responsibility* that this is true in large part because we are so busy communicating *our* needs to those around us.[3]

Learning to be sensitive to the needs of others begins in the home. Is there a sister whose feelings have been hurt? A brother who is unhappy because he feels his siblings have left him out? Those issues must be addressed, the relationships set right. In our house, in accordance with Ephesians 4:26, we don't let the sun go down on our anger. We never allow our children to go to bed with unresolved issues either between them or with us.

How can we encourage empathy and kindness in our children? Here are a few ideas:

- Assign pairs of children as "buddies" for a day. Have them play together or look out for each other on an outing. Or have them work together doing specific chores to encourage teamwork and bonding. For instance, an older and a younger child might work together on cleaning the room of the younger child.
- Teach your children to extend their kindness beyond the family. Is there a friend of the family they might encourage with a note or a flower from your garden? Is there some way they can minister to a church member who is ill or otherwise in need?
- Encourage your children to keep their own prayer/blessings notebook. They can record specific prayer requests for family and friends and also note special answers to prayer.
- Consider "adopting" an elderly church member. Visit him or her once a month with your children. Take flowers or a freshly baked treat.
- Make it known at your church that your family is available to minister to new mothers. Your older children can help you care for the family's children, and you can all work together to prepare meals or treats for that family.
- Get your children involved in planning birthday or other special day celebrations for one another. An eleven-year-old has more great birthday party ideas than anyone! Give her a budget and let her plan the games, goodies, and refreshments as an act of love for the younger sibling.

Encourage Teamwork

Being able to work with others as a contributing member of a team is a critical life skill and one that we have an opportunity to teach our children as we homeschool. One of the many positive aspects of having siblings is the "strength in numbers" factor. When children have a common goal and stick together in their efforts to achieve it, the likelihood of reaching that goal rises exponentially. If all my children agree they want to go swimming, for example, they are much more likely to get to go than if one or two want to go swimming and the others want to read or play computer games.

We are constantly stressing teamwork with our children. We make them accountable for one another. They know that if one person fails to do his or her part, all will suffer. At the community swimming pool, for example, the kids know they are to stay together.

"Now what are the rules at the swimming pool?" their dad asks on the way there, just as a reminder.

"Stay together and don't run," the children chorus.

"And what happens if you don't?"

"We have to leave."

"That's right," Dad says. "Remember, you're a team."

This approach encourages children to look out for one another and supervise themselves.

Younger siblings look up to older ones as role models. Make sure your older children are aware of their responsibility to their younger brothers and sisters. Encourage them to spend time with their younger siblings and treat them as special; they will have wonderful friends for life. But be sensitive, too, to the older child's need for time away from younger siblings. Seek balance. While we may truly need an older child's help with younger children, a tag-along brother or sister can be burdensome.

Ideas to encourage teamwork in your children:

- Have older children listen to a younger child read. A beginning reader takes up a lot of time. Share that experience with the siblings.
- Have play items all ages can enjoy, and encourage your children to play together. All of my children love LEGOs and trains and will frequently work together to make interesting structures.
- Encourage open-ended art activities, like drawing, that children of all ages can do together. There is no right or wrong way to create!
- Have your middle children work with the youngest ones. For example, your five-year-old can count blocks and sort them by color with your two-year-old.

Banish the Battle

No matter how hard you work at encouraging teamwork, fights are going to happen. Call it human nature. When sibling skirmishes erupt at your house, you're left with damage control. Try out the following ideas:

- If fighting between siblings appears to be out of control, separate them for a time to cool off. When tempers are calmed, encourage them to use dialogue to work out their conflict.
- If their fighting is disturbing others in the household, have them settle their conflict elsewhere. Our first house had a cramped, bare, kind of scary laundry room away from the rest of the house. When our children fought, we told them they would have to go to the laundry room to finish their fight. Somehow they always managed to resolve their conflict before they reached the door!
- If your children are equally at fault for some misdeed, have them hold each other's hand and serve a time-out together. When we

used this method with our children, they would complain bitterly—at first. But by the time their "punishment" was over, they would be giggling, once again good friends.

- Mark 3:25 tells us a divided house cannot stand. Build a structure with your children out of blocks, LEGOs, or other building materials. Then break it in half, illustrating the effect of their quarreling.

- If two children are chronically fighting, try this: Have them write out a list of all the things they are grateful for in the other sibling. Encourage them to make a poster or banner displaying this information to honor that sibling.

- Matthew 5:25 advises us to settle matters quickly with our adversary. Make it known that if your children resolve their squabbles quickly, the consequences for their misdeeds will be lessened.

- Finally, teach your children the principle of Matthew 18:15-17. Before involving other parties, make sure they speak first to the one who sins against them. Make them responsible for beginning the restoration process.

No Favors, No Favorites

One of the brothers in the old comedy duo the Smothers Brothers frequently complained to the other, "Mom always liked you best." In almost every family with multiple children, favoritism is a problem—if not in fact, then in the perception of one or more of the children. Barbara, an Illinois homeschooler, shares this insight: "Favoritism, I think, is often most present in the eyes of one who feels slighted. My parents treated the four of us individually, I don't think out of favoritism, but because each of us had different individual needs, personalities, strengths, and weaknesses. One of my brothers in particular complained of favoritism in his own disfavor, but he was always unwilling to behave in ways that earned him privileges that the rest of us had. In his eyes it was favoritism. In reality, at least to some extent, some of it was his own reward."

In every family, each child is an individual. Because this is true, treating every child equally doesn't mean treating each one the same. We may be looking for similar outcomes in our children as far as their spiritual, intellectual, and character growth; how we get there will probably differ from child to child.

Every child is unique, different from every other child. Different means different, not better. In God's scheme of things, there is no first place or second place or favored place. There is only the right place—the place he wants us for his divine purposes. He doesn't play favorites; he loves each of us equally and uniquely.

Montana homeschooler Tina has an ongoing opportunity to teach this concept as she struggles with her second child, who always feels left out and not loved enough. "It has taken patience, love, and prayer," Tina says, "but [my daughter] is finally learning to see herself through God's eyes."

It is easy to say we should celebrate our children's differences, but it may be difficult to practice. A homeschooling mom from Maine says, "My son taught himself to read at age four. My daughter is still learning at age six. She definitely feels the pressure to lean to read, and this upsets her. I try not to put too much pressure on her, but it's hard on all of us." Another homeschooler, Kim, shares, "My son is so very different from my daughter. We need to remind ourselves that God put a diversity of gifts into each person."

Says Kate Theriot of the Homeschooler's Curriculum Swap, "I recognize that as mothers we have different feelings for different children. When I feel a high level of affection for one particular child, I start thinking of each child separately and how much I love that child and his individual characteristics. That levels out the playing field of my emotions. But I never 'play favorites' that I'm aware of. If my kids tell me I am, I stop and look at the situation. Usually it's just a ploy to try to get me to give in to the one accusing me of favoritism. But I do try to watch how I respond to each one. I pay attention to my reactions, and I make sure that I don't give one child more affection or attention than I give the other."

Kat, a California homeschooler, provides another helpful perspective. "They all think we favor the other," she says, "so there doesn't seem to be an answer. But I try to look at things from their perspective, to under-stand *why* they think the other is getting favored." Kat also says that reminding her girls of the Golden Rule helps. She encourages them to stop thinking about themselves and think instead about what would make their sister happy. "This works most of the time," she says, "because they start treating the sister so well, they always get reciprocal behavior from the sister."

Sometimes I'm tempted to compare my children one against the other: One spoke clearly at an early age. Another is still hard to understand at the age of four. One read early. Another waited until she was over six.

Then I remember my own experience. I am from a large family, and we all attended the same elementary school and often had the same teach-ers as we progressed through the grades. As the youngest, I got compared to all seven of my siblings. "Your brother Don was much better in math," a teacher would tell me. Or, "Your sister Eleanor was a much better writer." I didn't need to hear those comparisons! In the end, we are all unique, each with our own gifts. We exhibit the marvelous diversity of our creative God.

I don't encourage competition between my children. Their talents and abilities are unique. Their gifts may not become evident until they are older, but the uniqueness is there from the beginning. I encourage you to let your children complement each other. Help them stretch each other in directions they need to go. Expect excellence from each child, but remember that each excellence will be unique.

Our only sure benchmark is the Word of God. Is each member of my family becoming more Christlike? Are we all growing into mature relationships with the Lord? That's the kind of progress I'm most looking for. It's the principal reason I choose to homeschool.

Toddler Tribulations

When my son Daniel was about eighteen months old, he had what I called an "annoyance circuit." He would make the rounds of the house, getting into one kind of mischief after another: pulling books off their shelves, trying to climb into the kitchen sink, putting objects in the toilet—including, once, a running hair dryer.

That summer at a garage sale I found a large dog cage that I couldn't resist for some future pet. In the meantime, I fantasized (and *only* fantasized!) about putting Daniel in the cage during the hours I was trying to teach the older kids. I even invented a name for this practice: CAGE (confined arena of gated enrichment). Homeschoolers do tend to have rich fantasy lives!

Sibling conflict notwithstanding, my older children were never the challenge to homeschooling that the babies and toddlers were. The younger ones' goal in life seemed to be to disrupt everything else I was trying to do.

When my friend Denise realized how much work a toddler added to homeschooling, she wondered if she'd made a big mistake to keep her children at home. "I cried a lot," she says. "I yelled at God because it was his idea to homeschool. I told him that he didn't know what he was doing. I'm sure I looked like an ant raising her fist into the air!"

In spite of the difficulties of homeschooling with little ones underfoot, my very little ones have taught me some of my most valuable lessons. They are a constant reminder that our house is first a home, then a school. They teach us to share. They remind us to practice flexibility. And they provide more that a few occasions of laughter and fun. For example, our son, Danny, loves to recite the Pledge of Allegiance. He holds up various objects and nags us until we recite the words with him. We have "pledged allegiance" to rakes and pencils and even to forks at the dinner table.

When interruptions from my littlest ones aggravate me, I have to ask myself, "Why am I here? To keep the house clean or to train my children?" These interruptions, if we view them properly, are really opportunities: for your child to have more of you and for you to learn much about patience, focus, kindness, and family cooperation.

Still, trying to teach a math concept or direct a science project with a little one constantly underfoot is challenging. How do we keep our older kids learning and our younger ones happy at the same time?

Homeschooler Kim, who has three younger children—ages three, two, and one—finds that the more occupied she keeps the little ones, the less trouble they get into. "After all," she quips, "it is a child left to himself who will bring his mother shame!"

Linda Dobson, author of *Home Schooling the Early Years,* uses what she refers to as "tactics of inclusion and diversion" to manage younger children during the school day.[4] To *include* my toddler while I'm working on long division with my older children, for instance, I might give him math manipulatives to play with. During a social studies lesson, I might give him a scaled-down art project or a picture to color that correlates with the older child's lesson. To *divert* him while I'm concentrating on an older child, I might allow him to play a computer game or watch a carefully selected video. (I do try to use that particular tactic on a limited basis.)

To give your younger children the attention they crave, make it a point to do something special with them first thing in the day. Perhaps while the older children are reading silently, you can play a game or put together a puzzle or read a story and snuggle with the littlest ones first. Then they'll be content, at least for a while, when you have to focus your attention away from them.

As for the rest of the day, plan for interruptions. Having an hour to do a project with your older children would be glorious—and is probably an unattainable dream for now. So count on working in fifteen-minute spurts throughout the day. Give instruction, then give the older children independent work so you can swing back to the younger children.

Barbara Fackler, a homeschooler in Illinois, remembers that when her son was younger, giving him something to do that he felt was important work kept him occupied for long periods of time. "Sometimes as a toddler he would work on solving mazes or sorting buttons by color for me," she says. "He stayed busy and felt helpful, and I had time to complete my own work undisturbed. Early on he learned that he could not be entertained all the time. We had scheduled times when he knew he was expected to play on his own, and if he had nothing he found interesting, I gave him a 'job.'"

Last year, when my son Daniel was two, we organized a number of his toys into five boxes. Each day, when the school day began, he got to choose one of these boxes to play with. He was excited to open his special "school boxes," and they occupied him for quite a while. As he grows older, I add developmentally appropriate items to each box. For instance, I recently marked a set of five index cards with one, two, three, four, and five dots and placed them in a bag with colorful plastic chips for him to match to the cards. He also has multicolored plastic bears to sort into colorful cups.

Another thing we did was make "Danny-Do Cards." Each card listed an activity that an older child could do with Daniel. They were simple but interactive and educational. For example, one card read, "Play 'Head, Shoulders, Knees and Toes.'" Another said, "Name the colors on the color poster with Daniel." I put fifteen cards on a ring and switched them around regularly. This idea worked splendidly! The older children enjoyed having something concrete to do with the two-year-old instead of simply being told, "Go watch your brother." Daniel benefited from the wisdom and knowledge of his older sisters, and I had a much smoother morning while trying to teach phonics to another child.

For ideas to include in your own version of Danny-Do Cards, consult June Oberlander's book for parents of babies and preschoolers, *Slow and Steady, Get Me Ready*. This wonderful resource provides 260 weekly developmental activities for children from birth to age five (Bio-Alpha, P.O. Box 7190, Fairfax Station, VA 22039). For example, at the twenty-week level, the timeless game of pat-a-cake encourages the baby's awareness of his or her hands. At the two year, forty-nine week level, helping the toddler practice pushing a ball with his or her foot is a developmentally appropriate activity. In the fourth and fifth years, in a relaxed manner, letter sounds and numbers may be introduced.

Here's a list of other suggestions to help you get through the school day if you have babies and toddlers to take care of as well:

- Designate a special play area near your homeschool classroom where your baby or toddler is expected to stay during school time. Keeping your little one there may be difficult at first, but ultimately, your child will appreciate the security of knowing what to expect during this time of day.

- Furnish the play area with special "school stuff" for your toddlers and preschoolers. You might fill a school bag with coloring books, markers, and special toys, for example, and allow your toddler to have access to those things only during school time.

- Fill inexpensive dishpans with children's board books, again accessible only during the school day. Your toddler can carry them around and be responsible for putting them away.

- Use nap time as prime instructional time with your nonnappers.
- Don't waste high-chair time. Confining a toddler to a high chair for a twenty-minute snack and coloring session might be one of the most productive times of day for your older children.
- Get a good baby carrier or sling and "wear" your infant. This keeps your baby close to your heart while leaving your hands free to help other children.
- Make wise use of gates and doors in your home to make certain areas off-limits during school time. Lots of children with access to many rooms make for confusion and anarchy!
- Keep a playpen out in your classroom area. On occasion, give your toddler fifteen minutes to play quietly in the playpen, within your sight.
- Throughout the day, have each older child take fifteen minutes with the younger children. Encourage them to use this time pro-ductively—playing, reading a story, or playing a game. Make your own version of our Danny-Do Cards, discussed above. Or an older child might take the youngest child for a walk in the stroller down the block while you work with the child or chil-dren in the middle.
- Send one child to preschool for a season to break up the stress of trying to meet too many needs at once. This solution needs to be balanced against the added burden of transportation and other preschool parent participation, however.
- Trade baby-sitting, or set up a cooperative teaching arrangement with another homeschooler. You might take a friend's kids one morning every week for art experiences, while she takes your kids one afternoon a week for a writing workshop.
- Take advantage of dad's availability in the evenings or on week-

ends. Have him do the longer read-alouds, for example, when you simply can't get them done during the day.

Sometimes the only solution to the problem of managing infants and toddlers while you are trying to school the older children is patience. The young ones will grow up and be in another phase before you know it. Don't make yourself crazy trying to change something that can't be changed. Even if you could, you would be wishing away an entire part of life. Embrace it, and work with the challenge.

Don't forget that the relationships you are cultivating as you home-school are what really count: parent to God, child to God, parent to child, child to child. In the home environment, children are schooled in all these relationships. Preserving, embracing, and empowering these relationships is far more important than whether you cover a certain subject at a certain age.

Valerie Bendt, author of *How to Create Your Own Unit Study* (Common Sense Press, 1997) and *Reading Made Easy* (Bendt Family Ministries, 2000), sent me a draft of her article called "Making the Most of the Preschool Years." She writes, "Our children don't need special programs. They need us. These little ones are so precious. It's important that we give them lots of hugs, cuddles, and books read on laps. It's important for them, and it's important for us. They won't be little forever. Let's not one day regret that we did not spend more time enjoying our preschoolers."

More Practical Pointers to Settle the Family Circus

- Help your children cultivate servant hearts. This starts by letting them see you serving others out of love, then helping them to be aware of the needs of others.

- Give them opportunities to practice teamwork. Give them big projects to work on together, and reward team behavior.
- Butt out! Let your children practice fighting with respect and integrity.
- Respect your children's differences, and rejoice in the opportunity you have to teach and train them as individuals.
- Enjoy your little ones while you can. This season will be over before you know it, and you'll wish you had a baby to cuddle again.

Siblings who don't get along and toddlers who never seem to stop are special challenges for homeschooling moms. But they also offer opportunities to teach our children valuable conflict resolution skills and practical ways to help one another. Who knows—maybe our children will someday be best friends!

CHAPTER TEN

What's a Daddy to Do?

The Impact of Homeschooling on Your Marriage

*H*oney, we really should think about fixing the side of the house before the rains set in," I told my husband shortly after our family had moved into a new residence.

"You mean that strip where the siding doesn't quite meet the roof?" he asked.

I nodded. "I'm afraid we might develop a major leak if we don't get it taken care of. It shouldn't be too hard," I added brightly.

Mark rolled his eyes. "Spoken like someone who doesn't have to do it," he teased. "You're right though. I do need to get on it."

As does any older house, ours needed a number of repairs. Mark got to many of them in the first few months after we moved in, but somehow that problem on the north side of the house kept getting put off.

For weeks my husband and I had the same conversation over dinner: "That strip on the side of the house really needs some attention," I'd say. "Yeah, I know," he would mutter, and the matter would be tabled for the day.

A few days later, he would bring it up: "You know, I really should work on the side of the house this weekend. Do we have anything planned?"

Finally we set a date for Mark to do the required repairs. "I'll take the kids out for the morning so you can have uninterrupted work time," I told him that morning. He made a quick trip to the hardware store while the rest of us got ready for a morning at the children's museum. By the time we backed out of the driveway, he was dragging the ladder from the garage.

Several hours and four worn-out children later, Mark greeted us with a cheery wave as we pulled back into the driveway. "I'm almost done!" he called. "Man, I'm glad I get to check that project off my list."

"Good for you, honey! Let me get the kids inside and you can show me."

I got the kids unloaded from the van and settled in the house, then hurried back outside and around the corner to the north side of the house. Mark was nowhere in sight. And when I looked up to check out his repair job, the gap between the roof overhang and the siding was still there!

Then I heard him calling, "Honey, are you out here? Come take a look." Confused, I followed his voice around the house to its south side, where Mark stood staring up at the eaves.

"Mark?"

"Well, what do you think?" He sounded very pleased with himself. "No leaks in the Field house this spring! We should be nice and snug now."

My mouth dropped open. There on the *south* side of the house, a newly painted plank ran true and square between the siding and the eaves.

"Honey?" my husband asked, his voice puzzled.

I started to laugh. "Oh, Mark. All these months I've been talking about the *north* side of the house and—"

"I've been talking about the south side!" he finished for me, slapping himself on the forehead and joining me in laughter. "I can't believe it. For months we've been having the same conversation and missing each other entirely!"

Eventually the repairs to the north side of the house were finished as well, but the episode got me to thinking: How often in our marriages, fig-uratively speaking, are we focusing on different sides of the house when we think we're focusing on the same side? For a marriage to be effective, both husband and wife must understand clearly their common mission, goals, and intentions. This is particularly true when it comes to homeschooling.

In our family, we have a mission statement, a brief paragraph that encompasses the reasons we choose to be together as a family (see chapter 8). When we have family decisions to make—taking on a new commit-ment, for instance—we ask ourselves if the commitment fits in with our family mission. If it does, we give ourselves to it wholeheartedly. The simple paragraph gives our family a focal point. It ensures that Mark and I are focusing on the same side of the house.

Our decision to homeschool wasn't *my* decision, it was *our* decision, made together after thinking about it in terms of our family mission and praying about it individually and together. In fact, without my husband, our homeschool makes no sense. Even though I am the one who stays home with the kids every day, Mark is an integral part of the homeschool-ing endeavor. His prayers and perseverance are the engine that powers our homeschool journey. We are living this lifestyle together.

Homeschooling and Your Marriage

I like the way a speaker I heard in the mid 1980s illustrated the family—as a suspended mobile. One piece of a mobile cannot move, even in a minor way, without affecting every other piece. In the family system, what has an impact on one family member has an impact on all. The daily adventure of homeschooling is no exception; it touches every area of family life. In a sense, it *becomes* family life. If you've been teaching your children at home for even a short time, you know that homeschooling affects not just the relationships between you and your children, but their relationships with one another, the relationship between you and your husband, and his relationship with the kids.

Mothers are not the only ones who sacrifice when a family homeschools. Fathers make considerable sacrifices as well. They devote space, time, and energy to their family. They have as little time for outside pursuits as we do.

A homeschool lifestyle is rigorous for everyone and can challenge even a strong marriage. Children often make the loudest demands, but a squeaky wheel is a minor concern if the engine is about to quit. Your husband has interests beyond homeschooling. So should you, and after your relationship with God, your marriage should be at the top of your list. It is imperative that we don't homeschool at the expense of our marriage relationship.

Children can suck us dry. If we have nothing left to give our husbands, our marriage will suffer. Our spouse may become resentful. Then the family itself is compromised. When the family is compromised, so is the homeschool. In other words, a healthy relationship between you and your husband is key to the success of your homeschooling journey. If you want your homeschool to thrive, nurture your marriage.

Beverly, a Maryland homeschooler, is very clear on this issue: "I can only say that if homeschooling negatively impacted our marriage, I would quit. Our marriage is far more important than my children's education at home. There are other ways for our kids to learn and grow."

A well-balanced homeschooling experience can actually be good for a marriage. When again in your married life will you endeavor together to accomplish such a task? Texas homeschooler Gayle believes that homeschooling has a positive impact on her marriage as she and her husband are drawn together in their love and concern for the well-being of their children. "Our homeschooling gives us a sense of shared responsibility and shared achievement," she says.

My friend Norma, too, notes that the vision she and her husband share for raising their children has strengthened their marriage. In my own marriage, homeschooling has increased our unity and commitment. Another homeschooler says homeschooling "keeps us family-focused."

Ellen Stanclift, who homeschools in Maine, says that because she is home, she and her husband are able to spend more time together than they might otherwise. "In many of the dual-career couples we know, there is so little emotional energy left over for one another," she says. "We're able to make time with one another a priority. We both share a strong commitment to the success of our marriage as well as to our family goals, and this shared vision has brought us even closer together." Still, Ellen admits that she and her husband aren't immune to the pitfalls that other marriages face. "Open communication, we've learned, is key!"

Her point is well made. Effective communication about issues relating to family life and homeschooling is essential for keeping your marriage strong. Common sense rules apply: You are not out to win an argument. You are out to have your hearts united in a common goal.

"What Am I Supposed to Do?"

When I speak to groups of men and women about homeschooling, inevitably a husband will raise his hand and ask, "What am I supposed to do in our homeschool?"

In my surveys for this book, homeschooling mothers, too, were often unsure about their husband's role. Many wished he would take a more active interest. A few wanted him less involved. Most admitted that they were still trying to work out how their husbands fit in the scheme of their homeschooling day.

I believe a father's contribution to homeschooling begins with selfless dedication to his family and respect and esteem for his wife's work in homemaking and homeschooling. These two things will do more to ensure the success of our homeschools than any number of model pyramids built over the weekend.

In return, we need to value and appreciate our husband's faithfulness and responsibility to his task of earning the livelihood that makes it possible for us to stay home. A dad doesn't have to be the fairy-tale-perfect father who works all day, teaches algebra to the kids at night, and takes his daughters to ballet classes or builds tree houses on the weekends in order to be contributing significantly to the family homeschool.

I forget that sometimes, especially when I'm feeling overwhelmed by my myriad roles and responsibilities. When the pressures of homeschooling begin to close in on me, I wish my husband were more involved on a practical level with my efforts to educate our children. That's when I have to take time out to remind myself exactly how much he *does* do to support our homeschool.

Without Mark, I would not be spending my days with my children, teaching, guiding, and caring for them as only I am able. For one thing, he gets up every weekday morning and goes to work to provide for his family. Faithfully. Whether he feels like it or not. If not for his commitment to homeschooling, we would both be working outside the home to make ends meet. If not for his willingness to embrace our lifestyle of relative simplicity, doing without many of the things that other men enjoy, our children would be in someone else's classroom. As a consequence, our family life would not have the strength and richness we now enjoy.

Mark is our chief encourager—both mine and the children's. He listens to my complaints, allows me to vent my frustration without judgment, gives me opportunities to be alone for reflection or study, and does more than an average amount of household work so that my time is not monopolized by chores and cooking. As for the children, he inquires as to their progress, listens to their endless stories and narration, helps them study their Bible verses, and helps them finish the work we have not completed during the day.

Another way my husband supports our homeschooling efforts is by adding structure and accountability to our day. The children know that the bulk of their work must be completed before their daddy comes home. At bedtime, even when I'm too tired to care much whether the kids' teeth get brushed, Mark helps encourage healthy habits by taking charge of their nighttime routine.

Many dads play important roles in the life of their homeschool. Here's a sampling of responses from the moms who filled out my homeschool survey. Perhaps you'll recognize your husband in one or more of these descriptions. If you do, let him know how much you appreciate and count on his support. Sometimes we get so caught up in our own roles that we forget to say thank you.

When Kate Theriot of the Homeschooler's Curriculum Swap first began homeschooling, she knew God was "loudly and clearly" calling her to the endeavor. Her husband was more reluctant, but because he was concerned about a number of issues regarding their two older children, he was willing to give homeschooling a try. Now he's Kate's biggest cheerleader.

"After the first year, I felt as if I had accomplished nothing," Kate says. "But my husband gushed over how much calmer and more mature the kids were, [how much] happier and more self-confident. Whenever I've been down and feeling like a failure, he's been there to tell me I'm doing a great job. When I've needed help, he hasn't criticized; he has supported me and jumped right in to help."

My friend Norma's husband supports her homeschooling efforts in several tangible ways. He is the "school principal" and the evening teacher. "He begins reading aloud to us—biographies, historical fiction, or just plain fun books—after he's eaten dinner," Norma says. "The children finish eating, fold clean laundry, or do mechanical types of schoolwork while they listen." Dad is also the homeschool science teacher. Fascinated with science as well as knowledgeable about it, he is able to engage and excite his students in ways Norma could not.

Norma's husband also works with any child who hasn't finished his or her assigned work or who has math corrections to do. In addition, he's active in his children's 4-H club, which meets once a month on Saturdays. "My husband spends eleven hours away from home each weekday. He purposely leaves for work at 5:45 A.M. so he can be home at 5:00 P.M. to spend more time with us," says Norma, well aware of and grateful for the sacrifices he makes.

Shari, a mother of seven, homeschools in Illinois. Her husband, too, is the "school principal," handling all discipline issues at the family "School House on the Rock." If the kids don't show proper respect for their teacher, Shari sends them directly to the principal. "He also functions as the lifeboat for mom," Shari says, "rescuing" her when the kids are having trouble understanding a new concept. He always manages to have a new, inventive way of getting the concept across, she says.

Illinois homeschooler Barbara can also count on her husband as an extra teacher in the homeschool. "As math and science progressed beyond my ability even to grade papers well, he took over those subject areas," she says. Now he chooses the curricula for those areas, teaches, schedules science labs, and does all the grading. Because he is "the best editor in the house," he also does the final edit on all papers and book reports. In order to accommodate his work schedule, Barbara keeps their homeschool schedule flexible; sometimes the kids don't get science lessons for a week. A small price to pay for dad's hands-on involvement in the homeschool, in Barbara's opinion.

Another homeschooling mom shares, "I'm not good at everything, and there were areas where I was not succeeding in getting information across.

I told [my husband] that rather than critique me, he could make a contribution. And he has! His style and emphasis are different from mine, so even when we cover the same territory, it looks fresh to the kids."

In some families the father provides needed accountability. All assignments are turned in to him, and children are accountable to him for getting everything done. A father who is willing to be in control in this way can foster the development and maintenance of good habits in his children. A faithful father who works hard and follows through on his commitments is also a wonderful role model.

The more that homeschooling is seen as a lifestyle, the easier it is for fathers to be involved because learning can be incorporated into everything they do. Having a child stand by while dad does home repairs, taking a child along for a trip to the hardware store, or working on a building project with a child can be valuable ways for fathers to be involved in homeschooling. Life, after all, is learning.

Denise, a homeschooler from Illinois, says that her husband supports her best by helping her see the long-term benefits and goals of their homeschooling efforts. "I get bogged down with the here-and-now daily grind," she says, "but he helps me see the big picture."

I have a note hanging on my refrigerator that reminds me constantly to keep my eyes on the big picture: "I'm both proud and appreciative of your work with the children at school," it reads. "It's hard sometimes, but God will bless it for us. Love, Mark."

God will bless it. It isn't all up to us.

When You're Left to Do It Alone

Many of us are blessed to have the full support of our husbands in our efforts to homeschool. But what if your husband opposes your desire to begin or continue homeschooling or is lukewarm about the whole idea? At the opposite extreme, what if he wants to control every aspect of your homeschool?

Sometimes in the homeschooling family, the wife is ready to step out in faith on a new path for her family. She simply cannot wait for her husband to take the lead. She confidently strides ahead, leaving her husband in the dust—and inviting disaster. "Every kingdom divided against itself will be ruined," Matthew warned in his gospel, "and every city or household divided against itself will not stand" (Matthew 12:25).

"If your husband is dead set against home teaching his children, it is safe to assume God doesn't think you ought to do it either," says author and homeschooler Luanne Shackelford. "Ladies, if you want the blessing of the Lord on this endeavor, don't go over your husband's head."[1]

As wives, we must submit to our husbands' leadership. We must seek together to do God's will. If you and your husband are not of one mind— if you are not looking at the same side of the house—then homeschooling is not God's will for your family at this particular time. To continue forward in opposition to your husband is to risk your marriage.

Sometimes husbands don't say no to homeschool, but they're not enthusiastic about it either. One of the saddest and most frequent comments I hear from homeschooling mothers goes something like this: "My husband has nothing to do with our homeschool. I'd rather do it myself than keep asking for and receiving a halfhearted effort on his part." Many of my survey respondents complained that their husbands' involvement in their homeschool doesn't stay regular; it just kind of fizzles out.

If your husband is gone for twelve hours out of the day, every day, the actual contribution he can make to your homeschool will be limited. If this is the case in your family, make sure you have some kind of support system and take regular breaks from your routine.

One homeschooling mom with an unsupportive, uninvolved husband recommends that other mothers in her position find support from a church group, counselor, a homeschool group, or whatever means of connecting with others she can find. "I could not do everything alone for fourteen hours each day," she says. "It was too lonely, long, and difficult. It drained me." She also encourages homeschooling moms who are left alone to their task to nurture themselves. "To deal with my husband's lack of help, I had to look within and find the answers there," she says. "It was not always an easy process. It still can be hard."

Sometimes husbands don't get involved in the homeschool because they don't know how. They might make a halfhearted attempt to help out, feel uncomfortable in their role, and then step back, basically leaving their wives with the entire load. If that's the case for you, review the special section for dads below and see if your husband might enjoy trying out some of the ideas there.

The Other Extreme

While some spouses are unsupportive, others want to control everything about homeschooling. It must be done their way or not at all; there is no compromise. This is not a healthy arrangement! Homeschooling moms who find themselves in this situation must lovingly, patiently express their views and concerns to their husbands—and then pray!

The best advertisement to husbands for homeschooling is the one we find in 1 Peter 3:1-2: winning them over without words by our behavior "when they see the purity and reverence of [our] lives." A controlling husband who sees his wife quietly and reverently going about the work of teaching his children cannot help but grow in confidence in her ability and her heart commitment. With that confidence may come some loosening of his need to control and a new commitment to seek agreement with you on how things should be done.

Whether a spouse is unsupportive or overcontrolling, wives have an incredible responsibility with regard to the hearts of their children toward their father. The way I view and respect my husband is the way my children learn to view and respect him. In the natural course of learning to understand lines of authority, their attitudes toward daddy become their attitudes toward God, because children translate those attitudes in their relationship with the Lord. If I am not honoring and respecting my husband, I am teaching my children to dishonor him and to dishonor God. Help your children keep their hearts turned toward their father. Honor him, and God will honor you.

Ideas Especially for Dads

Dads, don't feel inadequate or guilty if you can't afford to spend the time and energy that Harry Homeschooler spends on regularly scheduled hands-on teaching. Even a simple contribution to family life—washing dishes or changing a diaper, for instance—speaks volumes about your love and commitment to your family.

One homeschooling dad I heard about has taken on the role of school janitor, making sure the family room/classroom is cleaned every weekend so his wife and kids can have a fresh start on Mondays. It's a small thing but thoughtful, caring, and supportive. When small things are done out of a spirit of loving servanthood, your wife and children will know—even if you're not available to teach math or carpentry. Here's a list of other practical ways you can help out your wife in your homeschool:

- Take care of the legal aspects of home education. Make it your responsibility to assure that your homeschool complies with state law. Have a plan to deal with legal challenges, should you ever face them. Have a plan for your children's education if one parent dies.

- Be available to modify your homeschool study space as needs dictate. This might require moving furniture, building shelves, or upgrading lighting.
- Go to homeschool meetings and your state convention with your wife whenever possible. It is worth getting a baby-sitter for that time so you can both stay enthused and energized for homeschooling.
- Take time to listen to your wife, without criticism or comment. Allow her to vent her frustrations.
- Appreciate the many roles your wife plays as a homeschooling mom, and have reasonable expectations. Your house will not always be clean, and your meals will probably not be gourmet, but your children will be growing, learning, and changing every day under her loving care.
- Give your wife time alone, perhaps to go to the library to do lesson plans or catch a wind of inspiration, or to get her hair cut or shop for personal items.
- Call home during the day to see how the kids are behaving. Be available by phone for your wife to reach you in tough situations.
- Bring dinner home one night a week, or schedule a regular night to cook so your spouse can count on it.
- Lead family council meetings once a month to iron out family, chore, or homeschooling problems.
- Make sure your wife has quiet times alone to read Scripture and focus on devotions.
- Be patient in the evening, and show interest in the children's schoolwork.
- Review daily school and chore reports, and work on deficiencies with the children.
- Get involved with dinner-time discussions of history or literature.

- Teach a subject in the evenings or on the weekend. Math, science, and physical education are popular choices for fathers. If you have gifts in music, logic, or some other area, share your knowledge with your children. Bible and character lessons from dad provide a great example of spiritual leadership in the family.
- Teach the kids about fishing, camping, car maintenance skills, or other activities you may be gifted in.
- Listen to kids recite Bible memory verses.
- Help organize the work load at home by enlisting the children for household chores. Make chore assignments, and teach the kids how to do their jobs.
- Cheerfully watch babies and toddlers to give mom a break.
- Play with the kids! Take them outside for active play, or play a board game with them. These are the times your children are most likely to open up and share.
- Help with bedtime routines and baths.
- Read aloud to the children.

If you are too busy to do any of the above, make sure your wife has your unconditional love, support, and encouragement, and make sure she knows you are praying for her as she continues the task of preparing your children for adulthood.

Getting Your Man Involved

Cynthia Ulrich Tobias's book *"You Can't Make Me" (But I Can Be Persuaded)* is about dealing with strong-willed children, but her advice makes sense when dealing with an unsupportive spouse as well. You can't make anyone else do anything, Tobias says. So don't back others into a corner and leave them no choice; don't tell them what they will or will not do; don't insist that something can't be done; don't demand that they obey without question.

Although you can't make others do what you want them to do, you *can* persuade them to your point of view. How? Value their ability to see the world from a unique perspective, says Tobias; find ways to inspire them to change the world; ask them for their input, and recognize their uniqueness even if it bothers you.[2]

Everyone wants to be valued and recognized for his or her unique contributions. Wives, keep that perspective in mind as you review the following ideas for getting a reluctant husband involved in your family life and your homeschool.

- *Be positive.* Janet, who homeschools in Illinois, recommends *not* pointing out the things your husband isn't doing. A reluctant spouse is more likely to be won over by a gentle spirit than by nagging. (Remember the principle of 1 Peter 3:1-2.) "Be positive and start with small steps," Janet says. She is also careful not to overwhelm her husband with details when he's so depleted at the end of his workday that he probably won't hear her anyway.

- *Help keep him informed about home education.* Give him things to read. For some reason, Chris Klicka's book *The Right Choice* (Gresham, Oreg.: Noble Publishing, 1993) strikes a chord with men, perhaps because it is written by a man. This is a good resource for men who are deliberating the pros and cons of homeschooling.

- *Encourage his spiritual growth.* Pray for him. Give him time and space for devotions, attending men's retreats, and having some blessed solitude. Don't usurp his role in the home—let him lead. We empower our husbands to be spiritual leaders by letting them lead and being willing to follow.

- *Give him your admiration.* "Admiration is one of man's deepest and most important needs," says best-selling author Gary Smalley. "That's probably why scriptures teach wives to admire their husbands (Ephesians 5:33)."[3] Respect and admiration encourage our husbands' leadership.

- *Demonstrate your homeschool skills.* Let your husband see you teaching and enjoying your children, even if you are not formally homeschooling. As he observes you doing this on a casual basis, it will go a long way toward alleviating any fears he may have about your ability to homeschool.

Finally, be a "safe place" for your husband. In the sometimes overwhelming task of homeschooling our children, we can forget that our spouse needs a refuge as much as we do.

"A safe place? How can I possibly be a refuge for my husband?" you might protest. "I'm exhausted by the time he gets home. Homeschool refugee is more like it!"

After a hectic day of homeschooling, particularly if things haven't gone as smoothly as we might have wished, we don't always feel at our best. How *do* we become a refuge for our husbands to come home to?

It starts with accepting our husbands where they are and as they are.

Sometimes we paint grandiose pictures of how we want our husbands to be and then seek to impose those unrealistic expectations on them. Sometimes we're fuzzy about exactly who we want them to be—but we know they're not it. According to Maranatha Chapman, author and speaker to women's gatherings, we set ourselves up for disappointment, and our husbands for discouragement and frustration, with the fantasy-driven standards we expect them to meet. "They [the husbands] feel nothing they do is ever good enough," Chapman writes, "or they feel we would prefer them to be someone they're not."[4]

The irony is that a frustrated, discouraged man is not likely to jump into an environment in which he expects to meet even more frustration and discouragement. His natural inclination is to withdraw in self-protection. Women often complain about their husbands' unwillingness to share their hearts, says Chapman, but in her experience, the problem is more often of the wife's making than the husband's. A disappointed wife rarely hides her disappointment. She complains. She nags. She whines. She is as far from being a safe place as is a lion's den. Why would any sane man expose his heart in such a situation?

Proverbs has a lot to say about whiny wives: "Better to live on a corner of the roof than share a house with a quarrelsome wife" (25:24); "A quarrelsome wife is like a constant dripping on a rainy day; restraining her is like restraining the wind or grasping oil with the hand" (27:15-16). A wife who pouts because her husband doesn't meet her fairy-tale-perfect standards is not a safe place for him to be. Love him as he is. Accept him where he is. Make it safe for him to share his heart.

For some very practical ways to be a refuge for your husband, thoughtfully consider the following comments and questions:

1. The house. I have long ago abandoned the idea of a spotless house, but even I don't like coming home to a messy one. Clear a path through the clutter. To make your husband's homecoming more pleasant and enjoyable, take a few minutes to at least pick up a little before he arrives.

2. Noise. Can you hear your husband when he arrives home, or is it too noisy? My husband hates coming home to blaring music or a blasting television. What does yours prefer? It doesn't take a lot to plan to shut down the electronic noise before his arrival. Little things like this can mean a great deal.

3. Your attitude and appearance. Are you ready for your husband when he comes home from work? I am not saying you need to put on fresh clothing, but you may need to don a fresh attitude. Are you in a warm, welcoming frame of mind when your husband comes home? If not, consider setting aside ten minutes to wash your face and brush your hair before he arrives. *Don't* sit on the porch waiting to dump your troubles on him! (I've done that. A peaceful, cheerful evening it was not!)

4. Your children's greeting. Does your husband want to see the children right away, or does he want a few minutes to read the mail and decompress from his workday? Have you asked him what he prefers? Some fathers love to be greeted with squeals, hugs, and kisses, and others need some peace and quiet first.

5. Your greeting. Be ready to listen, not just talk. I know you haven't seen or spoken to an adult all day, but he hasn't seen or spoken to *you* all day. He won't ever have a chance to pour his heart out to you if you don't let him get a word in edgewise!

6. The evening meal. Does your husband want you to have dinner ready when he arrives, or would he rather come home, relax, and take a few minutes to switch gears before meal mayhem sets in? With small children, dinner can be less than peaceful. What approach would be the most relaxing for your husband? Some mothers feed their very young children before daddy comes home. What does your husband prefer, and what works best for your family? Have you asked him?

Having my husband tell me our home is a haven for him is a huge compliment. Make it your goal to have a peaceful home for everyone in your family—a safe, warm place filled with love.

Practical Pointers for Balancing Your Homeschool and Your Marriage

- Be a safe place for your husband. Strive to be the woman of Proverbs 31:11-12: "Her husband has full confidence is her and lacks nothing of value. She brings him good, not harm, all the days of her life."

- Work out the roles you and your husband will each play in your homeschool. Will he function more as the disciplinarian/principal or the encourager/accountability partner? Be flexible. Take the position that you will each do whatever needs to be done to make your homeschool work.

- If you haven't already done so, sit down with your husband and come to a mutual understanding of your vision for your family and your homeschool. Write out a mission statement based on your vision. (See chapter 8 for ideas about how to do this.)

- If you and your husband are not of one mind about a decision, pray that the Lord will reveal his will to both of you. There isn't anything about parenting or homeschooling that is so urgent you can't take the time to pray about it first.

- Be clear in your own mind about how you expect your husband to participate in your homeschool, and then communicate and negotiate your expectations. Just be sure they are realistic!

- If your husband is uninvolved, have him be your sounding board for making decisions related to homeschooling. Getting him on board this way may stir his interest and make him feel as if he is making a contribution even if he cannot be home much of the time.

- Pray for and encourage his spiritual growth. Let him lead in your home.

- Give him your admiration.

- Listen to him. Care about what he cares about. If he knows you'll listen and he knows you care, he'll share his heart.

- Let him see you teaching and enjoying your children, even if you are not formally homeschooling.
- Keep your husband informed and up to date about your homeschool. Share your ideas and fears, the new theories you read and the new ideas you want to try with your program. Give him reports on what you are doing, perhaps as a daily briefing over the dinner table or a review every weekend.
- Have your children present reports, presentations, and recitations to dad. This gives the children an audience and a chance to review material and keeps dad up to date with the homeschool program.
- Spend time discussing the overall health of your home, seeking God's Word and will. Ask God to give you and your spouse a heart and mind of agreement over the major issues in your marriage. Invite him into your home to inhabit your hearts and your lives.
- Avoid making decisions during the vulnerable times in your relationship—for instance, when you both are tired. Be especially gentle with one another during those times.
- Make time to be together to discuss your roles and responsibilities. The more clear your understanding of these matters, the less the potential for problems.
- Make sure your husband gets regular downtime.
- Make it a point to spend simple time together, perhaps to have a quiet conversation after the kids go to bed or to share a cup of coffee before the workday begins. Or you might go for a ride together in the car. Mark and I often load the kids into the backseats with coloring books or "travel bags" filled with things to do in the car (along with a few candy surprises!) and let them listen to one of their music tapes with the sound directed to the rear of

the van. With the children so engaged, we can actually have a conversation! Sometimes we send each other e-mails or leave notes or voice mail for each other during the day. I want my husband to feel a part of what goes on in our homeschool all day long.

- If your spouse is unenthused about homeschooling, continue to share your heart and your enthusiasm with him. Be considerate of the fact that husbands face challenges all day, but ask him to help you brainstorm ways he can be more involved.

- Don't try to define your husband's role in your home. God has already defined it. Pray that he will listen to God and develop his role in obedience to God's plan for fathers.

- If your spouse is in outright opposition to homeschooling, accept that it is not God's plan for your family right now. Continue to pray and seek God's will.

I'm grateful for the vision my husband and I share, for our family and our homeschool. We are a team. Without each other, we would not function effectively either as parents or homeschoolers. We have strengths and weaknesses; we compensate for one another and complement one another.

We are together serving God in our home.

CHAPTER ELEVEN

Sane Socialization

School Ties vs. Family Ties

I've thought about homeschooling," the mother of an active preschooler confides. "But my daughter really belongs in school. She's so fun loving and cheerful. I'm afraid she'd be awfully lonely if I kept her at home."

"My son's very quiet," says another mom. "We've been told that putting a child as shy as he is in a classroom with other kids is the best way to bring him out of his shell."

A third mom says with the air of a sage, "All kids need socialization; everyone knows that. If they don't go to school, how are they ever going to learn the social skills they'll need to get along in the world?"

As a homeschooling mom, I wish I had a dollar for every time I've heard the question "What about socialization?" The implication when someone brings up the topic is that I'm somehow depriving my children—perhaps even stunting their growth—by teaching them at home.

We've all heard the dire warnings:

"If they don't go to school, your children will never learn how to get along with people."

"You can't shelter them forever, you know."

"They won't know how to act in the real world."

"They'll never fit in!"

Do you worry sometimes that they might be right? Do you wonder if you're really doing right by your children by keeping them out of school? Take heart. Often these expressions of concern on the part of nonhome-schoolers are well intended, but they are also uninformed.

The point on which we all agree is that socialization is important. In order to flourish in a career or marriage, children need significant social skills, including the ability to:

- work in cooperation with others
- initiate and nurture interpersonal relationships
- interact with a wide range of people
- express feelings
- give and receive feedback
- interpret and use body language
- use tact and diplomacy
- recognize the uniqueness of individuals
- deal with conflict in an open, honest, and positive way
- resolve interpersonal conflicts
- help those with opposite viewpoints reach mutual agreements
- relate well to peers and supervisors
- treat others with respect
- demonstrate friendliness and politeness

The point on which we need *not* agree is that school is the only, or indeed even the best, place to learn those important social skills. The contention that kids can't learn social skills in any context but the classroom is a myth—one of several I will address in this chapter.

Myth 1: "Appropriate Social Behavior Is Best Learned in a School Setting"

We all want our children to learn how to get along with others, to treat the people they encounter with kindness and respect, to develop healthy friendships that will last through the years.

But the positive socialization that every caring parent desires for his or her children is *not* the socializing that happens when kids at school meet up with one another at their lockers to make small talk. Socialization and socializing are not the same. In fact, socializing got some of us into trouble when we were in school. How many times in your educational career did you hear the words "We do not come to school to socialize"?

Socialization goes deeper than feeling comfortable with one's peers. It's not just hanging around with other kids. It includes learning a worldview, adopting values, and practicing acceptable cultural behavior. It's about fellowship and ministry. Appropriate socialization prepares our children to be effective in the world. Inappropriate socialization, on the other hand, impairs any child's ability to effectively navigate the world.

What kind of socialization do children get in schools? When they are very young, they fight over toys. When they are kindergarten age, they parallel play—not really interacting, merely playing alongside one another. When they are older, they hang around in well-defined, perhaps even cruel groups until some adult tells them what to do. Homeschooled children, on the other hand, interact with family members of various ages to play games, work on projects, or simply talk with one another.

Every child's school experience is different, but bullying, ridicule, and a pecking order of pseudopower are far too common in classrooms and school common areas. It isn't an atmosphere conducive to the development of self-esteem; usually the opposite is true. Children experience stress, rivalry, competition, and unhealthy comparison to others.

Cornell University's Dr. Urie Bronfenbrenner, who has spent many years studying children in various societies, agrees. "The exposure of the child to group experience with peers tends, at least in contemporary American society, to undermine the socialization efforts of adults and to invite the emergence of egocentrism, aggression, and antisocial behavior. Once children are beyond the age of three, it is reasonable to expect the larger the peer group, the weaker will be the influence of the supervising adult. As the child approaches school age, group size can act as a catalyst in shifting the balance of power from adults to peers with corresponding impairment of developmental progress."[1]

Trying to fit in not only inhibits a healthy sense of self but may also inhibit the development of a child's skills and abilities. For example, in some schools it isn't cool to be smart. The child's choices are to downplay his or her intelligence in order to be seen as cool or to endure teasing and ostracism.

Isolated for long periods of time with their age mates and having only minor contact with significant adults, children become peer-dependent. They elevate their relationships with their friends over those with family members. They learn to value the unformed (and uninformed) opinions of other children over those of their parents and the church, and they also tend to overvalue their own, usually forced opinions.

On the other hand, "Homeschooled children tend to draw their primary social identity from their membership in a particular family rather than from their membership in a particular peer group," writes journalist William Mattox. In an article for the Knight-Ridder/Tribune News Service, Mattox quotes author, public school teacher, and homeschooling father David Guterson, observing that traditional schooling removes adults from the lives of children except "in an authoritarian role not entirely conducive to the forming of meaningful relationships."[2]

Children need and crave meaningful relationships with adults—parents first and then other adults who can show them what it means to be grown up. How can these relationships be fostered in a peer-oriented system?

In my own educational career, there were a few significant teachers, mostly in the later grades, who made an impact on me. I received their special attention in part because I was bright. Not all kids have the same opportunities I had; the average kid will be lucky to have any adult take a real interest in him or her.

Children already know how to be children. They must learn to be grownups, and it takes grownups to teach them. Healthy socialization isn't something a child catches, like a case of the flu. It is a process whereby someone intentionally seeks to inculcate a child with social rules, etiquette, values, and mores. That is a task most effectively accomplished at home.

"Like everything else a child learns, he or she learns socialization skills in the home first," says Lily, who homeschools in Oklahoma, pointing out that children were well socialized long before there were public schools.

Worldly wisdom tells us that children need to be independent from their parents and their parents' values. Separating from one's parents is seen as a necessary and even desirable part of growing up. As a result of this conventional wisdom, generations have ended up rootless and rudderless.

Researcher Jayn Carson, who has studied the structure and functioning of homeschool families, suggests there are "stabilizing forces" within homeschool family systems that "increase the amount of control the family has over…the socialization and education of their children."[3] By socializing our children in the context of a loving family, we have the opportunity to pour our values and beliefs into them. We need not leave them "rootless and rudderless."

As Christians, we have been given specific criteria for what constitutes healthy socialization. "You adulterous people, don't you know that friendship with the world is hatred toward God?" asked James in his epistle. "Anyone who chooses to be a friend of the world becomes an enemy of

God" (James 4:4). "Do not conform any longer to the pattern of this world, but be transformed by the renewing of your mind," the apostle Paul exhorted us (Romans 12:2).

We are to be "in the world, not of it"—"the world" meaning those who have abandoned God and established a value system apart from him. We live and move among the ungodly, but we do not have to be like them. We are called otherwise. What better way to prepare our kids to be "in the world but not of it" than to give them a sense of right and wrong and a solid foundation for decision making? What better training ground for adulthood than the home?

Homeschoolers challenge the notion that preschool or kindergarten is the proper time and place to launch children into complete socialization outside the home. Rather than normal and healthy, we see it as arbitrary and capricious.

Learning to get along with others, accept individual differences, and resolve and manage conflict begins at home. Children do not learn positive social behavior at school from their peers. In fact, as radio talk-show host Dr. Laura Schlessinger notes, "As the approval and attention of peers becomes more significant and powerful than that of adults, behavior problems inevitably appear. Studies show that the worst-behaved kids are those who spend the most time with other kids."[4]

Children learn appropriate socialization from close association with loving, committed adults who model appropriate social behavior for them day in and day out. In the homeschool, they learn it from us.

Myth 2: "Your Children Will Never Fit In"

In any discussion of socialization and the homeschool, the main concern of outsiders seems to be "How will your children ever fit in?" The implication is that homeschooled children are isolated geeks. "If we live according to God's direction the world will accuse us of being nonconformists, out of sync with society, or just plain weird," says Jonathan Lindvall of Bold Christian Living, an organization dedicated to the preservation of family values.[5]

But research into the socialization of homeschoolers does not support this widely held belief. *Time* magazine recently reported that "a slew" of doctoral dissertations has been written on the social adjustment of homeschoolers and quotes Mary Anne Pitman, a social anthropologist at the University of Cincinnati: "The preponderance of evidence is, they're fine."[6]

Journalist Isabel Lyman, writing in *USA Today*, expands on the issue: "In 1992, Larry Shyers of the University of Florida wrote a doctoral dissertation in which he challenged the notion that youngsters at home lag in social development. In his study, eight- to ten-year-old children were videotaped at play. Their behavior was observed by trained counselors who did not know which ones went to regular schools and which were homeschooled. The study found no big difference between the two groups in self-concept or assertiveness, which was measured by social development tests. However, the videotapes showed that youngsters who were taught at home by their parents had consistently fewer behavior problems."[7]

Nevertheless, as Christian homeschoolers we have a different perspective on "fitting in." Socialization is not about our children making merely superficial friends, but about their finding others with whom they can have meaningful fellowship or to whom they can minister and present the gospel of Jesus Christ.

Says Kate Theriot of the Homeschooler's Curriculum Swap, "We have told [our children] that throughout life, most people have only one or two very close friends at any time. The rest are acquaintances. We have encouraged them to cultivate those relationships that bring them the greatest enjoyment and to enjoy the others whenever the opportunity arises. The oldest has one very close friend, and my daughter has maybe two whom she would call very close."

What is of more value to a child: the acquaintance of many children or a few deep friendships that endure over time? Traditional school encourages the first, while homeschooling fosters the second.

Kate goes on to say that when her children have the desire to spend time with friends, she makes the effort to make that happen. But, she says, "We have found that our children are one another's best friends now. They can come up with the most creative play and have the best time without another soul around. They are fourteen, thirteen, nine, and seven and still play well together." Kate believes too that "any child…should be able to find profitable activity by himself," a view also held by Beverly, a Maryland homeschooler: "I think socialization is as much [about] learning to be alone and content as being with other people," she says. "With all the activities [children] have…when they don't have someone or something to entertain them, they get bored."

Some parents, perhaps feeling guilty about their children's lack of school socialization, go to an extreme to involve their children in outside activities. A homeschooling mom of twins in North Carolina shares, "My first year of homeschooling, I had the girls overinvolved. I think I was trying to compensate for their not being in school. And I wanted them to still see their friends, so I put them in all of these after-school activities. They hated most of them, and I was tired of driving them around. So the next year we cut way back [and did] only the things they really enjoyed doing. I had gained the confidence to see that they didn't need all that socialization."

Far from a lack of options, homeschoolers often have to choose the best from the many. April, who homeschools in Michigan, says, "Our primary socialization problem is not enough time in the day to do all the socializing [our children] would like to do!"

A woman once told me I was being cruel to my children because as homeschooled kids they would never know the joy of going to a prom. But many homeschoolers are creating a variety of unique and meaningful rites of passage for their children on their own. Homeschool support groups routinely host graduation ceremonies, and some families mark a child's coming of age with special celebrations. Besides, my recollection of the prom is that it was a place where kids drank illegally and did things in blatant disregard of their parents' wishes. It may not be such a bad thing that my kids never go to a prom!

Myth 3: "You're Not Preparing Your Children for the Real World"

I'm always amused when I read local newspaper coverage of a visit by a "real person" to a local school. Homeschooled children are around real people all the time! Yet we are often criticized for sheltering our children, making them ill prepared for life in the real world.

In many ways, homeschooling provides more real-world experience than a classroom does. In fact, traditional schools are far from the real world. Thinking back on your own education, when were you ever again so age-segregated as you were in school? A homeschooled child learns early on that the real world does not consist primarily of hanging out with one's peers. As journalist William Mattox notes, "Homeschooled children tend to interact more with people of different ages. This is actually more like the 'real world'—what businessperson's social interaction is largely restricted to those born in the same year?"[8]

In my surveys for this book, I asked homeschooling parents specifically how they were preparing their children for life in the real world. Some of their responses were passionate:

"What is more real world than our home?" asks Gayle, who home-schools in Texas. "What is more real world than watching mother do the household chores and helping daddy with his paperwork? What is more real world than being at home with mother and new baby sister around the clock? What is more real world than observing your parents firsthand going about the real-life activities in which adults participate? What is so real world about being in a room with twenty other people the same age as you? Where in the real world will that situation ever be replicated?"

Oklahoma homeschooler Lily believes that homeschooling gives a child the best possible perspective of what the real world is about. "My children see what my life is about, the work I do and the work their father does," she says. "My children learn kindness, compassion and tolerance, fairness, and justice by watching my husband and me interact with others. I've always found the microcosm of the public/private school world a bit odd. In the real world, we learn to form our views of people by meeting and interacting with a variety of people, not because we're mandated to accept or be tolerant of them. In the real world if you're roughed up or have money/property stolen by another, then you deal with it through the law and choose not to interact with that person again! In the real world, work-ers are expected to do their work independently and have self-discipline, and daily life involves preparing meals, doing laundry, keeping the house clean, and balancing the budget. Live it and learn it!"

In our own family, we can't help but talk about the real world. We are ardent news hounds and enjoy discussing current events with our children. Because my husband is currently in the criminal justice system and I previ-ously served as a criminal prosecutor, we have seen the worst of society. We have shared many of our experiences with our children, and our observations have provided a backdrop against which to discuss issues of truth and error, right and wrong. If we hide the world from them, how will they form their opinions about it?

As much as homeschool critics might portray us as "too heavenly minded to be any earthly good," our children are not huddled in the basement memorizing the book of Leviticus. They are ministering to others, engaging in creative pursuits, and taking plenty of time to have fun. They aren't simply preparing for the real world; they're part of it.

Myth 4: "Sheltering Your Kids Is Bad for Them"

Can you recall a single instance in Scripture where the term *shelter* is used negatively?

Neither can I. The Lord himself is referred to as a shelter, and David longed to rest in the shelter of his wings (Psalm 61:3-4). I want that for my children. And I want them to be able to depend on mom and dad in the same way. The argument is made that we should purposely expose our children to evil in order to toughen them up for the real world, but I believe we are here to shelter them—to protect them until they are mature enough to protect themselves.

It is abundantly clear that we will answer to God for whether we have adequately protected and trained our children. Fathers are to bring up their children "in the training and instruction of the Lord" (Ephesians 6:4), and in the same spirit in which Jesus prayed that his disciples be protected from "the evil one," we are to protect and shelter the ones we love (John 17:15). A loving shelter isn't a prison; it's a secure base from which to launch a child whose life, we pray, will be pleasing to the Lord.

Many leaders from the Bible spent a season of sheltering in preparation for a great work God had called them to. Timothy was sheltered from early childhood. John the Baptist led a sheltered life to the extreme. Sometimes a season of sheltering gives children an inner wisdom and discernment they would not acquire if all their time were frittered away in superficial friendships.

Parents do, however, sometimes *over*shelter their children. Protecting children so completely that we stifle their growth is as extreme as totally abandoning them to their peers in a traditional school system. Vickie and Jaymie Farris, authors of *A Mom Just Like You*, note the following regarding overprotected children they have observed: "Far too often, these young people were the very ones who fell into the hands of the world from which they had been so sheltered. Because they had never made their own decisions or learned the reasons behind their parents' decisions, they were ill equipped to deal with the temptations of the world around them."[9]

Releasing a child either too early or too late can be damaging. The Farrises caution us to release our children gradually and to maintain a balance between the rights and responsibilities we grant them. Both should increase as the child matures, and they should remain proportional. Oklahoma homeschooler Lily agrees: "As our children's socialization skills have developed, we've placed them in activities that match their [skill level]," she says. "Why frustrate a child with something he or she doesn't have the tools to handle?"

The Farrises go on to say that children need to be given opportunities to practice the principles you're teaching them. "Otherwise the principles will remain only theory, and your children will not learn how to put your standards into practice when you are not around."[10]

How do we go about releasing our children gradually, as the Farrises suggest? By gradually increasing the amount of freedom we give them socially. Begin by allowing them to entertain others in your home, where you can see them interacting with their friends, ascertain the level of friendship between them, and accurately assess the degree to which they are influenced by their peers.

Before a friend arrives, review the family rules with your child and make sure you have specific plans for activities. Children who are idle and/or poorly supervised are the ones who get into the most trouble. If a friend's visit doesn't work out well, for whatever reason, turn it into a learning opportunity by having your child brainstorm ways he or she could have handled the situation better or differently.

As your children mature, take them with you to visit in other families' homes. Before you go, once again remind them of your family rules. Also inquire as to your hosts' house rules and tell your children how you expect them to behave while you are in their home.

Next on the social continuum is allowing your children to visit in a home without your being there. We don't let our kids do this unless we know the family well, and even then we try to have two of them go together. I am always amazed when parents who have never met me or my husband drop their kids off at our home to play.

Are we being overprotective? I don't think so. In this day and age, if we do not protect our children, who will? Will they go "wild" when they get to adulthood, like the overprotected children Vickie and Jaymie Farris have observed? Perhaps you too know of a sheltered child who left home for college and began to drink deeply of worldly pleasures. If this is a concern, begin to talk to your children now about peer pressure and the negative consequences of experimenting with sex, drinking, smoking, drug use, and other risky behaviors. Get these issues out in the open so your kids can see what shallow substitutes they are for the real life and the real relationships you are providing for them in your home.

A junior high principal I interviewed for this book has two or three homeschoolers reenter his school every year. Their biggest adjustment, he says, is learning to handle teasing and nastiness and gain the ability to "just deal with it." Do I want my children to just deal with abusive behavior? In the context of their whole lives, kids are kids only for a short time. What's so wrong about wanting them to be safe from bullying for as long as possible?

A mom in Alabama who is raising adopted children has no apologies for sheltering them. Because they "have seen and lived though much more than most other children their age," she says, "we now try to shelter them as much as possible to help them regain some of that lost childhood."

Another homeschooling mom says of her own childhood, "I wish I had been more sheltered. I wouldn't have made the mistakes I made. My dad's favorite line is, 'You can't wrap [your kids] in cotton batting and protect them from the bumps in the road because cotton batting will catch on fire when it gets too hot.' Well, I'm wrapping them in the Word of God...and his 'lamb of God's wool' is just fine for my girls!"

Dare to shelter your children. But do it because God has given you responsibility for their training, their character, and their safety. Do it from a position of strength and love, not out of weakness and fear.

Practical Pointers for Sane Socialization

- Be clear about who you want your children to be when they reach maturity. Write down your goals for them. Pray for their spiritual, emotional, and social development.
- Make the family the basic unit of socialization. Seek to do things together rather than having family members splinter off into separate pursuits. Missouri homeschooler Trish sets this standard: "We participate in outside activities if the goal of the activity serves our family." Homeschoolers instinctively know that too

much outside influence tends to lead to attitude problems at home.

- Provide your children with exposure to many types of adults.
- Practice selective socialization rather than random socialization. Plan and supervise your children's social interactions.
- Seek out like-minded families and children. Invite them into your home as a family, and be friends with the entire family. Barbara, who homeschools in Illinois, overheard a friend of her son telling him it was too bad he had to spend his time with little kids and grownups. She was so pleased with his answer: "Listen, when you are with other kids you are stuck with just kids who are the same age and grade as you. When I am with other kids, or other people, I am with people I like to be with. I can choose who I spend my time with. You can't." Barbara says the friend ended up being envious rather than critical!
- Practice hospitality as a family. Invite church members, missionaries, international students, and other homeschooling families into your home.
- Provide a variety of social opportunities for your children outside the home. Tap into positive agents of socialization available in your community: neighbors, mentors, clubs, arts organizations, civic groups, volunteer opportunities. Trying to keep a well-rounded program, homeschooler Merre and her husband encourage their children to be involved in church activities, sports, music lessons, working for others, and volunteering in a cerebral palsy center, nursing homes, and a riding therapy program for people with Down syndrome.
- Distinguish between socializing (preparing the child to be popular among his or her peers) and socialization (the vehicle by

which the child learns a worldview, adopts a personal set of values, and practices acceptable cultural behavior).

Our culture would have us believe that relationships outside the family are of primary importance in our children's social development, but we know differently. Healthy socialization begins with loving parents who are rooted in strong values and who interact with their children in positive ways.

PART IV

personal issues and the homeschool

CHAPTER TWELVE

When Your World Falls Apart

Homeschooling Through Crises

D o you ever feel as if your life is just one crisis after another? I know I do. Sometimes I can barely remember what normal feels like.

From the beginning, our family has been no stranger to difficult times. We began our family life with two daughters born seventeen months apart. When my husband received a job offer in a different town, we made the decision that I would give up my law practice, which I dearly loved, to be a full-time mother in our new community.

I wasn't completely comfortable with the decision, and I soon discovered I was ill equipped for the job. Colicky babies? I had no idea how to deal with that! I also suffered significant depression from the loss of my work-related professional identity. My ego craved the attention I'd received as an attorney in the courtroom. I didn't like thinking of myself as just another lady on the street with a couple of kids.

But God is faithful; he brought my heart around to my home and even planted a desire for more children. Our eldest had been adopted, so adoption seemed a natural way to expand our family. We applied to adopt a baby girl from Korea.

While waiting for the adoption to be finalized, we learned that my husband's sister had been murdered by her estranged husband. Upon returning home on the day of her funeral, reeling from the turn of events, we received news that our baby girl, Grace, had been born in Korea and would soon be coming home to us.

At the time, we were homeschooling our two preschoolers. It seemed easy and fun—for me, a natural extension of being a full-time mommy. At that stage, I figured that when they reached the appropriate age, we'd ship them off to the homey little public school down the street.

Grace arrived in February. The transition wasn't easy for any of us. She had significant attachment issues, and I spent many months sleeping on the floor with her, holding her hand, until she felt secure in our home.

In September my oldest daughter started kindergarten. We live in a school district that is well funded and has many Christian teachers. Students always score above average on standardized testing. Yet, despite being in a superior school district, I knew within a few months that this road was not the right road for our family. For one thing, my daughter experienced significant peer dependence in her short time at the school. If her friends had decided to jump off a bridge, she would have gone along with it just to fit in. I shuddered to think what might happen as the stakes got higher.

I also realized we were missing too many teaching opportunities, not to mention opportunities simply to be together as a family. By the time Clare was released from school in the afternoon, the best part of her day had already passed, and we had not been with her to share in it.

And so we came home to school.

Meanwhile, we were still dealing with Grace's insecurities. Her early losses have manifested themselves in other ways over the years—ways that have proved to be a challenge to the process of homeschooling.

With the arrival from Korea of our fourth child, a boy, we finally saw our quiver filled. We were delighted to have Daniel join our family just in time for the Christmas season. When a slew of out-of-town relatives arrived for the holiday—and to meet the new addition to our family—I had the bright idea to take our older children and their cousins to the roller rink while Grandma and Grandpa got to know our baby son. On my first lap around the rink, I fell and broke my arm in four places, an accident that required seven hours of reconstructive surgery and six months of intensive physical therapy. Six months of four kids and one arm!

On top of those crises, in the last few years we have lived through Grandpa's prostate cancer, my own breast cancer scare, the discovery of my early-stage heart disease, and my sister's significant illnesses. One of our most recent emotional disruptions was the departure of an infant for whom our family had provided foster care. Every one of us had fallen in love him, and giving him up broke our hearts.

But life and lessons go on. Through all of our life crises, some predictable and some completely unexpected, God has been faithful to sustain us. I expect he will continue to do so for the crises still to come.

"The Norm" Is Never Normal

What crises have you had to face? A dear homeschooling saint I know suffered the death of her six-week-old son the same month she discovered her husband was having an affair. They ultimately divorced. She is one of my personal heroes because she has continued to homeschool and live out her beliefs through every difficulty. In fact, she sees many benefits to keeping up with homeschool during crisis times. "My kids didn't feel 'shipped off' someplace while their family was falling apart," she says. "Being right where things were happening actually helped them deal with it on the spot." In addition, she believes that crying together and supporting one another "helped us get over it all faster."

In our personal homeschooling journey, there have been only snippets of time here and there during which we have had an ideal environment and experience. The norm is that life is rarely normal. The ideal is just that— an ideal. God doesn't promise an idyllic life when we walk in faith; what he does promise is to walk beside us.

Still, new homeschoolers often approach their adventure with unrealistic expectations. We expect our school-at-home to be like humorist Garrison Keillor's Lake Wobegon, featured on National Public Radio's *Prairie Home Companion*, where "the women are strong, the men are good-looking, and the children are above average." Where does this town exist? Only in the mind of a very creative writer!

At the time I began teaching the children at home, my image of what life would be like came from my exposure to a few homeschooling families and, mostly, to books and articles I had read. I had formed in my mind a picture of the perfect homeschooling family: the father an unwavering spiritual leader, the mother an exemplary Titus 2 woman, the children brilliant and well behaved. Homeschooling—and life—would flow smoothly from one day into the next.

It was all a mirage. Rarely, except for fleeting moments between crises, does this ideal exist. Life is full of annoyances, if not catastrophes. Some are quickly solved, and some last a long time. They include the predictable stages of family life, like babies and colic or adolescence and confusion. They include great sorrows, like the death or debilitating illness of loved ones.

What does a homeschooling mom do when she's diagnosed with a chronic illness, or when her child is diagnosed with a learning disorder? How does she continue homeschooling in the midst of a cross-country move for her husband's job transfer? What does she do if he loses his job?

And how on earth does a mom who's been teaching her children at home cope if her husband decides he no longer wants to be married? Several years ago when I served as a referral attorney for the Home School Legal Defense Association, I would regularly receive calls from home-schooling moms whose marriages were ending but whose hearts' desire was to continue to teach their children at home. They wanted to know what legal grounds and financial recourse they had to be able to continue in their chosen calling.

Believe it or not, many families successfully homeschool through all these types of challenges. Perhaps their stories will encourage you to continue your homeschool journey even through the inevitable ups and downs of life.

Surviving a Change in Employment

A change in the employment status of either parent can cause major stress for the homeschooling family. If the change involves a geographical move as well, tensions can mount even higher. Still, these can be times of family growth and learning. The homeschoolers who safely navigate crises or disruptions to family life are those who are able to see beyond the event to the opportunities it provides.

Beverly, a homeschooler in Maryland, admits that homeschooling while her husband was changing jobs was extremely stressful, but they found ways to make the transition work for them. One example: "He went on a training trip to Boston for three weeks," she says. "Midway through this time, we went to visit him. We took time off our regular studies and learned about Boston, Paul Revere, and the Revolutionary War." Out of an unwelcome disruption to life as she knew it, Beverly created an opportunity for her children to experience history in a whole new way.

It takes time to adjust to a major change in the status quo. One homeschooling mom was shocked to find out how difficult it was to have her husband around the house when he left the traditional workplace to begin a home business. The fact that the family income dropped by 75 percent was only the beginning. "I suddenly felt extra watched and scrutinized," she says. "The children were unhappy because now there were two people to watch and correct them all day. We had to train [my husband] not to interrupt our schooling."

Children can learn important life lessons from the way we handle crises. Kat, a homeschooler from California, recalls the lessons her family learned when her husband lost his job. "God provided everything we needed," she says. "The children helped [their daddy] with depression, and we learned such valuable lessons about God's provision for us."

When it's mom who changes her work status, the family goes into another kind of transition. My friend Cathy took a part-time job on top of homeschooling. "I buried myself in my job," she says. "Rather than focusing on what I should have been, I kept busy, busy, busy." She knew her family wasn't getting her best, and neither was her job; she was too stretched to be excellent at anything. Eventually she burned out and quit her job. She is now happy to be home full time, concentrating on her family and her teaching.

Managing Relocation

I left the full-time practice of law when my first two children were two years old and six months old. We moved to a new town where my husband began a new job, and I became a full-time mother. I am grateful the Lord gave me an opportunity to adjust to full-time motherhood before adding homeschooling to the equation. Others are not so fortunate.

Although teaching your children at home during the upheaval of relocation may seem daunting, homeschooling offers significant advantages over moving your children from one school district to another. However inconsistent your educational program might seem in the midst of packing, cleaning, and accomplishing the myriad tasks associated with moving, it will still be more consistent and less stressful than what your child would experience having to deal with new facilities, teachers, friends, and curriculum in a public or private school setting. Continuing to homeschool your children can give them a real sense of security at a time when they are having to leave behind the home and friends they have known.

Lily, who homeschooled during a state-to-state move to Oklahoma, comments that continuing her children's educational program "gave them a sense of continuity." To help her kids know what to expect when they got to their new state, she also took advantage of the opportunity to incorporate information about Oklahoma into her curriculum.

Consider the things related to a cross-country move that a homeschooler can teach her children: the history and geography of the new location, organizational skills as they help sort items into moving boxes and write out labels, valuable life skill lessons as they observe how mom handles such mundane tasks as transferring utilities, having mail forwarded, and establishing contacts in their new community. Kat in California turned her family's move into an entire unit study.

A note about curriculum during the transition from one home to another: Moving requires a great deal of flexibility in your educational program. While you're packing up, don't feel guilty about focusing on real-life skills instead of textbook learning. For one thing, your textbooks may not be accessible. Take a break from books and teach your children practical skills.

Be sure to pack all your school materials in one load to make it easier to find them in the new location. Upon arrival, put a priority on setting up the bedrooms, the kitchen, and then the school area. While you are attending to the thousands of matters of resettling your family, your children will at least have ready access to their textbooks and other educational materials.

Homeschooler Connie reminds us to check the legal requirements for homeschools in the new state well before the actual move. Contact the Home School Legal Defense Association at www.hslda.org for referral information. (The address is P.O. Box 3000, Purcellville, VA 20134. Phone: 540-338-5600.) "We have moved three times in our homeschooling experience," Connie says. "There are new laws in every state that have to be investigated. Thanks to Home School Legal Defense, we have had great moves with no hassle whatsoever."

Coping with Illness

The stories of courageous mothers homeschooling from their sick beds are true! In our own family, life went on after the arrival of our fourth child and my roller-skating fall. My children pitched in like champions and learned much about family togetherness and life skills.

Janet, a homeschooling mom who suffers from chronic illness, says, "My entire life has been a crisis to some extent. I am in constant pain, and it seems that there is one disaster after another happening to my family." Rather than despairing and throwing in the towel, she trusts God to use her trials to make her stronger. "A homeschooling parent needs to be strong, believe in herself, and know that God loves her."

Barbara, a homeschooler in Illinois, notes, "By God's grace we can handle anything that comes our way. There are always people [willing] to help out and things that can be put on hold until time is easier to manage. Remember, few things are so urgent that the world would stop if they were not completed today." Wise words for those dealing with chronic physical problems.

One homeschooling mom from Nebraska has a recurrent disc problem that every couple of years puts her flat on her back for weeks at a time. When she's out of commission, her children take care of the daily responsibilities. "They do all the cooking, laundry, and cleaning," she says. "We don't always get schoolwork done during these times, but [my children] are learning important life skills. They all know how to run a home and cook. And they learn about self-sacrifice."

A homeschooler who suffers from long-term illness faces special challenges. She may have to rely on the support of others to provide her children with outside enrichment activities. But her faithfulness to continue in a deep relationship with her children will speak volumes to them about her level of commitment to her task.

Homeschooling through a season of serious illness on the part of a family friend or close relatives presents different challenges. A mom who homeschools in Maryland "packed school into a crate" and drove 250 miles with her children to help care for her dad after he had surgery. "We did a 'lighter' version of school, but still got quite a bit accomplished," she says. "I think the fact that we were homeschooling...made it easier to deal with the situation. And [the children] were more than willing to go and assist Grandpa while he was recovering."

Beverly, in Maryland, recalls the time that a very close friend, a woman she considers her homeschool mentor, was extremely ill. "I helped take care of one of her children, took her to the hospital, visited her in the hospital," Beverly says. Though she continued homeschooling throughout her friend's illness, she reduced the work load both for herself and her kids, concentrating on reading, math, and piano. Their most important lessons during that time, she says, were about prayer.

Oklahoma homeschooler Lily believes her children were fortunate to be able to spend time with their father during his recovery from a major auto accident. They did their lessons in the same room where their father was recovering, continuing their studies "while keeping an eye on their father," she says. "It gave them such a sense of security to be able to check on him and see how he was doing.... My father died when I was young, and there was so much pressure for me to get back to school as soon as possible—before I'd had an opportunity to deal with all my emotions. I'm thankful that if my children were in a similar situation, they would still be able to continue learning in their own time and space with the security of being in a loving environment."

Pregnancy and the birth of a child can place incredible demands on the time and energy levels of a homeschooling mom. One homeschooler from Illinois who in the last year both had a new baby and relocated with her family says there were times when she felt guilty that she wasn't doing more. But when she looks at how much her children have grown academically, she realizes that relinquishing some of her control over their education was a good experience all around. "Learning became child led rather than parent led," she says. "[My children] explored their passions. They became much more independent learners and took ownership of what they learned. This past year has shaped my idea of how we will homeschool in the future."

How does the illness of a child affect homeschooling? In my city, when a child is ill and unable to attend his or her classes, the school district sends an in-home tutor to work with the child each day. One high schooler I knew before I began homeschooling had a tutor who worked with her each day for about an hour and a half. After the tutor left, she completed assignments on her own. That was her school day. I was always amazed at the efficiency of this system: The child stayed home and dealt with her illness while still receiving an excellent education. As homeschoolers, we deal with the challenge of a seriously ill child in much the same way.

Vicki, a mom from Minnesota, says her child's illness was one reason she started homeschooling. She is able to pace her teaching to her child's energy level. "We take time off when necessary with absolutely *no* guilt," she says.

Having one child out of several confined in a hospital is another kind of challenge. One California homeschooler's solution was to leave her older children at home to work on "a mixture of fun and independent study things" while she visited her child in the hospital.

Illness, whether our own, our child's, or that of another loved one, is never a welcome disruption in our lives. Dealing with it in the midst of homeschooling is not easy, but it always provides opportunities for personal and family growth.

Wrestling with Special Needs

What if your child has been diagnosed with special needs, or you suspect a learning disability or some other problem that makes learning a challenge for him or her? For a homeschooler without special training, teaching a child with special needs can be daunting.

On the other hand, a special-needs child may be better served by loving parents than by anyone else. Margaret, a homeschooler who answered a survey for this book, has two hearing-impaired children. Sending them off to school made her feel out of control of her children's upbringing and education. "I believed that, especially because of their speech and language problems, they needed the one-on-one attention that I alone could provide," she says. She also decided that if she concentrated on Jane's speech and language for a year, she could accomplish much more than any preschool could.

"I never planned to homeschool," says Missouri homeschooler Trish. "Our sons were on the application list for a developmentally oriented private school from a young age, and I planned to return to teaching." But her husband was transferred to a new city when their older son was ready for kindergarten. Because he narrowly missed the criteria for an official ADHD diagnosis, the public school wouldn't serve her son's special needs. And the best private school in the city wasn't set up to serve him. "We brought him home to learn," says Trish, "and our younger son no longer wanted to attend preschool because we had so much fun at home.

"Basically we are managing the ADHD without medication, so I deal with a human tornado 24/7," Trish says. She does feel fortunate that her husband handles the bedtime rituals, allowing her to retire with a good book each night at nine o'clock.

Trish never doubts her decision to homeschool, but she feels sad that public and private schools don't offer a more diverse educational experience. "[Addressing] developmental issues has been discarded in favor of full-time child care from age four," she says. "Differences in learning styles aren't addressed in a typical classroom. The model child is sociable, attractive, and compliant. Woe to the grabby child with a kinesthetic learning style. Woe to the funny-looking introvert who will someday grow into her features. I mourn that I must be a renegade to provide the education that my children deserve."

During the writing of this book, we learned that one of our children has a slight speech delay and another has mild ADD. We are still prayerfully digesting these diagnoses and trying to educate ourselves on the best ways to handle them. These problems are minor in comparison to the profound needs that challenge many parents, but the experience has given me a deeper appreciation for those who wrestle with their children's special needs.

If you know or suspect your child has a learning problem, I recommend a wise book written by Sharon Hensley: *Home Schooling Children with Special Needs: Turning Challenges into Opportunities.* "No matter what we call the difficulty our child has," says Hensley, "we all need *accurate knowledge* about the difference (difficulty, disability), we all need to *accept* our children as unique creations of God, and we all need to take *appropriate action* to teach our children and help them achieve their fullest potential."[1]

Hensley cautions parents to distinguish between a disability and a weakness; a child may have a weakness in math or spelling that isn't a disability. Likewise, she cautions labeling an underachiever as learning disabled. An underachiever, she says, will do poorly in all subjects unless something catches his interest, while the child with a weakness or a disability in a particular area will do poorly just in that area. "In order to have a learning disability," she explains, "a person must demonstrate three things: average intelligence, below average achievement *and* evidence of interference in either receiving, processing or reproducing information."[2]

Average intelligence is indicated by an IQ score. Below average achievement might be indicated by poor scores on achievement tests such as the Iowa Test of Basic Skills. If a child truly has a disability, poor achievement must be coupled with evidence of interference: visual system disorders, motor system disorders, auditory system (language) disorders, or attention system disorders.

Your first stop for information and resources about learning challenges must be NATHHAN (National Challenged Homeschoolers Associated Network). NATHHAN has a newsletter, a directory of families with similar situations, and an extensive lending library. Visit their Web site at http://www.NATHHAN.com, send an e-mail to nathanews@aol.com, or write to NATHHAN News, P.O. Box 39, Porthill, ID 83853.

A great resource for ADHD children and other energetic learners is *How to Get Your Child off the Refrigerator and on to Learning: Homeschooling Highly Distractible, ADHD, or Just Plain Fidgety Kids* by Carol Barnier. (For a copy, contact Emerald Books, P.O. Box 536, Lynnwood, WA 98046.) Barnier presents the humorous but effective methods she uses to deal with her own children and shares learning games and techniques for working with behavioral issues.

Working Through Grief

The death of a loved one could well be the most difficult crisis most of us will ever face. During the darkest days of our grieving, it may seem nearly impossible to focus on anything except our sorrow. How do we continue homeschooling in the midst of our grief?

Missouri homeschooler Trish advises moms to lower their expectations during times of deep depression. "[Your children] are learning every day, even if you're reading together in bed," she says. Some moms do minimal hands-on schooling during times they are dealing with grief and the depression that grief sometimes initiates. Instead, they take their children on lots of field trips, enriching their lives without having to call on personal resources that are already stretched thin.

The structure homeschooling provides can actually help a grieving family get through a crisis time. One Arizona homeschooler continued to teach her children at home after her mother's sudden death, even while she was still grieving. "It was good for me, as I *had* to focus on something and *had* to get out of bed in the morning," she says. She did make adjustments in her teaching style, allowing herself more flexibility than she had in the past. And as she worked through her grief, some of those adjustments became permanent changes in her approach to homeschooling.

"I was much more aware of eternity and what is really important," she says. "My mom left a lot of things undone, and I realized that none of them really mattered. I was able to apply this to myself: 'Will it really matter if I never crochet this afghan? Will it really matter if my girls learn their state capitals in fifth grade instead of fourth grade?' I realized [that] most of my stress was self-imposed. No one was requesting that I do the majority of the things I was stressed about."

If our children see us cope with the personal crises of our lives, continuing to put one foot in front of the other in faith, they will learn that problems can be met and surmounted. They may also learn *how*. Ellen, a homeschooler from Maine, tells this story: "In the fall of 1998, my father passed away following a very long illness. Ten days later, I miscarried our much-wanted third baby. We were all devastated. I can't imagine what life would have been like for my children had they needed to go 'be cheerful' in public school all day. We cried together, did a lot of praying, cuddled, read large numbers of wonderful books, took long walks, and just supported each other through the time of trial. While the math books didn't get opened every day during that period, we grew in countless ways as a family. We talked about our losses, as well as about happier times. We spoke of the future, and all the things we wanted to do. That time was very painful for us, but in the same way, the lessons we learned are irreplaceable."

This is the way it works: We are building our children's character while God is shaping ours.

Learning from Crises

Crises test our faith, sharpen our focus, force us to prioritize. They teach us to slow down, and they teach us to hold on to the things most dear to us. "Consider it pure joy, my brothers, whenever you face trials of many kinds," James 1:2-3 exhorts us, "because you know that the testing of your faith develops perseverance." If there is one thing a homeschooler needs, it is perseverance! The fruit of our labor is sometimes long to ripen.

I am not exactly thrilled when a crisis occurs in my life, but I no longer dread the prospect. Every crisis provides an opportunity for me to grow, to develop patience, to practice faith. Those times in which we have no choice but to trust God are the times in which he reveals his wisdom and imparts his peace. Our troubles lead us to focus on God and his Word and to trust him in all of life's circumstances.

"Have I not commanded you?" he gently reminds us in Joshua 1:9. "Be strong and courageous. Do not be terrified; do not be discouraged, for the LORD your God will be with you wherever you go." What a marvelous promise!

In the midst of every crisis, God is near. He is present to us every day; he waits for us to reach out to him. He is a God of comfort. Though he will stretch us further than we believed we could ever be stretched, he will never give us a greater load than we can bear (see 1 Corinthians 10:13).

"We are hard pressed on every side, but not crushed; perplexed, but not in despair; persecuted, but not abandoned; struck down, but not destroyed," Paul wrote in his second letter to the Corinthians (4:8-9). Although our bodies are "jars of clay," they hold "the light of the knowledge of the glory of God" and express "the all-surpassing power" of God (2 Corinthians 4:6-7). Our faith in that light and power can sustain us in times of crises.

How do we gain access to God's power? Jesus himself told us in John 15:4: "Remain in me, and I will remain in you. No branch can bear fruit by itself; it must remain in the vine. Neither can you bear fruit unless you remain in me." Crises teach us that when we yield to God, he will see us through any situation. He is a God of abundance, the source of abundant strength, abundant joy, abundant wisdom. As long as we stay connected to the vine, we will flourish. When we fall away from the vine, we will wither and die—whether the times are good or bad.

Our children learn a great deal from observing our response to crises. Crises give them an opportunity to observe our faith in action. As they see us meet our trials head-on and work through them, their own faith is strengthened. They see that life goes on, even in the midst of less than ideal circumstances. They learn that problems need not defeat us—even if they slow us down a bit.

More Practical Pointers to Survive Homeschooling During Crises

- Accept the fact that you will sometimes feel overwhelmed. It's normal. It's okay. If you persevere, by God's grace the feeling will pass.
- Seek out the advice and support of others who have faced the same challenges you are facing. Whatever it is, you're not the first to go through it. You aren't alone.
- Make sure you address your own health care issues.
- Allow yourself to change directions in your homeschool during a time of crisis. If you're feeling overwhelmed, lighten up the academic load and spend time reading books together. Concentrate on your relationships with your children. If your curriculum isn't working, don't be afraid to try a different approach. Give your children more independent, child-directed studies. (Refer to chapter 4 for specific ideas.)

When we find ourselves saying, "This is too hard," when we come to the end of our own ability to cope with crises and we turn them over to God, then he can begin to work in us. Crises are an opportunity for great personal growth—if we will but persevere.

CHAPTER THIRTEEN

"You're Going to Ruin Those Kids!"

Dealing with Disapproval

Y ou're going to ruin those kids."

The dire prediction came from a well-intentioned relative after my husband and I announced our intention to homeschool. The words pierced my heart and touched a deep-seated insecurity.

I did not approach motherhood with confidence. My own mother suffered from chronic depression and my father was a weekend alcoholic, so I didn't have much in the way of role models. When I contemplated raising children, my greatest fear was that I would "mess them up" because my own childhood had been so messed up. The warning words of that relative haunted me.

To be fair to those relatives who initially questioned my choice, I admit I have not always made wise decisions. There were entire eras of my life when I lived and thought as a fool. I have a history with my relatives, and they remember every fault and foible, every stumble and wrong move. They may have been truly concerned that I was making yet another unwise decision.

When my husband and I first started raising our children, we just wanted "normal kids." As we progressed in our parenting and continued to seek God's wisdom, however, we found we had a hard time deciding what a normal kid was. As we looked around us, we saw that a lot of so-called normal kids had no faith base, were highly disrespectful of their parents and of anyone in authority, were marginal scholars, and possessed bad attitudes. If this defined normal, we decided, we didn't want it after all. We wanted something different.

It was that seeking after something different that put some of my relatives and colleagues into a tailspin of concern. Would we do a good job if we weren't doing the job the way it had always been done?

Not everyone disapproved of our decision. After all, we live in a society in which many schools are failing miserably. Children in our culture as a general rule lack guidance and supervision. School violence is on the rise. Schools and children are the topic of much debate. Against this backdrop, homeschoolers are admired in some circles for their dedication and sacrifice. In others, though, we are mistrusted and perceived as oddballs. And many people simply don't know *what* to think of us. They hear that homeschooling might be bad for kids but have insufficient information for an educated opinion.

The fact that we are choosing an alternative form of education for our children opens us up to both scrutiny and criticism, which can be unnerving, to say the least. Disapproval can shake up even the most grounded person. Stephen Covey, best known for his book *The Seven Habits of Highly Effective People,* calls the effect "spiritual vertigo." The absence of values in the culture at large can alter our moral and ethical sense and cause us to doubt our decisions. He likens the feeling to the vertigo a pilot experiences when flying without instruments through a cloud bank. He can't receive ground reference, and he can't use his instincts because the inner ear is disoriented.

Similarly, when we encounter extremely powerful influences in life, such as a dominant culture, charismatic people, or dynamic group movements, we become disoriented. Our moral compass is thrown off, and we don't even know it. The needle that in less turbulent times pointed easily to true north—to the set of principles that normally govern us in our lives—is being jerked about by the powerful electric and magnetic fields of a storm.[1]

To deal with this spiritual vertigo, I believe we must take a proactive approach to the misunderstanding, disapproval, and outright hostility that our decision to educate our children at home sometimes engenders.

Our first line of defense is to remind ourselves, as often as necessary, that we are accountable to God—not to anyone else—for how we raise our kids. As my friend Becky says, "God told us to homeschool. When he tells us not to, we'll change our ways."

Our second line of defense is to educate ourselves. Why do people disapprove of homeschooling? Could some of their concerns be legitimate? If so, and if we were called to, could we answer those concerns? First Peter 3:15 exhorts us to "always be prepared to give an answer to everyone who asks you to give the reason for the hope that you have." While Peter's interest was that we be able to articulate to others the reasons for our faith in Christ, his words are good advice for homeschoolers as well.

Having an answer for the world's concerns about homeschooling is not so much for our detractors as it is for ourselves. When the disapproval of others shakes our sense of certainty about our calling, there is no better way to regain our balance than to understand our reasons for the hope that we have.

Legitimate Concerns?

People disapprove of homeschooling for a variety of reasons. Katherine Pfleger, writing for *The New Republic*, expresses a concern that "well-meaning

parents who lack the know-how, time, or resources to be effective teachers—or worse, parents who actually have malignant motives for keeping
their kids out of school—will deprive their children of needed social skills
and a decent education."[2]

In light of a study released by the Home School Legal Defense Association in 1999, Pfleger's concerns about homeschoolers receiving a "decent
education" seem unwarranted. National testing expert Lawrence Rudner
coordinated efforts to administer the Iowa Test of Basic Skills to more than
twenty thousand homeschooled students. The results? Homeschooled students in grades one through four scored an average of one grade level
higher than their peers in public and private schools. At the eighth-grade
level, homeschooled students performed *four* grade levels above the
national average. Interestingly, students who had been taught entirely at
home scored the highest.[3]

Pfleger's concerns that parents who teach their children at home will
deprive them of needed social skills have been addressed in chapter 11. The
evidence is that homeschooled children are not only well adjusted socially
but as a whole have consistently fewer behavior problems than children
educated in the traditional manner. Socialization provided by homeschooling, rather than being isolating and stultifying, can be positive and healthy.

Pfleger may have a legitimate concern about parents who keep their
children home from school for less than healthy reasons, however. I'm
aware of parents who have pulled a delinquent child out of school in order
to avoid his or her expulsion, for instance, deceptively claiming they were
going to homeschool the child when in reality they had no plans to do so.

One junior high principal I interviewed says the most egregious abuse
of homeschooling he's seen is parents pulling a child out of school for their
own convenience—to baby-sit younger children, for instance. One homeschooling father he had dealt with, a roofer, purportedly took his son out
of school to educate him at home but instead put him to work as his assis-

tant. Situations such as these make all homeschoolers look bad and may ultimately diminish our freedoms.

Some people object to homeschooling because they see it as a conclave of the religious right. Indeed, this was my own prejudice prior to becoming educated about the subject. A small group of homeschoolers truly are religious fanatics who want to isolate themselves and their families from the world in an unhealthy way. Any approach that clings to legalism and is not immersed in integrity and the desire to provide the best educational experience for a child is dangerous and irresponsible.

The common misperception that homeschools are the exclusive domain of conservative Christians took form in the 1980s, when changes in tax regulations brought about the closure of hundreds of small Christian schools. Mary Griffith, in her book *The Homeschooling Handbook,* explains that "parents who had turned to private church schools as a refuge from the worldly orientation of public schools suddenly found homeschooling their only acceptable option.... This new wave of Christian homeschoolers was so large that the popular image of homeschoolers became the caricature of the intensely religious family isolating their children from the world to protect them from the evils of evolution and sex education."[4]

Certainly our desire to see our children grow in the grace and knowledge of Jesus Christ is one of the reasons we homeschool. But this is not the case for every parent who makes the homeschooling choice. The fact is, homeschools today run the gamut of religions from Christian to Islamic to Jewish. Others are purely secular. Black professionals, worried by the lack of safe, effective public schools for their children, are a fast-growing group of homeschoolers.[5] Parents who educate their children at home represent a broad spectrum of Americans who are seeking something better for their children than what public and private school systems have to offer.

Study after study on the effectiveness of homeschooling yields overwhelmingly positive feedback. Dozens of books on homeschooling are available in secular as well as religious bookstores, and the media are report-ing more and more positive stories about homeschooling. As a result, public perception of homeschools is slowly changing. A Phi Delta Kappa/Gallup poll in 1985 reported that 16 percent of those surveyed approved of homeschooling, while 73 percent disapproved. By 1997, the numbers were up another twenty points (to 36 percent) for those who approved and down sixteen points (to 57 percent) for those who disap-proved.[6] In the wake of the unprecedented school violence we have wit-nessed in schools in the last several years, from strictly a school safety perspective, it would be interesting to see the results of a similar poll today.

Homeschoolers stand to gain ground and acceptance in the current cli-mate because there is no legitimate research to prove otherwise. If you are a homeschooler dealing with the disapproval of relatives and others, be encouraged. They may come around yet!

I believe that some people object to homeschooling because they are envious. "I wish I could homeschool," I've had people say to me, "but I am not a super mom. I couldn't do it." All I can do in a case such as this is to openly share my struggles. You don't have to be a super mom to edu-cate your kids at home. I know, because I'm not. God uses ordinary people, calling and equipping us to do a job we sometimes feel is beyond our ability. We rest in the faith that he never calls us to do more than we are able.

Finally, there are opponents of homeschooling who truly have funda-mental philosophical differences with those of us who have made this lifestyle choice. Perhaps they have studied the issue and have an informed position, based on their own philosophical system, against homeschooling. These are the people with whom I graciously agree to disagree. Trying to win them over to my side would be a waste of time since their convictions are based on an entirely different system of beliefs. Their minds are already made up—and so is mine!

Walking the Walk

It's understandable that you should want the people you most care about to approve of your decision to homeschool. I believe many people who disapprove of our lifestyle choice do so simply because they are uninformed. If this is the case for you, and your relatives and loved ones are receptive, share the research you've done on homeschooling in an effort to put their concerns to rest. You might want to give disapproving relatives a copy of an article that positively portrays homeschooling, for example, or a well-researched book such as my own *Field Guide to Homeschooling* (Grand Rapids: Fleming Revell, 1998).

Before being too hard on relatives for their negativity, consider carefully their point of view. Imagine how you would feel if your children, once they had children of their own, adopted a completely different parenting approach from yours—an approach that might be considered "radical." You can now begin to understand how your relatives might feel about your decision to homeschool. Be respectful as they express their concerns. If you are truly homeschooling out of your convictions, their concerns will fade as they see the proof in the pudding.

We must carefully avoid shoving our convictions about homeschooling down anyone's throat. While 1 Peter 3:15 does exhort us to "be prepared to give an answer to everyone who asks you to give the reason for the hope that you have," we are cautioned to do so "with gentleness and respect, keeping a clear conscience, so that those who speak maliciously against your good behavior in Christ may be ashamed of their slander" (verses 15-16).

When answering our critics, we must be "wise as a serpent and gentle as a dove," cautions Tina, a homeschooler from Montana. "Let your actions speak louder than [your] words." She doesn't talk her contentious relatives to death, Tina says; she and her family simply "live the life."

Don't forget that the work of conviction is the Holy Spirit's—not ours. Our call, as Tina reminds us, is to live our lives as an example of faithfulness. In fact, says Mary Griffith in *The Homeschooling Handbook,* cutting back on "evangelizing" may even lead your critics to cut back on their negative comments. And as the novelty of the idea wears off and your homeschooling efforts bear fruit, you'll likely hear even less from them.[7]

Reach a truce with your relatives. Keep communication open. Listen to their concerns. Share your choices and your goals. Don't allow fighting on the subject, especially in front of your children. Follow the example of Suzanne, a homeschooler in Illinois, who in the face of criticism tries "to smile and walk away." Then go home and live out your convictions. The best defense for our choice to homeschool is to live our lives in such a way that others can have no legitimate complaints about it.

Our family lifestyle is the highly visible fruit of our convictions and beliefs. Walking the walk of a Christian homeschooler will always be more productive than arguing with our neighbors about why our children aren't in school. Author Debra Bell calls this our "homeschool witness." Our family lifestyle, she says, ought to be a "voluntary public relations campaign" to the communities in which we live.[8]

From a practical perspective, do whatever you can to keep the neighbors out of your business. If you live next door to hostile neighbors, monitor the hours your kids are allowed to play outside. Don't otherwise annoy the neighbors with loud pets, loud music, or an overly messy yard. Make sure your contact with them is friendly and polite.

While serving as a referral attorney for the Home School Legal Defense Association, I dealt with parents who were experiencing some legal difficulty relative to homeschooling. In almost every instance when a family was reported to child welfare services, it was *not* specifically for their efforts to homeschool. Perhaps a well-intentioned (or sometimes ill-intentioned) neighbor had contacted child welfare authorities about a dirty, unkempt child being out in the yard during the day. In the course of an ensuing investigation (required by law), the homeschooling would come to light. The initial complaint almost always began because a neighbor disapproved of something he or she saw and then reported the family.

Knowing that our whole program could be undermined by some superficial observation of a neighbor makes it especially important that we live our lives above reproach. What other people see in our families will do more to help or harm the cause of home education than anything we may verbalize or advocate. People want to see us living a life that makes sense in light of our convictions.

With very little effort, homeschoolers can build positive relationships within their communities. You might sponsor a homeschooling information day at your public library so citizens can come to ask questions and get information about homeschooling. Or you might invite the public to homeschool project fairs, science fairs, and geography fairs. Newspapers are generally cooperative and will be happy to place notices and press releases of these events.

You might also have your children participate in traditional school competitions such as geography bees, Battle of the Books, and spelling bees. Several homeschoolers have won competitions at the national level in these events. Such awards can only be good for the cause of homeschooling.

My very best advice for homeschoolers who meet with disapproval for their choice to teach their children at home is to follow a principle I learned in law school: "Let the thing speak for itself." In Latin it's called *res ipsa loquitur*, and in legal terms it refers to circumstances in which the truth of the matter is so obvious there is no need for discussion of its merits.

The mother-in-law of my friend Denise is a public school teacher who "doesn't generally approve of homeschooling." "We just stayed very low key about it," says Denise, "and through the years she has seen my sons grow academically and spiritually." Recently, her mother-in-law told her that she's been "boasting to her colleagues" about what a great job she's doing educating the boys at home. "For us the silent witness is best," Denise shares. "Our kids speak of homeschooling to [their] friends and [their friends'] parents in ways we couldn't even put into words."

Merre, a homeschooler in Missouri, lets members of the extended family see what's going on in her family's homeschool by inviting them to special programs and presentations. "One year," she says, "our twelve-year-old son, who was studying medieval history, prepared a meal, costumes, entertainment, invitations, and a brief history report for the extended family." The evening was "a delight to all and made a very positive impression." You might think about inviting neighbors to such special events as well.

Those of us who homeschool diligently and with integrity are rarely recognized for the sacrifices we make for our family. We live in a culture that devalues children and motherhood and has little real interest in family issues—except, of course, during an election year.

In an article entitled "Parent Support, Not Child Care," journalist Barbara Dafoe contends that parents everywhere are "flunking the most basic tests." "In a survey by the Carnegie Foundation, 90 percent of a national sample of public school teachers say a lack of parental support is a problem in their classroom," she writes. "Librarians [recently] gathered at a national convention to draft a new policy to deal with the problem of parents who send unattended children to the library after school. Day-care workers complain to Ann Landers that all too often parents hand over their children with empty stomachs and full diapers."[9]

Adds author Susan Schaeffer Macaulay, homeschooling mom and daughter of Francis and Edith Schaeffer, "There has never been a generation when children have so desperately needed their parents' time, thoughtful creativity, and friendship."[10]

It's hard to imagine why anyone would disapprove of our choice to educate our children at home when we are extending time, creativity, and friendship to our children in such abundance. Homeschoolers truly are practicing the ultimate in parental involvement.

In the end, I've discovered, it doesn't really matter what anybody outside my family thinks about our school at home. In the words of Shari, a homeschooler from Illinois, "I know in my heart [that] God has called me to do this. If I teach God's Word, when the kids are old, they won't depart from it. What a great insurance policy!" When we are truly at peace with our decision to teach our children at home, the criticism of others may shake us, but it will not move us.

There was a time when the question "Do your kids know they are different?" made me cringe. When I hear that question now, I check my defensiveness and reply with all the enthusiasm I can muster, "I hope so!" When I see examples of who they might be *without* my daily guidance and input to their lives, I am grateful that my kids are different. I hope you feel the same way about yours.

Finding Support

When you're feeling disapproval from others for your decision to homeschool, seek out the company of those who support and nurture your choice. Go where you need to go for encouragement: your husband, your relatives and friends, your homeschool support group, perhaps an online support community. Each issue of *The Teaching Home* magazine lists statewide support groups. You can contact them to be put in touch with a local group. The Home School Legal Defense Association (HSLDA) also maintains a listing of support groups on their Internet site at http://www.hslda.org.

Homeschooling magazines can offer encouragement, too. Here's a list of possibilities:

Home School Digest
P.O. Box 374
Covert, MI 49043
616-764-1710
http://www.homeschooldigest.com
(See my regular column, "Field Notes.")

Growing Without Schooling
Holt Associates
2269 Massachusetts Ave.
Cambridge, MA 02140
617-864-3100
e-mail: holtgws@aol.com
Web site: www.holtgws.com

Home Education Magazine
P.O. Box 1587
Palmer, AK 99645-1587
907-746-1336
e-mail: HomeEdMag@aol.com
Web site: www.home-ed-magazine.com

Home Schooling Today
P.O. Box 1608
Fort Collins, CO 80522-1608
954-962-1930
e-mail: hstodaymag@aol.com

Practical Homeschooling
Home Life

Box 1250
Fenton, MO 63026-1850
800-346-6322
e-mail: PHSCustSvc@aol.com
Web site: www.home-school.com

The Teaching Home
P.O. Box 20219
Portland, OR 97294
503-253-9633

Homeschool support on the Internet is available at the following sites:

Homeschooler's Curriculum Swap
http://theswap.com

Crosswalk: Home Schooling
http://homeschool.crosswalk.com

Kaleidoscapes Discussion Board
http://www.kaleidoscapes.com/wwboard

Christian Homeschool Forum
http://www.gocin.com/homeschool

Eclectic Homeschoolers
http://eho.org

Whatever you need to do to feel supported when the disapproval of others is getting you down, do it! You'll find new strength to "keep on keeping on" as you realize you're not alone on your journey. Others have survived disapproval. You will too.

More Practical Pointers for Dealing with Disapproval

- Strive for excellence. Encourage your children to be the best they can be. Don't give your critics an opportunity to criticize!
- Invite skeptical relatives to participate in your homeschool. They might read to the children, for instance, or teach a craft. Share with them a taste of your life.
- Challenge critics to sit in on classes in a public school for a day to observe what children there are exposed to.
- Highlight the advantages of homeschooling with friends and relatives. Talk about the exciting field trips you are taking or a special study unit you've devised. Be enthusiastic. You may have waged World War III over math facts with your kids this morning, but this afternoon you have the opportunity to influence someone's attitude toward homeschooling. Convey the joy and satisfaction of your calling, not just the frustration.
- Know the laws that relate to homeschooling in your state and obey them. "Voluntary registration" is a matter of preference, but mandatory state requirements must be met. Respect authority, even if you don't agree; to fail to comply with state requirements amounts to civil disobedience. Besides, how really onerous is the law if you are doing a creditable job of educating your children?
- Don't denigrate the public schools or school systems. For one thing, your kids may need the support of public school teachers and administrators in the future for letters of reference, intern-

ships, or other opportunities. Engender their respect for your efforts. To engage in criticism only fuels the fire of prejudice against homeschoolers.

- Avoid making statements that imply you're "above" the public school system. "I would never send my kids to public school," for instance. (What if your husband died? Do you really want to have to eat crow?) Or, "I don't let my kids play with just *anyone*." Many parents practice selective socialization. You don't have to broadcast it; just do it.

- Let the world see Christ in your home and your homeschool. This is the best work you can do for the homeschooling movement and ultimately the best way to change critics into supporters.

Disapproval is never fun, but we can use it to clarify our values and strengthen our resolve. If we avoid defensiveness, build positive relationships in our communities, and teach our children well, "the thing will speak for itself." Who can argue with success?

CHAPTER FOURTEEN

To Walk and Not Grow Weary

Handling Discouragement

I'm tired of being the mom," I announced to my husband one morning early on in our homeschooling journey. "I quit."

"What?" he said, incredulous. I could almost see the pictures filling his head: hungry, crying children, a filthy house, dour-faced child welfare social workers swarming through the front door.

"Oh, I don't mean forever," I reassured him. "Just for today." I stopped, thought about it a moment longer, and changed my mind. "Well, maybe a couple of days…"

If you're a homeschooling mom, I have no doubt you understand what I was feeling. I don't know anyone who homeschools who hasn't had a bad day. It comes with the territory. Maybe the children are fighting. Maybe they have the attention span of gnats. Maybe they are challenging you at every turn. Invariably, the house is a mess.

Bad days used to throw me into a tailspin. I questioned *everything*. Had I made the right decision to homeschool? Was I using the right curriculum? Were my children going to be maladjusted? Was I ever going to have a clean house again? On really bad days I wondered whatever had possessed me to give up a job I loved to raise all these kids!

With a few years of homeschooling under my belt, I began to realize that bad days were part of the package. Not just the homeschooling package, but life in general. I realized I'd been looking at my former life as an attorney through rose-colored glasses, and when I finally set those glasses aside I remembered that parts of that life were far from ideal. I remembered days I'd despised my work, days I'd come home stressed out and longing for the simple pleasures of home.

In homeschooling as in the rest of life, nothing is ever simple and nothing is all pleasure. It's when I start thinking that teaching my kids at home *ought* to be simple and pleasurable that I get discouraged. My unrealistic expectations and presumptions cloud my thinking.

A Spiritual Issue

When I find myself wondering whether this homeschooling journey is really worth the time and energy I'm pouring into it, when I'm feeling discouraged or disillusioned, when I'm tempted to call the whole thing quits, the first thing I do is remind myself exactly what it is I'm doing and why I'm doing it.

Reviewing our family mission statement helps me in that process (see chapter 8). My husband and I homeschool because God called us to homeschool. We homeschool because we're accountable for the way our children turn out. Taking charge of our children's education, raising them "in the nurture and admonition of the Lord" (Ephesians 6:4, KJV), training them to be effective adults—all are goals that we have determined are important for our family.

Once I'm clear again about my reasons for embarking on the homeschooling journey and I understand what is at stake should I allow discouragement to sidetrack or stop me, I'm ready for some serious soul searching. Discouragement, I believe, is a spiritual issue. The number-one cause for discouragement in our lives and in our homeschooling journey is spiritual stagnation. When we neglect our relationship with God, we become disconnected from our ultimate source of strength, joy, and peace. Without that connection, how can we expect to manifest power and peace in our lives?

If discouragement is a spiritual problem, then our best weapon in the fight against it is to nurture our spiritual lives, immersing ourselves in Scripture and prayer. As we seek God's heart and reestablish our connection with him, we'll find what we need to reconnect with our vision for our family and our children. With that vision, we'll find the strength we need to stay the course to which we've been called.

Living the life of faith is a daily discipline. "Sometimes it can be overwhelming if you start looking too far ahead," says a mom who homeschools twins in North Carolina. "If we take one step at a time on our path, we will get to our goal." Those steps are not always easy; we don't always know exactly where we're going, and sometimes the path we step onto is rocky and treacherous. But we have God's promise that his Word will be a lamp to our feet and a light to our path as we make our way in the dark (see Psalm 119:105).

Our faith is not an emotion. It is a decision we make. Meditating on God's Word and character helps to strengthen the decision daily. We can replace our doubt and discouragement when we train our minds according to Philippians 4:8-9: "Whatever is true, whatever is noble, whatever is right, whatever is pure, whatever is lovely, whatever is admirable—if anything is excellent or praiseworthy—think about such things. Whatever you have learned or received or heard from me, or seen in me—put it into practice. And the God of peace will be with you." When we feel ourselves wavering, we need to run to the Word to renew our minds and to fill our hearts with his promises, remembering that nothing—"neither height nor depth, nor anything else in all creation"—can separate us from the love of God in Christ Jesus our Lord (Romans 8:39).

I like to keep a three-ring binder with alphabetical tabs where I can write down Bible verses that apply to an emotion or problem I'm struggling with. For instance, under *A* I might have verses that refer to anger: "Everyone should be quick to listen, slow to speak and slow to become angry, for man's anger does not bring about the righteous life that God desires" (James 1:19-20). "A patient man has great understanding, but a quick-tempered man displays folly" (Proverbs 14:29).

Under *B* I might have verses that deal with bitterness, such as Ephesians 4:31: "Get rid of all bitterness, rage and anger." One of my life verses, Psalm 113:9, is also under *B* in my notebook: "He settles the barren woman in her home as a happy mother of children. Praise the LORD."

Written in my own hand, these verses are a wealth of encouragement in difficult times. I can look at them time and time again for refreshment and encouragement, and I also have them on hand to share with a friend who might be experiencing the same problems.

Renewing ourselves spiritually doesn't have to take grand gestures and massive amounts of time—although those would be great! We can take small slices of time in our lives to renew and refresh ourselves:

- Keep Bibles and devotional materials handy to take advantage of unexpected time. Not to be disrespectful, but we even keep a Bible and a daily devotional in our bathroom. We also keep materials near our bed and by our favorite chair. I hang scriptures and praise songs over the kitchen sink so I can meditate on them while I do my chores.

- Keeping a journal has been an extraordinary blessing for me. I have kept fancy bound journals written in only with fountain pens, and I have kept spiral-bound notebooks in pencil and marker. It doesn't matter. For the past year or so I have been keeping my journal on the computer, taking an extra five minutes after I've finished working to record my thoughts and prayers for the day. Keeping a journal provides a place to pour out your prayers, your feelings, your hopes, and your dreams. Rereading your entries after a life crisis has passed is also a tremendous testimony to God's faithfulness.

• Can't get out for a Bible study? How about hosting one in your home? It doesn't have to be huge. I regularly meet with three or four women from my church who also homeschool. In the winter we meet at my home for tea and a topic, like reverencing our husbands or loving our children. In the summer we meet at a park so the children can play while we talk and go through a Bible study.

• Can't get up early for devotions? God doesn't care what time we pray. We can offer small prayers throughout the day. If early morning or late night do not work for you for a slice of Bible reading, designate a half-hour in the afternoon as your devotional time. Even if your children no longer nap, they can take that time for their own devotions or silent reading time.

Other ways to nurture our spiritual lives include reading encouraging books, listening to uplifting tapes, and being part of a healthy, Bible-believing church community. Fellowship with other Christian homeschoolers can also strengthen our faith; make sure you attend a homeschooling seminar at least once a year, and make it a practice to go to support group meetings and mom's nights out with fellow homeschoolers. One homeschooling mom from Nebraska shares that in every case when she's felt like giving up, "God [has been] faithful to put someone in my path who…convinced me we were doing the right thing."

"The LORD will guide you always," promised the prophet Isaiah (Isaiah 58:11). "He will satisfy your needs in a sun-scorched land and will strengthen your frame. You will be like a well-watered garden, like a spring whose waters never fail."

More Reasons for Discouragement

Even when I'm doing all I can to stay connected to my source of strength, other things can rob me of my sense that all is well in my homeschool and my life. Sometimes, for instance, I try to do too much—more than anyone else would ever expect of me. I've been known to have unrealistic expectations of my children, too, in areas of behavior and academic achievement. When my efforts at discipline are inconsistent and my kids are bouncing off the walls or when I can't seem to get a new concept across in a way they understand, I'd give almost anything to send them off to school and let someone else deal with them for a while!

I find that when I'm not taking care of myself—too little sleep, maybe, or too much junk food—my energy is low and my motivation practically nonexistent. That's fertile ground for discouragement. And sometimes I simply slip into negativity, and nothing anyone says or does could cheer me up. I remind myself of one of my daughters, who regularly cries, "This is too hard for me!"

During those times I once again turn to scripture:

"You, O God, are my fortress, my loving God" (Psalm 59:17).

"Be on your guard; stand firm in the faith; be men of courage; be strong. Do everything in love" (1 Corinthians 16:13-14).

"Strengthen the feeble hands, steady the knees that give way; say to those with fearful hearts, 'Be strong, do not fear; your God will come, he will come with vengeance; with divine retribution he will come to save you'" (Isaiah 35:3-4).

"Look to the LORD and his strength; seek his face always" (Psalm 105:4).

Another cause of discouragement among homeschoolers is worry about whether we're doing enough for our kids. We've taken on a huge responsibility in the education of our children. We are accountable to no less an authority than God. Are we meeting his standards? Are we doing right by our children?

Maybe their progress seems slow. Would they be doing better if someone else were teaching them? Perhaps we feel we aren't covering enough bases with our curriculum. Another year has passed, and we've not yet begun to study a foreign language, our physical education program is nearly nonexistent, and we've barely scratched the surface of art and music. The rate at which the body of knowledge in the world continues to expand is alarming. When we contemplate all there is in the world to learn, let alone teach our children, we can easily feel overwhelmed.

On the other hand, there are days when we jam an entire day's formal study into the morning, dash off to the museum for the afternoon, and then drag home for piano lessons and an evening of church activities. Those days, too, can leave us feeling tired, discouraged, and overwhelmed. We *did* a lot, but did our frantic activity really do any good?

When it comes to preparing our children for adulthood, how much is enough? There simply is no way for us to master all knowledge. What we *can* do is teach our children how to learn and how to love learning. With the proper tools and the ability to learn independently, they will always be able to gain the information they need when they need it.

Comparison: The Ultimate Joy Killer

I know of few more potent joy killers than our very human tendency to compare ourselves to others. Reading homeschooling magazines and literature can be encouraging and inspiring, but sometimes what they inspire for me is the comparison game. A magazine arrives with a picture-perfect family on the cover and a description of their homeschool inside. My heart sinks. We don't look like that. I haven't made time to make the girls matching jumpers. We haven't ever dissected a cow's eyeball. We don't use the new teaching method featured in the issue.

The minute we meet or hear about Suzy Perfect Homeschooler, we begin to make comparisons: Is she doing more than I am? Is she using a better curriculum? Are her kids learning more? Are they better behaved than my kids are? The answers we come up with are usually not in our favor. Doubt sets in. Discouragement follows.

In her book *The Ultimate Guide to Home Schooling*, homeschooler Debra Bell maintains she has to keep blinders on to stay content with her homeschool efforts and results. I know what she means. So many areas of comparison steal my contentment:

- Mary's children are so well behaved and polite.
- Judy has the newest, spiffiest curriculum. Her husband makes a lot of money.
- Lisa teaches her three daughters in a sunny room large enough to house an entire preschool, complete with a playhouse, a well-stocked play store, several large tables, a reading area with comfy pillows, and a video-viewing enclave.
- Sally has a van big enough to transport the entire neighborhood to youth group at church.

Comparing ourselves to others is unhealthy in many respects. For one thing, it keeps us from focusing on the real standard—Christ himself. "For those God foreknew he also predestined to be conformed to the likeness of his Son," we read in Romans 8:29. We are called to be conformed to Christ's image alone and no one else's.

Comparison also keeps us from celebrating our uniqueness. If only we had as much room in our house as they do, we tell ourselves. If only we could afford the curriculum they use. If only my husband were home as much as hers is!

"If onlys" rob us of contentment. The fact is, our house is our house. We have the income we have. Our husbands are home as often as they are home. We are a one-of-a-kind family who has made the choices right for us. Celebrate your uniqueness! To remind yourselves just how unique your family is, fill in the blanks after the sentence starters below with the first thing that comes to mind.

We are _____.

We believe _____.

We dream _____.

We want _____.

We worry about _____.

We wonder about _____.

We weep for _____.

We support _____.

David praises God in Psalm 139:14 because he is "fearfully and wonderfully made." So should we celebrate our own uniqueness. As families, we, too, are fearfully and wonderfully made.

Judging yourself, your children, or your homeschool on the basis of comparisons with others who have different needs, desires, and standards than your own is unproductive and self-destructive. When you're tempted to make comparisons, instead of contrasting "you" and "them," try contrasting "then" and "now"—that is, where you have been compared to where you are. In our homeschool I use scope and sequence charts and a guided curriculum in part because it gives me a benchmark to measure my children's progress. And while traits like self-control and confidence and a deeper walk with the Lord aren't as easy to measure as academic achievement, we know when our children have made progress in those areas. We can take pride in all our children's accomplishments—and our own as well—without having to compare ourselves to anyone else (see Galatians 6:4).

Does avoiding comparisons mean we shouldn't try to emulate the good we see in other homeschool families? Far from it. There is a distinct difference between imitation and comparison, and Scripture encourages us to follow the good examples of others. The apostle Paul, in particular, had much to say on this matter: "You became imitators of us and of the Lord," he praised the Thessalonians (1 Thessalonians 1:6). "Join with others in following my example, brothers, and take note of those who live according to the pattern we gave you," he exhorted the believers at Philippi (Philippians 3:17). "Be imitators of God, therefore, as dearly loved children," he wrote the Ephesians, "and live a life of love, just as Christ loved us and gave himself up for us as a fragrant offering and sacrifice to God" (Ephesians 5:1-2).

Emulating the good in others has limits, however. The Bible tells us we are to be conformed to the image of Jesus (Romans 8:29), not that of Suzy Perfect Homeschooler. Sometimes we get so caught up in following the latest homeschooling expert or the latest educational fad that we cannot hear what God is telling us. But when we give authority to a fad or an expert, we take it away from the Lord and the Holy Spirit.

What makes another homeschooler worthy of emulation? Ask yourself these questions:

- Does her family please God?
- Does each family member have a lively relationship with Jesus?
- Do they exhibit Christlike character in their dealings with others?

Only when we can answer yes to these important questions should we seek to imitate another homeschooler in any way.

Practice Joy

One of the best ways to dispense with discouragement in your life is to practice joy. How? By learning to love your life *just as it is.* "If onlys," as I said earlier in this chapter, are certain joy killers. *If only* this kid wasn't colicky, we think. *If only* my daughter weren't two years old.

I've found joy with a colicky baby by bundling him up, rocking him close to my heart, and singing "Jesus Loves Me." I've found joy with a two-year-old who was driving me crazy by setting her on my lap and praying with her: "I thank God for your spirit, your wonderful laugh, your beautiful smile. I pray that Jesus will help you obey today."

God never promised us that life would be all sunshine and happiness. We know as Christians that we are not entitled to "the good life." By God's grace, he gives us what he gives us. When we reach the point where we really believe that the good life is the life we have, we'll find that discouragement isn't an issue in our life or in our homeschool.

Joy comes in tiny segments. If we deal with life as it comes, moment by moment, one step at a time, we'll find it. Now is all God asks us to handle. "Do not worry about tomorrow," he says, "for tomorrow will worry about itself. Each day has enough trouble of its own" (Matthew 6:34). Take each day's challenges one step at a time—one moment at a time if you have to. Find joy in the now.

Practical Pointers for Dispensing with Discouragement

- Encourage someone else. I often get phone calls from other discouraged moms when I, myself, am discouraged. By the time I finish giving the other person a pep talk, I almost always feel better myself. Hebrews 3:13 tells us, "Encourage one another daily." Doing so lightens the load for two hearts, not just one.

- Take comfort in author Debra Bell's observation in *The Ultimate Guide to Home Schooling* that frustration, discouragement, and ambivalence are common emotions among homeschoolers. You are not alone!

- Visit your local school for a reality check. As a taxpayer, you have the right. Ask to sit in on classes for a few days. Observe the children, their interactions, and their use of time. It will be refreshing for you to go home. Barbara, a homeschooler in Illinois, says that "any flicker of doubt" that she is doing the right thing for her children by educating them at home is cured by observing a school board meeting or finding out what neighbor children are learning and not learning in their schools. "What we are able to offer in our homeschool is so much better suited to our son that we have not wavered from the commitment," she says.

- Make sure you are getting adequate support and socialization. When people ask me the big question—"What about socialization?"—I usually respond as if they were referring to *me* instead of my children. "I try to get together with like-minded friends as often as I can," I'll say. The struggles of homeschoolers everywhere are remarkably similar. What a blessing to know that we are not alone!

- Look for, ask for, and pray for help. You are not a failure if you send a child off to a playgroup once a week so you can get some relief or some time to spend with your older children. It is not a sign of weakness to get a baby-sitter to help you whenever you can. A few times in recent years when my writing and speaking work load was whirring out of control, I made child care arrangements for my younger children. Having a trusted friend or relative take them a few hours a week allowed me to catch my breath and take care of other needs.

- Remember that God doesn't ask us to do more than we can do. Philippians 4:19 promises, "God will meet all your needs according to his glorious riches in Christ Jesus." According to *his* riches, not our desires or wants of the moment.

- *Don't* make a major decision about homeschooling on a bad day! Pray about any changes you think you might want to make, whether sending a child to school, withdrawing a child from school, or changing your teaching approach or curriculum. Talk potential changes over with your spouse, sleep on them, consult with a trusted friend. "We all have our share of bad days," says Ellen, a homeschooler from Maine. "We learn from those bad days, and we move on." That doesn't mean quitting, she emphasizes; it means looking for better ways to accomplish what needs to get done.

- Make a conscious choice to be joyful. First Thessalonians 5:16-18 tells us to "Be joyful always; pray continually; give thanks in all circumstances, for this is God's will for you in Christ Jesus." We can't praise God and complain at the same time. When we complain, we are telling God we don't like the job he is doing. So instead of raising your hand to shake your fist at God, try raising your hands to praise him instead.

- Thoughtfully answer the following questions to pinpoint specific causes of your frustration and discouragement. If you can do something about the situation, do it! If not, ask God for grace and patience and learn to love your life just as it is.

  1. Are you trying to be super mom? Do you know how to say no? Are you overly committed outside the family? Do you try

to keep your commitments family oriented? Can you be content to stay home more?

2. Is your home organized for school? Do you have a place for everything? Do you have a family schedule in place so your children know what to expect? Do you have adequate help with housework?

3. Do you have rules for your children's behavior? Do you enforce them consistently? Are your children growing in character? Do you monitor the time they spend watching television or playing on computers?

4. Does your day have too much or too little structure? Are you using the right approach and curriculum for your family? Is your program too academic at the expense of character and life skills training? Are you trying to push a child who isn't ready?

5. Are you getting the support you need from your husband? Do you have a support system of fellow travelers who understand your struggles? Are you remembering to have fun?

When you feel like giving up, remember who called you to homeschool your children. Reflect on the reasons you chose to answer. Nurture your spiritual life. Take care of yourself, avoid unhealthy comparisons, and relax and have fun. Tune in to God's Word and your children's hearts. And stay the course. Remember, God never leads where we cannot follow.

CHAPTER FIFTEEN

New Life in the Val-ley of Dry Bones

Learning from Burnout

I closed my eyes and leaned back in the tub with a groan and a sigh, willing myself to relax. I hadn't had the luxury of a solitary bath in months, and I wanted to enjoy it. But my nerves were so shot even the warm, inviting water failed to calm me.

I had been giving too much lately—at home, at church, with friends and acquaintances—and I had taken too little time to nurture and support myself. I was drained dry. I felt beyond caring about anyone or anything.

Later that morning I blew up at my daughter during her reading lesson. "Can't you remember anything?" I yelled. Her sweet face looked toward me as huge tears welled in her eyes. She ran off to her room, crying loudly. I didn't follow her. I resented her needing me, and I resented my own unmet needs. I couldn't do this anymore. Who was I trying to kid? I simply wasn't cut out for this mothering/teaching/being the good wife thing.

Needing New Breath

Burnout. We don't have to define it; we know it when we see it. Or more accurately, when we *feel* it: the dread, the joylessness, the physical exhaustion, the sense of inadequacy or even failure. We have no vision for our work. We're less and less interested in the subject matter we're teaching. We're short and impatient with the kids. According to Dr. Richard Swenson, author of *The Overload Syndrome,* we become self-protective to such a degree that we actually start resenting people for needing our help.[1]

Resentment and irritability have reared their ugly heads in my own family when I have felt overwhelmed by the task of homeschooling. I have found myself, out of self-preservation, hoarding my love and attention while inflicting my negative emotions on those I love the most. When I realize how I'm behaving, self-recrimination sets in, and I feel even more overwhelmed.

That's when I find myself thinking, *Maybe it's time to send the kids to school and end this grand experiment. Maybe it's time to wave the white flag and admit the naysayers were right.*

Burnout is the bleak side of homeschooling, and at some point, the experience of almost every veteran homeschooler. If we knew how common it was, if we were willing to talk about it more, perhaps we could help one another work through it. But the fact is, we don't want to talk about it. We don't want to be seen as failures. We feel a need to prove ourselves to other homeschoolers as well as to our skeptical relatives and the world at large. How are we doing? Great! Wonderful! What a joy our homeschooling journey is!

But pretending that everything is fine when it's not does nobody any good. If burnout is a problem in our efforts to homeschool, we need to face it and deal with it—or risk everything for which we've sacrificed. How many homeschools are abandoned before their time, I wonder, because a burned-out mom saw no other alternative?

If only we understood that every other homeschooling mom has experienced at least some of the same feelings. "I am laid low in the dust," lamented the psalmist in what might be the burned-out homeschooler's theme song (Psalm 119:25). *Laid low in the dust.* What a perfect description of burnout!

Burnout is the end-of-the line stop on the discouragement train. But it doesn't have to be the end of homeschooling. Far from being the death knell of our homeschooling journey, burnout can provide fertile ground for new growth in both our own and our children's lives. Consider the prophet Ezekiel's vision of the Valley of Dry Bones and take heart:

> The hand of the LORD was upon me, and he brought me out…and set me in the middle of a valley; it was full of bones. He led me back and forth among them, and I saw a great many bones on the floor of the valley, bones that were very dry. He asked me, "Son of man, can these bones live?" I said, "O Sovereign LORD, you alone know." Then he said to me, "Prophesy to these bones and say to them, 'Dry bones, hear the word of the LORD! This is that the Sovereign LORD says to these bones: I will make breath enter you, and you will come to life. I will attach tendons to you and make flesh come upon you and cover you with skin; I will put breath in you, and you will come to life. Then you will know that I am the LORD.'" (Ezekiel 37:1-6)

If God can breathe new life into a pile of dry bones, he can breathe new life into our dry and desperate spirits—if we let him.

The Lessons of Burnout

God wants to use us in bigger and better ways than we've ever imagined. To accomplish his plans, he arranges the circumstances of our lives to move us to a place where he *can* use us.

But God's plans aren't always our plans. We don't always want to move where he wants to take us. He might even have to move us kicking and screaming! But in the long run, we can be assured that his plans for us are always for our good. As Jeremiah 29:11 reminds us, "'I know the plans I have for you,' declares the LORD, 'plans to prosper you and not to harm you, plans to give you hope and a future.'"

God desires our personal growth, and we cannot grow without change. But change isn't easy. Often it's painful. Our human temptation is to run the other way as fast as we can. Yet submitting ourselves to the process God intends for us, committing ourselves to work through our pain rather than try to circumvent it, offers opportunities for growth no other experience can. The fact is, pain can be a powerful agent for good in our lives.

In the Field family homeschool, we've studied the plant cycle three times. Each time I'm impressed by the fact that a seed, before it sends shoots up through the earth, does some of its most important work underground. In the same way, our children grow in the darkness of a womb until they are born. Before a beautiful flower or a tiny baby emerges into the light, growth occurs in darkness. Before godly character emerges into the light, growth occurs in what has been called "the dark night of the soul."

In my own life, God has used seasons of burnout to draw me closer to him. He has arranged circumstances, through illness or exhaustion, in which I have been forced to take the time to renew my walk with him. Some of my sweetest times of fellowship with Jesus have been times when I've been forced to rest and read Scripture to knit both my health and my heart back to wholeness. Burnout requires me to surrender to God, to relinquish my own efforts and admit my total dependence on him.

God has also used my times of forced inactivity to restore my sense of wonder. It's ironic that the things that cause us the most distraction—namely our kids—can also help us learn to pay attention. Have you ever seen your child transfixed by the dust particles in a sunbeam? Or by a rainbow of light cast through a window across a floor? A child can study the phenomenon for half an hour without tiring of it: "Look, I have a rainbow on my arm!" And later: "Now it's on my forehead. Isn't it neat, Mommy?"

At the last full moon, we bundled up the children and went out to the yard to gaze at its beauty and recite together, "God bless the moon and God bless me." Never mind that it was twenty below zero with the wind-chill factor. We were sharing a sense of wonder at God's world.

One of my children turned to me in the car the other day and gushed, "Mommy, I love my life!" How many of us feel that way? How do we become blind to the wonders that are so joyously evident to our children? Could it be that we're just too busy and too distracted to contemplate anything long enough to truly see it?

My husband has coined a phrase that says it all when it comes to our lives as homeschoolers: "Parenting at the Speed of Light." The days seem to move so quickly and the demands seem so overwhelming that they crush us with their weight. We lose sight of our need to know and experience the heart of God. We lose sight of almost everything except the never-ending demands on our time and energy.

Hurrying through life diminishes the significance of everything we do. When we are trying to do too many things or juggle too many things, we are not really paying attention to anything. Burnout is calling us back to childlike wonder, urging us to pay attention, to seize the moment, to enjoy.

One way the Lord has used my own burnout is to encourage and comfort others who are in need. In 2 Corinthians 1:3-4, Paul offered praise to "the God of all comfort, who comforts us in all our troubles, so that we can comfort those in any trouble with the comfort we ourselves have received from God." If we allow God to comfort us in the middle of our suffering, we can become a bridge to comfort for others. When we take our eyes off ourselves and look for ways to minister to others, our burdens seem to lighten.

Burnout can help us understand and manage our feelings. Mothering is an emotional business, a matter of the heart. In addition, I've found that as I approach midlife, I have a whole new respect for hormones. One minute I'm up, and then the next I'm down.

When I was younger, I believed that my feelings were my reality. If I felt up, my life was wonderful. *I* was wonderful. If I felt down, my life was pitiful and I was worthless. I was a bad mother, a bad wife, a lousy Christian, a rotten friend. I remember retreating to the bathroom in defeat at times, where I would sit in the dark and hope no one would find me.

Then I would get some sleep, or my hormones would settle down, and a few days later my life was wonderful again.

Feelings are an important part of our experience as humans, but they are not *us*. Our feelings are just our feelings. They change. Only the love of God endures. Burnout calls us to recognize that and to base our sense of our own worth not on our feelings of the moment but on God's opinion of us. He finds us worthwhile even when we are feeling lousy. The simple truth we teach our children from the beginning is still so profound: God loves us so much he sent his one and only son into the world so that we might have life everlasting (see John 3:16). If I am worthy of that love, can I not muster the energy to begin to love myself?

In my work as an attorney, I often defended individuals who had been wrongly accused of crimes. I recall the drama and tension in the courtroom while we waited for a verdict. The relief we all felt when we heard the words "not guilty" was almost overwhelming.

When we are caught up in condemning ourselves, God longs for us to hear his not-guilty verdict. When we feel like a burned-out failure, it is not his condemnation pressing our spirits down. It is our own. God may *convict* us at times, but he never condemns us. The gulf between conviction and condemnation is huge. Conviction comes from the Lord. It comes with the power and promise of the Holy Spirit to help us repent and take appropriate action. Condemnation comes from the Enemy, whose goal is our discouragement and defeat.

The irony is that the more we seek to walk with God and desire to know him, the greater our self-condemnation when we think we have blown it. We set such high expectations of ourselves that our world comes crashing down around us when we fall short. Yet Romans 8:1 tells us, "There is now *no condemnation* for those who are in Christ Jesus" (emphasis mine).

God does not want to condemn us, especially when we are so eager to condemn ourselves. Instead, he longs to embrace us, to welcome us back to his heart, which is our source of strength, refuge, refreshment, and encouragement. God's grace is never used up, even when our human grace runs dry.

In the midst of burnout, I have the opportunity to learn in the most practical ways that with God all things are possible. In his power, I can accomplish all that he has called me to do. When I begin to feel overwhelmed, I stop, take a deep breath, and remind myself who gave me this family, my vision for family life, and the charge to raise my children well.

The reminder is particularly poignant for me. My husband and I had to jump through a lot of hoops to become adoptive parents, and there is no question that God's presence sustained and led us throughout the process. God gave us these children. He made me their primary caretaker and their teacher. He must think I am adequate to meet their needs. Who am I to doubt the judgment of almighty God?

Finding Your Way Out of Burnout

The dried bones in the valley of Ezekiel's vision needed muscle, skin, flesh, and breath to live again. What is the muscle, skin, and flesh that in the midst of burnout will make us whole again? What is the breath of life that will make us able to climb out of the valley of dry bones?

Our most valuable resource as we seek healing and spiritual renewal is prayer: taking our empty hearts to God and asking him to fill them, pouring out our desperation, reading Scripture prayerfully to give God an opportunity to respond. Sometimes I write out my prayers, describing my pain and suffering and reminding myself of God's past faithfulness, as David did in his Psalms: "Hear my prayer, O LORD; listen to my cry for mercy. In the day of my trouble I will call to you, for you will answer me.... You are great and do marvelous deeds; you alone are God" (Psalm 86:6-7,10).

When we don't have the will or the means to take care of ourselves, it is God we can count on. "The LORD is good to those whose hope is in him, to the one who seeks him; it is good to wait quietly for the salvation of the Lord," Lamentations 3:25-26 tells us.

When our bodies and spirits are weary God promises rest: "Come to me, all you who are weary and burdened, and I will give you rest" (Matthew 11:28). When we cannot be strong, he will be our strength: "My flesh and my heart may fail, but God is the strength of my heart and my portion forever" (Psalm 73:26). When our legs will no longer sustain us, he will carry us as he carried Israel: "You whom I have upheld since you were conceived, and have carried since your birth. Even to your old age and gray hairs I am he, I am he who will sustain you. I have made you and I will carry you" (Isaiah 46:3-4).

Using the power of Scripture and prayer, we can change our thoughts and change our lives. "Do not conform any longer to the pattern of this world," the apostle Paul urged, "but be transformed by the renewing of your mind" (Romans 12:2). "Take captive every thought to make it obedient to Christ" (2 Corinthians 10:5). We need not accept the cycle of self-doubt, self-hatred, and despair. With God's grace, we can train our minds to cultivate peace, joy, and gratitude instead.

It isn't easy, breathing new life into dry bones. Working through burnout requires patience and perseverance. "Forgetting what is behind and straining toward what is ahead," Paul encourages us in Philippians 3:13-14 to "press on toward the goal to win the prize for which God has called [us] heavenward in Jesus Christ." Our confidence in God "will be richly rewarded," adds Hebrews 10:35-36. "You need to persevere so that when you have done the will of God, you will receive what he has promised"— that is, Christ himself.

How we respond to life's pain determines the joy factor in our life. It also determines the way our children will respond to pain. If you never admit your pain and lead your kids to believe that life is always beautiful, they will be disillusioned when life throws them an inevitable curve. If you give up without working through your pain, they will learn to give up in the face of adversity. But show them that life is precious even though it has its ups and downs—show them that relying on the strength of your God, you can handle the ups and downs—and your kids will catch your quiet assurance and gain confidence that they too will be able to meet life's challenges.

What's the answer to burnout? Pray. Read Scripture. Spend time alone. Spend time with the people you love. Take time to laugh and time to play. Take time, period. Seek joy in small things. Take care of your body. Believe in your dreams. Give yourself permission to make mistakes. Love others. Love yourself. Forgive the ones you love for their imperfections. Most especially, forgive yourself.

Wait. Healing will come. The way out of burnout is not to go around it or bury it or ignore it. The way out of burnout is to deal with it—and then move on to whatever the Lord has planned for you next.

In the midst of your pain, remember: God is there. He's there when you blow it with the kids. He's there in the struggles of your marriage. He's there when you're ill or depressed and when family members are ill. He's there during every crisis. He's there to catch you when you fall.

I love Isaiah 40:11, both for its promise and its tone: "He gently leads those that have young."

He leads us. He does so gently. He understands the challenges of our journey, and his heart toward us is tender. When we reach the end of our own resources, when we lift up our hands to him and say, "I can't do this" or "I can't love this child who is driving me crazy!" he will do what we cannot. He is the God who heals wounded hearts and mends broken ones.

He is the God who fills our hearts when they are empty.

Avoiding Burnout

Many factors contribute to burnout among homeschoolers: overextending ourselves; issues with discipline; too much or too little structure; feeling overwhelmed with information and choices; criticism from outsiders; unrealistic expectations and self-criticism; lack of support; unexpected crises. Our first step is to identify the potential causes of burnout in our particular homeschooling journey. Earlier chapters in this book address many of these issues specifically and offer practical ideas for dealing with them before they get out of hand.

In my own homeschooling journey, my biggest obstacle has been myself—in particular, my self-expectations. Dr. Richard Swenson comments in his book *The Overload Syndrome* that when we "start to pretend that somehow we don't have limits, we get ourselves mired in painful consequences."[2] I know about those painful consequences. I have pushed myself to do more and give more than God or my husband or my children ever asked of me. I have suffered burnout from trying to do a job no one ever asked me to do: to be the perfect homeschooling mom, to fill all my roles in my family, my church, and my community perfectly.

Does God ask me to maintain an immaculate house or to sew every item of my family's clothing from scratch? Does he ask me to volunteer in my church or community in every capacity? Does he ask me to fill every minute of my day in frenetic activity until I am driven to exhaustion?

"Limits were God's intention from the beginning," Dr. Swenson says. "He is the Creator—the One without limits. We are the created—the ones with limits.... As the author of limits, God put them within us for our protection. We violate them at our peril."[3]

Believe me, I know. Not long ago I began to notice my heartbeats were irregular. I told myself it was probably a reaction to the thyroid medication I have taken for most of my life. I didn't want to think about the fact that I have a terrible family history of cardiac problems or that my mother died at the age of fifty-six. And I was in total denial about the fact that I had been meeting everyone else's needs and completely ignoring my own. Yes, I'd gained a lot of weight, but it didn't have anything to do with trying to meet my emotional needs with food, or so I tried to deceive myself. I didn't want to acknowledge that my spiritual life had slipped and my health had deteriorated.

I'm a very stubborn woman. The Lord knows this, and he used those irregular heartbeats to get my attention in a big-time way. The visit to my doctor and the round of testing he put me through was like a whack upside the head: My right coronary artery had substantial calcium deposits. If I didn't change my lifestyle, reduce my stress, and focus some attention on myself, my condition would only get worse. The cardiologist put it bluntly: "Do you want to live to see your grandchildren?" You don't want to hear that at age forty-three.

Stephen Covey, in his book *The Seven Habits of Highly Effective Families,* puts it this way: "In physics, 'entropy' means that anything left to itself will eventually disintegrate until it reaches its most elemental form. The dictionary defines entropy as 'the steady degradation of a system or society.' This happens in all of life and we all know it. Neglect your body, and it will deteriorate. Neglect your car, and it will deteriorate. Watch TV every available hour, and your mind will deteriorate. Anything that is not consciously attended to and renewed will break down, become disordered, and deteriorate."

Covey goes on to tell a story about two men seeking to cut down trees. One labored all day long with a dull saw and barely made any headway. The other took the time to sharpen his saw; his work went more quickly and easily. In the context of our lives, says Covey, "Sharpening the saw means attending regularly and consistently to renewal in all four dimensions of life," which he defines as physical, spiritual, social/emotional, and mental.[4]

How do we sharpen our saws in order to avoid burnout? What specific actions of self-care can we take to keep it at bay? The answer will be different for each of us. We have to figure out what replenishes us physically, spiritually, emotionally, and mentally and regularly incorporate those things into our schedules. What gives us energy? What fills us up? What makes us feel refreshed and revitalized?

I used to think the only way to recharge myself was to get away. "Bye honey—see you in a few weeks!" If I couldn't physically leave my homeschooling environment for an extended time, I thought, I was doomed to burnout. But life, as any homeschooling mom will tell you, is rarely conducive to solitary vacations!

God will never take us—or leave us—where his grace won't sustain us. He won't send us challenges that he won't also send us the strength to endure. Our charge is to stay fit in every area of our lives for the purpose of carrying out his plans. Yet the 24/7/365 nature of our life as homeschooling moms places incredible stress on our bodies, our minds and our hearts. We need to take care of ourselves, or we won't be there to take care of our families when they need us.

God gave me a wake-up call before it was too late. I'm taking better care of myself because I know that if I don't, I won't be around to see my children graduate, establish careers, and start families of their own. Much of what I've learned about managing my life as a homeschooling mom came out of crises like my heart problem. It's not the curriculum I recommend.

"An ounce of prevention," some wise person once said, "is worth a pound of cure." Don't allow yourself to get to the point where burnout is an actual threat to your life and your family. Identify the areas in your homeschooling experience in which you have the most difficulty, then look back to earlier chapters in this book that address those areas. Put into practice some of the ideas and suggestions at the end of each chapter. Here's an additional list of practical "burnout busters":

Practical Pointers for Avoiding Homeschool Burnout

- Nurture your spiritual life. Draw from the well of God's love. Lily, an Oklahoma homeschooler, advises, "Pray! Keep solid in the Word of God. Trust that he is guiding [you] in the right direction."

- Make time every day for Bible reading. Can't spare five minutes? Ten minutes? Keep a Bible in the bathroom and next to the rocking chair in the nursery. Locate a Bible on tape so you can listen even when your hands are busy. These short slices of Scripture will refill your spiritual well and help you want to dig deeper.

- Articulate your vision for homeschooling. If you've never had a vision, or think you might have once but can't remember what it was, now's the time to get it down on paper. Brainstorm with your husband—maybe even with your kids. Why do you homeschool? What's your mission? What are your goals for your children and your family? Are your current actions and time commitments consistent with your vision?

- Fellowship with other Christian homeschoolers. Isolation leads to a loss of objectivity about our situation. Ecclesiastes 4:9-10 says, "Two are better than one, because they have a good return for their work: If one falls down, his friend can help him up. But pity the man who falls and has no one to help him up!"

- Cultivate a "girls' night out" to share your struggles with others. Denise, a homeschooler in Illinois, refers to the time she shares with fellow homeschoolers, away from her kids, as a "wonderful gift" her husband gives her. "He will even make dinner for himself and the kids to allow me to go," she says.

- Take care of yourself physically. A homeschooling mother of four from Missouri writes, "I make getting a good night's sleep a top priority, often napping daily. I also take high-powered vitamins, walk and work out with weights daily, see friends, travel with my family, and have fun on a regular basis. This preserves my sanity. I work very, very hard to pace myself."

- Take a nap when your children are sleeping. This is not slothful. It's sanity! Even great athletes pace themselves to endure the event.

- Schedule an hour of quiet time every day. Get your young children accustomed to the practice so you can catch your breath and relax during that time. Read, crochet, or write letters—anything that helps you unwind.

- Reevaluate your time commitments. A mom who homeschools in Arizona writes that she knows she can't do everything her friends are doing. "All women are not created with the same amount of energy," she says. When she realizes she's bitten off more than she can chew, she drops an activity or commitment from her schedule as soon as practically possible.

- Figure out what comforts you, and do it! Take a hot bath. Take a half-hour for tea in the afternoon to regroup and recharge for the rest of the day. Join a health club, and use the facilities on a regular basis.

- On a difficult day, using moderation, connect to some cyber-support on the Internet.

- Take time to be alone. During my alone times, I go to bookstores and libraries.

- Create a sanctuary in your home where the children aren't allowed, perhaps your bedroom or a corner of the basement. When the kids are old enough to be alone for twenty minutes, you can send them off to another part of the house to play while you regroup in private.

- Collect words of encouragement. What words of God revive you? Are there certain scriptures that always encourage you? Write them out on cards, and hang them around your house. I have a shelf above my kitchen sink where I post prayers, the words to favorite songs, and encouraging Bible verses to refresh me while I tend to my kitchen duties.

- Learn something new. If motherhood brought you home from the work force, think about the things you wanted to pursue when you were working but didn't have time for. For me, it's writing.

- Do something creative. Personal hobbies are great for burnout. Knit, sew, paint, write. The rhythm and pace of the activity itself can relax you, and sometimes just looking at something you've created can replenish you.

- Break your routine. Have breakfast for dinner. Let the dishes go until morning. Let daddy teach one day and take a vacation day for yourself!

- Change your teaching approach. If you do a structured curriculum, try a unit study or have a game day or a game week. Kat, a California homeschooler, shares that she has learned to relax more in her teaching, to let go of the things she doesn't get to. "If I am worried about a specific subject or the standards that the schools have, I will burn out much more rapidly," she says. "I concentrate on my children's strengths and weaknesses (which are different for each child) and just take [my concerns about teaching] to God and leave them there. I know as long as I keep close to him, he won't leave me stranded or let me mess up."

- Take a break from homeschooling when you need it. You will be a better mom and teacher if you meet some of your own needs first. Elizabeth Prentiss, in her wise book *Stepping Heavenward,* reminds us, "The only true way to live in this world, constituted just as we are, is to make all our employments serve the one great end and aim of our existence, namely, to glorify God and to enjoy Him forever. But in order to do this we must be wise taskmasters, and not require of ourselves what we cannot possibly perform. Recreation we must have. Otherwise the strings of our soul, wound up to an unnatural tension, will break."[5]

- Have fun with your kids! Prentiss says that a mother "must learn to enter into the happy moods of her children at the very moment when her own heart is sad. It may be as religious an act for her to romp with them at that time," she says, "as to pray with them at others."[6] My friend Jana also advises taking time to play. When homeschooling responsibilities feel overwhelming, "It helps to focus on your delight in your children," she says. Remember how very short the time is that you'll have them home with you and "make the most of it.... Keep your sense of humor alive. Laughing helps a lot. Don't hesitate to take a day off and just play if you need it—even if it means doing summer school."

- Let go of chores and cleaning for a while. Enlist help from your husband and your children. Hire outside help.
- Put away the textbooks for a day. Or longer. Take the kids to a park or an amusement center. Spend time wandering aimlessly at the library. Take an unstructured field trip.
- Take long walks as a family.
- Keep a gratitude journal. Daily list the things in your life for which you are grateful—the blessings and answered prayers.
- Refocus on your original homeschooling vision. Are you homeschooling to preserve family closeness and to insulate your children from some of the garbage of popular culture? Lily, an Oklahoma homeschooler, says that every time she begins to feel overwhelmed, she stops and thanks God for the opportunity to educate her children at home. "I would be missing out on so much if they weren't here with me," she says.
- Praise your children for their academic progress and for the good things you see developing in their character. That encouragement may turn the whole family around.
- Share your passions with your child. Stay excited about your personal interests. Do you sew, stitch, or sculpt? Introduce these pleasurable pursuits to your children and teach them what you know. Your enthusiasm will rub off.

- Try this clarifying exercise: Fold a paper in half. On one side list those things that give you energy. On the other side, list the things that take away your energy. What can you do to balance these out?
- Have a mom's helper come for a few hours while you are at home.
- Swap baby-sitting once a month with another family to give mom and dad a night out.
- Do something together with your husband and children as a service project. One year my husband and I taught in the AWANA program while our children attended club. We were all together for the evening—living, loving, and serving the Lord.
- Remind yourself that in another year, life will be different. The children will be older. They will have abilities and self-care skills they don't have now. Sometimes the only solution to "problems" is to wait them out—or wait for them to grow up a little!

A Final Note: Before You Throw in the Towel

Did God call you to homeschool? If he did and you're contemplating sending your kids off to "regular" school, ask yourself what has changed: his call or your response to his call?

I agonized over whether to homeschool my children. I should feel that same anguish over whether to abandon the journey. What does God want for me and for my children at this time in our lives?

This past February, on Presidents' Day, I was enjoying having my husband home for the day by taking a little afternoon nap. I was beyond tired. I was "February-tired," something all homeschoolers can relate to. As I rested, I prayed my most earnest prayer for God to guide me in our plans for the next school year. I was seriously considering middle school for the oldest two. They wanted a change. I wanted a break. *Lord,* I asked, *could you be asking too much from me?*

When I got up, my daughters announced their intention to go for a walk to a friend's house, two blocks away. Even in our safe community, we require them to go in pairs if they are leaving the block. They took off for their visit, and I settled in on the couch to read some library books to the younger two.

A few minutes later I heard hysterical crying at the back of the house. The older two were talking in excited voices to my husband. He ran to the bedroom, grabbed his service revolver, and dashed out the door. I gathered Clare and Caitlin to my lap and heard them tell their story: a half block from home, a scraggly sixteen-year-old in an older model car had approached the girls and tried to get them into the car. They'd had the good sense to run.

When my husband, the police chief in our town, sent out a call for assistance on the police radio, the offender was stopped only a few blocks away. When they inventoried his car, they discovered children's toys, rope, and a knife. The offender was later tied to six other instances of attempted abduction.

To say this got my attention is an understatement. Feeling complacent about our mission to teach and train our children, we were given an opportunity to reexamine our priorities. This incident has forced us to rekindle our passion, and although we regret the trauma to our daughters, we are grateful for God's protective mercy and his incredible patience with our weaknesses.

Sometimes I want God to deliver me out of the fire of my difficulties when he desires instead to lead me through them. If I find that my longing to give up homeschooling is based on burnout rather than God's leading, I must persevere. God has called me, and I know in faith and from experience that he will equip me for the task. Isaiah 43:2 is his promise that I will survive: "When you walk through the fire, you will not be burned; the flames will not set you ablaze."

I keep a prayer journal in the notebook that I use for personal Bible study and sermon notes. In it, I have a page set aside for each of my family members on which I write my prayer requests for them. The list for my children includes their spiritual and character growth, their friends, their health, their future spouse, their ongoing protection, and any specific problems for which I believe they need encouragement and guidance. I also record on these pages praise for answered prayer. What joy to see God answer prayer in the life of my family!

Someday you and I will be done with the work of homeschooling. That job will end. But we will continue to have the job of praying fervently for our children. As long as we have breath, we will never finish the task of praying for our children. Whether we choose to continue homeschooling or not, we must start and finish every day of our parenthood with prayer.

If we remember that, we will have at our disposal, for every challenge that lies ahead in our homeschooling journey, the power of almighty God.

The Rewards of Homeschooling

An anonymous mom in Shari Henry's book *Homeschooling the Middle Years,* sums up her experience as a homeschooler this way: "Living with my daughters so intensely and knowing they are observing me is humbling, exhilarating, and enormously intimidating. I think homeschooling has inspired me to become a better person and a better mother. [It] has taught me volumes about the complexities of forging a life well lived while navigating a road less traveled."[1]

"Forging a life well lived while navigating a road less traveled"—the road of homeschooling—has brought me many unexpected blessings. Pearls, I like to think of them. Remember the parable Jesus told about pearls? "The kingdom of heaven is like a merchant looking for fine pearls. When he found one of great value, he went away and sold everything he had and bought it" (Matthew 13:45-46).

I believe the lessons we learn from homeschooling are like that pearl. When we recognize their true value, we are willing to do whatever we can to gain them. We make sacrifices because we know the lessons are beyond any price we might pay.

When I first became a mother, I dreamed of all the wonderful things I was going to do for my children. I was going to love them like no one else could. I would have unlimited patience and understanding. I would give them enriching life experiences and prepare healthy foods to nourish them. They would have a stable, joyous home.

I had no reason to believe my life as a mother would be any different from the picture I had envisioned. My life as an attorney during the many years I practiced law had made me believe in my power to order and control my world. If I told a witness to be seated, he sat. If I asked him questions, he answered. If he refused to answer, the presiding judge would compel him to. I decided who would go on the witness stand and how the trial would flow. At the end of the trial, I decided how I would appeal to the jury. Did I want to make them angry? Did I want to make them cry? I knew how to get the response I wanted.

Then God blessed me with my first two daughters, seventeen months apart. Guess what? The skills I learned in the courtroom didn't translate well to life at home.

I would say, "Be seated," and they would scream, "No!" If they didn't follow the rules, there was no stern judge to intervene and compel their compliance. In fact, they pretty much controlled the flow of my day. They had the ability, as I did with the jury, to make me angry or to make me cry, both of which they did with alarming skill and regularity!

Perhaps you have found yourselves on your knees, as I have, surrounded by colicky babies, dirty diapers and even dirtier houses, rebellious preteens, disorganized curriculum, hungry toddlers, and tired husbands. Maybe you have cried out to God, as I have, "This is not what I had planned!" My brain was too good to be spending my days managing the menial tasks that made up daily life with small children. I felt used and abused. Surely this wasn't where God wanted me!

But it was. As a homeschooling mom, I was in a place where God could teach me some things that I desperately needed to learn—the lessons I call my pearls of homeschooling.

A pearl is formed when an oyster reacts to a tiny piece of sand. God uses the same principle in my life as a mom and a homeschooler, using the irritants that seem to be a part of my daily experience to produce something of greater value than I ever could have imagined.

My dream of being a wonderful mother shifted as I faced the realities of motherhood. I knew that I was going to do some good and healthy things for my children, but also that along the way, I would inadvertently do some not-so-good and not-so-healthy things. What I wasn't prepared for at all was what my *children* would do for *me*. This has been the biggest surprise of my homeschooling journey as well: what my children have given me, what I have learned, and how I have grown in the process of training them.

What are some of the pearls I've gained through homeschooling?

P—peace

E—endurance

A—acceptance

R—restoration

L—lasting love

S—satisfaction with servanthood.

Peace. Homeschooling has required a surrender on my part of my need to control and orchestrate everything, to cease my striving and to let God's will unfold in my life instead. When I gave up my need to control, much of my anger and frustration dissipated. Homeschooling has brought me greater peace than any other experience in my life.

I wanted to do something grand and spectacular with my life. Most of my former colleagues are now either judges or involved in politics. That was where I was headed—because that was where I felt I could be in control. Having two kids in diapers so close together and then two more kids behind them taught me I'm not in control of anything.

It is no coincidence that each time Jesus defines what is great or significant in life, he is reaching to lift or embrace a child. If God has blessed us with children, he has given us a mission to change the world, one child at a time, starting with the children in our home. What could be more grand than that?

Endurance. Someone once said that mothering is not a sprint race—it's a marathon. If we want to reach the end, we need to learn to pace ourselves and increase our endurance. For me, focusing on God's enduring love has helped me endure in *my* love for my children; it has also helped me remain confident in my vision. "Persevere," said the writer of Hebrews, "so that when you have done the will of God, you will receive what he has promised" (10:36).

Part of endurance is pacing ourselves. Have you noticed in Scripture that Jesus never hurried? He didn't worry about programs, schedules, plans, and priorities. He did the work of the Father. He relinquished himself to be about his Father's business. That kept him in peace and gave him the strength to see his work through to the end.

Acceptance. Homeschooling has taught me that God accepts my imperfections. When even my children continually forgive me for failing, for losing it, for screaming at them in frustration, I know that God, too, forgives. Just as my children accept me in my weakness, so does God.

But it goes further. When I know that I am accepted, I can in turn accept the imperfections of my children and others around me. That's the neatest thing about God's love; it opens our hearts and allows us to extend his love and acceptance to others, even those who seem to irritate us the most.

Restoration. God has shepherded me safely through the rough spots of homeschooling: the doubts about my ability, the many character issues, the sheer volume of work. The times we've tried to tough it out on our own, without his guidance and strength, have been pure disaster; but relying on him, our family has weathered much. He continually restores us to wholeness and harmony.

We've had plenty of rough spots, among them a cancer scare, a planned adoption falling through, and cardiac problems at age forty-three—with four little children to worry about. "Okay, Lord, tell me how you want me to handle this," I'd pray. "Okay, Lord, tell me your point here—I don't get it. Why? Why me? Why us?" Desperate, begging for answers, crying for guidance: "Please, Lord, tell me what to do, and I'll do it."

Love me, God always answers. *Love your neighbors. That's all. I'll work out the rough spots.* And he does.

Lasting love. God's lasting love is a precious gift available to all, not simply to homeschoolers. But homeschooling has allowed me to see that love more clearly and to know it on the most personal level.

"Love is patient, love is kind," the apostle Paul tells us. "It does not envy, it does not boast, it is not proud. It is not rude, it is not self-seeking, it is not easily angered, it keeps no record of wrongs. Love does not delight in evil but rejoices with the truth. It always protects, always trusts, always hopes, always perseveres. Love never fails" (1 Corinthians 13:4-8). Through all the challenges of homeschooling, God has never given up on me. The challenge he leaves me with now is to love my family as he loves me.

I have wonderful, loving memories as a homeschooler that I would not have if my children were schooled traditionally. Being with them every day, I see them learn new things and discover new experiences. I find a joy and satisfaction in this sharing of our moments, hours, and days that I have found nowhere else—not arguing a case to a jury or writing a book or speaking to an audience. Without the small treasures of these everyday memories, my heart would be less full and my children's hearts would be less available to me. I would not give up these pearls for all the world has to offer.

Satisfaction with servanthood. I was raised and educated to be in charge of the world. But I never knew true happiness until I figured out some-where deep in my heart that my only true satisfaction would be found in servanthood. No other calling has brought such satisfaction as serving my Lord Jesus Christ and serving my family. What an unexpected pearl!

Those are some of my pearls—a small number of the precious lessons of homeschooling I've collected over the years. I wouldn't give them up for anything.

What are the pearls God has given you as a homeschooler? Were they handed to you in a fancy jewelry box with a gold bow on top, or were they hatched out of the sand and irritation of a nasty old oyster shell? Hard-earned as they are, would you ever give them up?

Think about it. Make a list of your pearls. Consider how the challenges of homeschooling produced them. You may find yourself thanking God as much for the rough spots as for the easy ones.

"Let us not be weary in well doing: for in due season
we shall reap, if we faint not."
GALATIANS 6:9, KJV

Notes

Chapter 1

1. James Dobson, Focus on the Family Ministry, *Fatigue and the Homemaker*, n.d., 9.

2. Ross Werland, "Beat the Clock," *Chicago Tribune*, 2 January 2000, 13.

3. "Beat the Clock," 13.

4. Richard A. Swenson, *The Overload Syndrome: Learning to Live Within Your Limits* (Colorado Springs, Colo.: NavPress, 1998), 34.

5. Luanne Shackelford and Susan White, *A Survivor's Guide to Home Schooling* (Westchester, Ill.: Crossway, 1988), 143.

6. Iris Krasnow, *Surrendering to Motherhood: Losing Your Mind, Finding Your Soul* (New York: Hyperion, 1997), 170.

7. Krasnow, *Surrendering to Motherhood*, 189.

8. Brother Lawrence, *The Practice of the Presence of God* (Springdale, Pa.: Whitaker House, 1982), 33.

9. Krasnow, *Surrendering to Motherhood*, 157.

Chapter 2

1. For lots of other ideas about mobilizing children for household chores, see my book *Life Skills for Kids* (Colorado Springs, Colo.: Shaw Books, 2000).

2. Debra Bell, *The Ultimate Guide to Homeschooling* (Nashville, Tenn.: Nelson, 1997), 147.

Chapter 3

1. Tedd Tripp, *Shepherding a Child's Heart* (Wapwallopen, Pa.: Shepherd Press, 1995), 11.

2. Tripp, *Shepherding a Child's Heart*, 13-4.

3. Tripp, *Shepherding a Child's Heart,* 20.

4. Pat Holt and Grace Ketterman, *When You Feel Like Screaming: Help for Frustrated Mothers* (Wheaton, Ill.: Shaw, 1998), 3-4.

5. Robert Rosenthal and Lenore Jacobson, *Pygmalion in the Classroom: Teacher Expectation and Pupils' Intellectual Development* (Holt, Rinehart & Winston, 1968), 117.

6. Kym Wright, *Living Life on Purpose* (Conyers, Ga.: alWright Publishing, 1998), 58.

7. Michael Pearl and Debi Pearl, *No Greater Joy* (Pleasantville, Tenn.: The Church at Cane Creek, 1997), 22.

8. Pearl and Pearl, *No Greater Joy,* 41-2.

9. Elizabeth Crary, *Pick Up Your Socks* (Seattle, Wash.: Parenting Press, 1990), 40.

Chapter 4

1. Quoted in Diana Waring, *Beyond Survival: A Guide to Abundant-Life Homeschooling* (Lynnwood, Wash.: Emerald Books, 1996), 11.

2. Mary Griffith, *The Homeschooling Handbook: From Preschool to High School: A Parent's Guide* (Rocklin, Calif.: Prima Publishing, 1997), 64-5.

3. Cheri Fuller, *Motivating Your Kids from Crayons to Career* (Tulsa, Okla.: Honor Books, 1990), 114.

4. Fuller, *Motivating Your Kids,* 107-8.

5. Fuller, *Motivating Your Kids,* 111-2.

Chapter 5

1. Mary Griffith, *The Homeschooling Handbook: From Preschool to High School: A Parent's Guide* (Rocklin, Calif.: Prima Publishing, 1997), 70.

Chapter 6

1. Raymond Moore and Dorothy Moore, *Home Style Teaching: A Handbook for Parents and Teachers* (Waco, Tex.: Word, 1984), 36.

2. Moore and Moore, *Home Style Teaching,* 36.

3. Moore and Moore, *Home Style Teaching,* 36.

4. Moore and Moore, *Home Style Teaching,* 36.

5. Kay Kuzma, "Teaching Values," in *The Homeschool Manual,* ed. Ted Wade (Bridgeman, Mich.: Gazelle Publications, 1995), 147.

6. Kuzma, "Teaching Values," 147-8.

7. Kuzma, "Teaching Values," 147.

8. Kuzma, "Teaching Values," 148.

9. Kuzma, "Teaching Values," 149.

10. Kuzma, "Teaching Values," 149.

11. These were first published in my book *Life Skills for Kids* (Colorado Springs, Colo.: Shaw Books, 2000).

12. American Dietetic Association, "Position Paper: Dietary Guidance for Healthy Children Aged 2 to 11 Years," *Journal of American Dietetic Association* 99 (1999): 93-101.

13. James Dobson, Focus on the Family Ministry, *Fatigue and the Homemaker,* n.d., 9.

Chapter 7

1. Elisabeth Elliot, *The Gatekeeper* (Lincoln, Nebr.: Back to the Bible, 2000), 1-2.

Chapter 8

1. Quoted in Linda Dobson, *Homeschooling Book of Answers: The 88 Most Important Questions Answered by Homeschooling's Most Respected Voices* (Rocklin, Calif.: Prima Publishing, 1998), 95.

2. Daniel Golden, "Home-Schooled Kids Defy Stereotypes," *Wall Street Journal,* 11 February 2000, A1.

3. Brian D. Ray, *Home Education Across the United States* (Purcellville, Va.: Home School Legal Defense Association and National Home Education Research Institute, 1997).

4. *1998 Report Card on the Ethics of American Youth: Survey Data on Youth Violence* (Josephson Institute of Ethics, May 1999), www.josephsoninstitute.org.

5. James Dobson, *The New Hide or Seek* (Grand Rapids, Mich.: Revell, 1999), 222.

6. Home School Legal Defense Association, *Homeschool Court Report* (December 1990, 2-7), quoted in Deborah McIntire and Robert Windham, *Home Schooling: Answers to Questions Parents Most Often Ask* (Cypress, Calif.: Creative Teaching Press, 1995), 19.

7. McIntire and Windham, *Home Schooling,* 19.

Chapter 9

1. John Gottman with Nan Silver, *Why Marriages Succeed or Fail: What You Can Learn from the Breakthrough Research to Make Your Marriage Last* (New York: Simon & Schuster, 1994), 28.

2. Bob Barnes, *Ready for Responsibility: How to Equip Your Children for Work and Marriage* (Grand Rapids, Mich.: Zondervan, 1997), 139.

3. Barnes, *Ready for Responsibility,* 100.

4. Linda Dobson, *Home Schooling the Early Years* (Rocklin, Calif.: Prima Publishing, 1999), 267.

Chapter 10

1. Luanne Shackelford and Susan White, *A Survivor's Guide to Home Schooling* (Westchester, Ill.: Crossway, 1988), 21.

2. Cynthia Ulrich Tobias, *"You Can't Make Me" (But I Can Be Persuaded)* (Colorado Springs, Colo.: WaterBrook, 1999), 167.

3. Gary Smalley, *Hidden Keys of a Loving, Lasting Marriage: A Valuable Guide to Knowing, Understanding and Loving Each Other* (Grand Rapids, Mich.: Zondervan, 1988), 201-3.

4. Maranatha Chapman, "Being a Safe Place for Your Husband," *An Encouraging Word* 31, 14-5.

Chapter 11

1. Urie Bronfenbrenner, *The Ecology of Human Development* (Cambridge, Mass.: Harvard University Press, 1979), 194-5.

2. William R. Mattox, "Are Homeschooled Children Socially Deprived?" Knight Ridder/Tribune News Service, 3 March 1999.

3. *Marching to the Beat of Their Own Drum* (Purcellville, Va.: Home School Legal Defense Association), 11.

4. Laura Schlessinger, *Parenthood by Proxy: Don't Have Them If You Won't Raise Them* (New York: HarperCollins, 2000), 170.

5. Jonathan Lindvall, *Sheltering Children*, audiotape (Springville, Calif.: Bold Christian Living, 1995).

6. Francine Russo, "Homeschool Report Card," *Time*, 13 September 1999, C10.

7. Isabel Lyman, "What's Behind the Growth in Homeschooling," *USA Today* magazine 127, no. 2620 (September 1998): 64.

8. Mattox, "Are Homeschooled Children Socially Deprived?"

9. Vickie Farris and Jayme Farris, *A Mom Just Like You: [The Home Schooling Mother]* (Sisters, Oreg.: Loyal Publishing, 2000), 231.

10. Farris and Farris, *A Mom Just Like You*, 232-3.

Chapter 12

1. Sharon Hensley, *Home Schooling Children with Special Needs: Turning Challenges into Opportunities* (Gresham, Oreg.: Noble Publishing, 1995), 18.

2. Hensley, *Homeschooling Children with Special Needs*, 27.

Chapter 13

1. Stephen Covey, *Seven Habits of Highly Effective Families: Building a Beautiful Family Culture in a Turbulent World* (New York: Golden Books, 1997), 127.

2. Katherine Pfleger, "School's Out," *The New Republic*, 6 April 1998, 11.

3. Nancy Mitchell, "Homeschooled Children Score Well on National Test," Knight Ridder/Tribune News Service, 25 March 1999.

4. Mary Griffith, *The Homeschooling Handbook: From Preschool to High School: A Parent's Guide* (Rocklin, Calif.: Prima Publishing, 1997), xix.

5. "Learning Around the Kitchen Table," *The Economist,* 6 June 1998, 28.

6. "Learning Around the Kitchen Table," 28.

7. Griffith, *The Homeschooling Handbook,* 189.

8. Debra Bell, *The Ultimate Guide to Homeschooling* (Nashville, Tenn.: Nelson, 1997), 299.

9. Barbara Dafoe, "Parent Support, Not Child Care," *New Perspectives Quarterly,* summer 1998, 73.

10. Susan Schaeffer Macaulay, *For the Children's Sake: Foundations of Education for Home and School* (Westchester, Ill., Crossway, 1984), 15.

Chapter 15

1. Richard A. Swenson, *The Overload Syndrome: Learning to Live Within Your Limits* (Colorado Springs, Colo.: NavPress, 1998), 48.

2. Swenson, *The Overload Syndrome,* 26-7.

3. Swenson, *The Overload Syndrome,* 27-8.

4. Stephen Covey, *Seven Habits of Highly Effective Families* (New York: Golden Books, 1998), 276-7.

5. Elizabeth Prentiss, *Stepping Heavenward* (Amityville, N.Y.: Calvary Press, 1998), 105-6.

6. Prentiss, *Stepping Heavenward,* 331.

Afterword

1. Shari Henry, *Homeschooling, the Middle Years: Your Complete Guide to Successfully Homeschooling the 8- to 12-Year-Old Child* (Rocklin, Calif.: Prima Publishing, 1999), 71.

About the Author

Christine M. Field practiced law for eight years before becoming a full-time stay-at-home mom. She and her husband live and homeschool their four children in Wheaton, Illinois, where her husband serves as chief of police. Three of their four children are adopted, one through a private adoption and two from Korea. Christine is the author of four other books, including *Life Skills for Kids, Coming Home to Raise Your Children, Should You Adopt?* and *A Field Guide to Homeschooling.* She writes columns for several magazines, including *Homeschool Digest* and *Open Arms* magazine. Her work appears regularly in *Hearts at Home* magazine and others, and her articles on life skills have appeared in *Focus on the Family* magazine and *Single Parent Family.* Christine enjoys speaking to groups, from small fellowships to large conventions. If you would like to share your stories of homeschooling survival, e-mail Christine at FieldFamily@HomeFieldAdvantage.org or visit her Web site at www.HomeFieldAdvantage.org. Her mailing address is The Home Field Advantage, P.O. Box 261, Wheaton, IL 60189-0261.